T0350395

Deep Natural Language Processing and AI Applications for Industry 5.0

Poonam Tanwar
Manav Rachna International Institute of Research and Studies, India

Arti Saxena
Manav Rachna International Institute of Research and Studies, India

C. Priya
Vels Institute of Science, Technology, and Advanced Studies, India

A volume in the Advances in Computational
Intelligence and Robotics (ACIR) Book Series

Published in the United States of America by
    IGI Global
    Engineering Science Reference (an imprint of IGI Global)
    701 E. Chocolate Avenue
    Hershey PA, USA 17033
    Tel: 717-533-8845
    Fax: 717-533-8661
    E-mail: cust@igi-global.com
    Web site: http://www.igi-global.com

Library of Congress Cataloging-in-Publication Data

Names: Tanwar, Poonam, 1979- editor. | Saxena, Arti, 1984- editor. | Priya,
    C., 1979- editor.
Title: Deep natural language processing and AI applications for industry
    5.0 / Poonam Tanwar, Arti Saxena, and C. Priya, editors.
Description: Hershey, PA : Engineering Science Reference, [2021] | Includes
    bibliographical references and index. | Summary: "This book is a
    collection of contributed chapters of latest research findings, ideas,
    and applications in the fields of Natural Language Processing and their
    applications, Computational Linguistics, Deep NLP, Web Analysis,
    Sentiments analysis for business and industry"-- Provided by publisher.
Identifiers: LCCN 2021013796 (print) | LCCN 2021013797 (ebook) | ISBN
    9781799877288 (h/c) | ISBN 9781799877295 (s/c) | ISBN 9781799877301
    (ebook)
Subjects: LCSH: Natural language processing (Computer science) | Industry
    4.0.
Classification: LCC QA76.9.N38 D43 2021 (print) | LCC QA76.9.N38 (ebook)
    | DDC 006.3/5--dc23
LC record available at https://lccn.loc.gov/2021013796
LC ebook record available at https://lccn.loc.gov/2021013797

This book is published in the IGI Global book series Advances in Computational Intelligence and Robotics (ACIR) (ISSN: 2327-0411; eISSN: 2327-042X)

British Cataloguing in Publication Data
A Cataloguing in Publication record for this book is available from the British Library.

All work contributed to this book is new, previously-unpublished material. The views expressed in this book are those of the authors, but not necessarily of the publisher.

For electronic access to this publication, please contact: eresources@igi-global.com.

Advances in Computational Intelligence and Robotics (ACIR) Book Series

Ivan Giannoccaro
University of Salento, Italy

ISSN:2327-0411
EISSN:2327-042X

MISSION

While intelligence is traditionally a term applied to humans and human cognition, technology has progressed in such a way to allow for the development of intelligent systems able to simulate many human traits. With this new era of simulated and artificial intelligence, much research is needed in order to continue to advance the field and also to evaluate the ethical and societal concerns of the existence of artificial life and machine learning.

The **Advances in Computational Intelligence and Robotics (ACIR) Book Series** encourages scholarly discourse on all topics pertaining to evolutionary computing, artificial life, computational intelligence, machine learning, and robotics. ACIR presents the latest research being conducted on diverse topics in intelligence technologies with the goal of advancing knowledge and applications in this rapidly evolving field.

COVERAGE

- Adaptive and Complex Systems
- Robotics
- Synthetic Emotions
- Artificial Life
- Computational Intelligence
- Agent technologies
- Cognitive Informatics
- Cyborgs
- Automated Reasoning
- Brain Simulation

IGI Global is currently accepting manuscripts for publication within this series. To submit a proposal for a volume in this series, please contact our Acquisition Editors at Acquisitions@igi-global.com or visit: http://www.igi-global.com/publish/.

Titles in this Series

For a list of additional titles in this series, please visit: www.igi-global.com/book-series

Genetic Algorithms and Applications for Stock Trading Optimization
Vivek Kapoor (Devi Ahilya University, India) and Shubhamoy Dey (Indian Institute of Management, Indore, India)
Engineering Science Reference • © 2021 • 315pp • H/C (ISBN: 9781799841050) • US $225.00

Handbook of Research on Innovations and Applications of AI, IoT, and Cognitive Technologies
Jingyuan Zhao (University of Toronto, Canada) and V. Vinoth Kumar (MVJ College of Engineering, India)
Engineering Science Reference • © 2021 • 400pp • H/C (ISBN: 9781799868705) • US $325.00

Decision Support Systems and Industrial IoT in Smart Grid, Factories, and Cities
Ismail Butun (Chalmers University of Technology, Sweden & Konya Food and Agriculture University, Turkey & Royal University of Technology, Sweden)
Engineering Science Reference • © 2021 • 285pp • H/C (ISBN: 9781799874683) • US $245.00

AI Tools and Electronic Virtual Assistants for Improved Business Performance
Christian Graham (University of Maine, USA)
Business Science Reference • © 2021 • 300pp • H/C (ISBN: 9781799838418) • US $245.00

Transforming the Internet of Things for Next-Generation Smart Systems
Bhavya Alankar (Jamia Hamdard, India) Harleen Kaur (Hamdard University, India) and Ritu Chauhan (Amity University, India)
Engineering Science Reference • © 2021 • 173pp • H/C (ISBN: 9781799875413) • US $245.00

Handbook of Research on Machine Learning Techniques for Pattern Recognition and Information Security
Mohit Dua (National Institute of Technology, Kurukshetra, India) and Ankit Kumar Jain (National Institute of Technology, Kurukshetra, India)
Engineering Science Reference • © 2021 • 355pp • H/C (ISBN: 9781799832997) • US $295.00

Driving Innovation and Productivity Through Sustainable Automation
Ardavan Amini (EsseSystems, UK) Stephen Bushell (Bushell Investment Group, UK) and Arshad Mahmood (Birmingham City University, UK)
Engineering Science Reference • © 2021 • 275pp • H/C (ISBN: 9781799858799) • US $245.00

701 East Chocolate Avenue, Hershey, PA 17033, USA
Tel: 717-533-8845 x100 • Fax: 717-533-8661
E-Mail: cust@igi-global.com • www.igi-global.com

Table of Contents

Preface..xii

Chapter 1
Recent Trends in Deepfake Detection...1
  Kerenalli Sudarshana, GITAM School of Technology, Bengaluru, India
  Mylarareddy C., GITAM School of Technology, Bengaluru, India

Chapter 2
Text Mining Using Twitter Data...29
  Falak Bhardwaj, Manav Rachna International Institute of Research and Studies, India
  Pulkit Arora, Manav Rachna International Institute of Research and Studies, India
  Gaurav Agrawal, Manav Rachna International Institute of Research and Studies, India

Chapter 3
Analysis Report for Statistics in the Twitter Network 50
  Parvathi R., Vellore Institute of Technology, Chennai, India
  Yamani Sai Asish, Vellore Institute of Technology, Chennai, India
  Pattabiraman V., Vellore Institute of Technology, Chennai, India

Chapter 4
Chemical Named Entity Recognition Using Deep Learning Techniques: A Review............................59
  Hema R., Department of Computer Science, University of Madras, India
  Ajantha Devi, AP3 Solutions, India

Chapter 5
Mathematical Information Retrieval Trends and Techniques 74
  Pankaj Dadure, National Institute of Technology, Silchar, India
  Partha Pakray, National Institute of Technology, Silchar, India
  Sivaji Bandyopadhyay, National Institute of Technology, Silchar, India

Chapter 6
Language Processing and Python 93
  Belsini Glad Shiya V., Agurchand Manmull Jain College, India
  Sharmila K., VISTAS, India

Chapter 7
Creditworthiness Assessment Using Natural Language Processing 120
    Somya Goyal, Delhi Technological University, India
    Arti Saxena, Manav Rachna International Institute of Research and Studies, India

Chapter 8
NLP for Chatbot Application: Tools and Techniques Used for Chatbot Application, NLP
Techniques for Chatbot, Implementation 142
    Shyamala Devi Nithyanandam, VISTAS, India
    Sharmila Kasinathan, VISTAS, India
    Devi Radhakrishnan, VISTAS, India
    Jebathangam Jebapandian, VISTAS, India

Chapter 9
Significance of Natural Language Processing in Data Analysis Using Business Intelligence 169
    Jayashree Rajesh, School of Computing Sciences, VISTAS, India
    Priya Chitti Babu, School of Computing Sciences, VISTAS, India

Chapter 10
Deep NLP in the Healthcare Industry: Applied Machine Learning and Artificial Intelligence in
Rheumatoid Arthritis 189
    Krishnachalitha K. C., Department of Computer Science, VISTAS, India
    C. Priya, VISTAS, India

Chapter 11
Information Retrieval in Business Industry Using Blockchain Technology and Artificial
Intelligence 204
    Sheela K., Department of Computer Science, VISTAS, Chennai, India
    Priya C., Department of Computer Science, VISTAS, Chennai, India

Compilation of References 220

About the Contributors 235

Index 239

Detailed Table of Contents

Preface..xii

Chapter 1
Recent Trends in Deepfake Detection.. 1
Kerenalli Sudarshana, GITAM School of Technology, Bengaluru, India
Mylarareddy C., GITAM School of Technology, Bengaluru, India

Almost 59% of the world's population is on the internet, and in 2020, globally, there were more than 3.81 billion individual social network users. Eighty-six percent of the internet users were fooled to spread fake news. The advanced artificial intelligence (AI) algorithms can generate fake digital content that appears to be realistic. The generated content can deceive the users into believing it is real. These fabricated contents are termed deepfakes. The common category of deepfakes is video deepfakes. The deep learning techniques, such as auto-encoders and generative adversarial network (GAN), generate near realistic digital content. The content generated poses a serious threat to the multiple dimensions of human life and civil society. This chapter provides a comprehensive discussion on deepfake generation, detection techniques, deepfake generation tools, datasets, applications, and research trends.

Chapter 2
Text Mining Using Twitter Data... 29
Falak Bhardwaj, Manav Rachna International Institute of Research and Studies, India
Pulkit Arora, Manav Rachna International Institute of Research and Studies, India
Gaurav Agrawal, Manav Rachna International Institute of Research and Studies, India

The microblogging social networking service Twitter has been abuzz around the globe in the last decade. A number of allegations as well as exculpation of different types are being held against it. The list of pros and cons of social networks is huge. India on one hand had an abundance of internet access in last half of the decade. The growth of social media and its influence on people have affected the society in both good as well as in bad way. The following research was done in the month of September and October. The research was carried out on 13 lakh tweets approximately, collected over the course of a month from September to October providing insights about the different attributes of general tweets available on Twitter API for analysis. Insights include the hashtags, account mentions, sentiment, polarity, subject, and object of a tweet. The topics like Rhea Chakraborty and Sushant Singh Rajput, PM Narendra Modi's Birthday, IPL 2020 overshadowed the topics like COVID-19 and women's security.

Chapter 3
Analysis Report for Statistics in the Twitter Network 50
    Parvathi R., Vellore Institute of Technology, Chennai, India
    Yamani Sai Asish, Vellore Institute of Technology, Chennai, India
    Pattabiraman V., Vellore Institute of Technology, Chennai, India

Twitter is the most popular social networking service across the world. In Twitter, the messages are known as tweets. Tweets are mainly text-based posts that can be up to 140 characters long which can reach the author's subscribers. These subscribers are also known as followers. Such subscriptions form a direct connection. But these connections are not always symmetric. In this study, the authors have assumed that if two nodes are connected, then the tweet is propagated between them without any other conditions. But using sentiment analysis, the general opinion of people about various things can be figured. The Twitter data set analyzed includes almost 20k nodes and 33k edges, where the visualization is done with software called Gephi. Later a deep dive analysis is done by calculating some of the metrics such as degree centrality and closeness centrality for the obtained Twitter network. Using this analysis, it is easy to find the influencers in the Twitter network and also the various groups involved in the network.

Chapter 4
Chemical Named Entity Recognition Using Deep Learning Techniques: A Review 59
    Hema R., Department of Computer Science, University of Madras, India
    Ajantha Devi, AP3 Solutions, India

Chemical entities can be represented in different forms like chemical names, chemical formulae, and chemical structures. Because of the different classification frameworks for chemical names, the task of distinguishing proof or extraction of chemical elements with less ambiguous is considered a major test. Compound named entity recognition (NER) is the initial phase in any chemical-related data extraction strategy. The majority of the chemical NER is done utilizing dictionary-based, rule-based, and machine learning procedures. Recently, deep learning methods have evolved, and, in this chapter, the authors sketch out the various deep learning techniques applied for chemical NER. First, the authors introduced the fundamental concepts of chemical named entity recognition, the textual contents of chemical documents, and how these chemicals are represented in chemical literature. The chapter concludes with the strengths and weaknesses of the above methods and also the types of the chemical entities extracted.

Chapter 5
Mathematical Information Retrieval Trends and Techniques 74
    Pankaj Dadure, National Institute of Technology, Silchar, India
    Partha Pakray, National Institute of Technology, Silchar, India
    Sivaji Bandyopadhyay, National Institute of Technology, Silchar, India

Mathematical formulas are widely used to express ideas and fundamental principles of science, technology, engineering, and mathematics. The rapidly growing research in science and engineering leads to a generation of a huge number of scientific documents which contain both textual as well as mathematical terms. In a scientific document, the sense of mathematical formulae is conveyed through the context and the symbolic structure which follows the strong domain specific conventions. In contrast to textual information, developed mathematical information retrieval systems have demonstrated the unique and elite indexing and matching approaches which are beneficial to the retrieval of formulae and scientific term. This chapter discusses the recent advancement in formula-based search engines, various formula representation styles and indexing techniques, benefits of formula-based search engines in various future applications like plagiarism detection, math recommendation system, etc.

Chapter 6
Language Processing and Python 93
Belsini Glad Shiya V., Agurchand Manmull Jain College, India
Sharmila K., VISTAS, India

Natural language processing is the communication between the humans and the computers. It is the field of computer science which incorporates artificial intelligence and linguistics where machine learning algorithms are used to analyze and process the enormous variety of data. This chapter delivers the fundamental concepts of language processing in Python such as text and word operations. It also gives the details about the preference of Python language for language processing and its advantages. It specifies the basic concept of variables, list, operators, looping statements in Python and explains how it can be implemented in language processing. It also specifies how a structured program can be written using Python, categorizing and tagging of words, how an information can be extracted from a text, syntactic and semantic analysis, and NLP applications. It also concentrates some of the research applications where NLP is applied and the challenges of NLP processing in the real-time area of applications.

Chapter 7
Creditworthiness Assessment Using Natural Language Processing 120
Somya Goyal, Delhi Technological University, India
Arti Saxena, Manav Rachna International Institute of Research and Studies, India

NLP is a wide and quickly developing segment of today's new digital technology, which falls under the domain of artificial intelligence. Alternative approaches for qualifying and quantifying an individual's creditworthiness have emerged in recent years as a result of recent advancements in AI. Banks and creditors may use AI to rate potential borrowers' creditworthiness based on alternative data, such as social media messages and internet usage, such as which websites people visit and what they buy from e-commerce stores. These digital footprints may show whether or not an individual is able to repay their debts. In this chapter, how the approaches of NLP could offer financial solutions to unbanked communities is explored. This chapter includes the use of various machine learning algorithms and deep learning to find the most accurate credit score of a user. Since NLP is less intrusive than providing direct access to a person's entire contact list or a social media site, it is a more accessible way to measure risk while still having the potential to target a larger audience.

Chapter 8
NLP for Chatbot Application: Tools and Techniques Used for Chatbot Application, NLP
Techniques for Chatbot, Implementation 142
Shyamala Devi Nithyanandam, VISTAS, India
Sharmila Kasinathan, VISTAS, India
Devi Radhakrishnan, VISTAS, India
Jebathangam Jebapandian, VISTAS, India

The chatbot is one of the increasing number applications in the era of conversational series. It is a virtual application that can efficiently interact with any human being using the deep natural language processing skills. In NLP, for chatbot application, the various techniques needed for chatbot using NLTK tool are explained and implemented. The process of converting the text to numerical value is called text embedding. In NLTK tool, various text embedding tools are available such as TF-IDF vectorization and bag of words. Deep NLP is an efficient way to implement the chatbot. Thus the chatbot is implemented with sequence-to-sequence networks.

Chapter 9

Significance of Natural Language Processing in Data Analysis Using Business Intelligence 169
    Jayashree Rajesh, School of Computing Sciences, VISTAS, India
    Priya Chitti Babu, School of Computing Sciences, VISTAS, India

In the current machine-centric world, humans expect a lot from machines right from waking us up. We expect them to do activities like reminding us on traffic, tracking of appointments, etc. The smart devices we have with us are creating a constructive impact on our day-to-day lives. Many of us have not thought about the communication between ourselves and the devices we have and the language we use for communication. Natural language processing runs behind all these activities and is currently playing a vital role with respect to the communication with humans with the use of virtual assistants like Alexa, Siri, and search engines like Bing, Google, etc. This implies that we are talking with the machines as if they are human. The advanced natural language processing techniques have drastically modified the way to discover and interact with data. In the recent world, the same advanced techniques are primarily used in the data analysis using NLP in business intelligence tools. This chapter elaborates the significance of natural language processing in business intelligence.

Chapter 10

Deep NLP in the Healthcare Industry: Applied Machine Learning and Artificial Intelligence in Rheumatoid Arthritis 189
    Krishnachalitha K. C., Department of Computer Science, VISTAS, India
    C. Priya, VISTAS, India

A reliable provocative issue which impacts the joints by harming the body's tissue is called rheumatoid arthritis. The ID of rheumatoid arthritis by hand, particularly during its unanticipated turn of events or pre-expressive stages, requires an extraordinary construction analysis. The standard end technique for rheumatoid arthritis (RA) calls for the assessment of hands and feet radiographs. Still, for clinical experts, it winds up being an unconventional endeavor considering the way that regularly the right completion of the disease relies on the exposure of unfathomably subtle changes for the typical eye. In this work, the authors built a design using convolutional neural networks (CNN) and reinforcement learning technique for detecting RA from hand and wrist MRI. For this, they took 564 cases (real information) which provided a precision of 100%. Compared to the existing system, the system showed a high performance with very good results. This model is highly recommended to detect rheumatoid arthritis automatically without human intervention.

Chapter 11
Information Retrieval in Business Industry Using Blockchain Technology and Artificial
Intelligence..204
Sheela K., Department of Computer Science, VISTAS, Chennai, India
Priya C., Department of Computer Science, VISTAS, Chennai, India

Industry 5.0 promotes automation in an optimized way. Collaboration with blockchain technology and artificial intelligence helps to enrich Industry 5.0 with its quantifiers and qualifiers. In the business industry, information plays an iconic role. When we consider the issues of storage and retrieval, we need to think about blockchain technology where the data will be stored and shared in a secure way. Here, the data will be distributed across the network in an encrypted format; hence, the original data can be viewed only by the owner of the data. Blockchain stores the information in the form of blocks. Every block has three sections. The first section holds the hash value of the previous block, the second one holds the information to be stored in a block, and the third one holds the hash value of an upcoming block. It does not allow an intruder to hack or modify the data without user's knowledge as these blocks are interconnected on both the sides with their hashes. This synergy of technologies brings supremacy in the field of business industries which will be discussed in this chapter.

Compilation of References 220

About the Contributors 235

Index..239

Preface

To sustain and stay at the top of the market and give absolute comfort to consumers, industries are using different strategies and technologies. NLP is the technology that is penetrating widely in the market, irrespective of the industry and domains. It is extensively applied in businesses today and it is the buzz-word in every engineer's life. In short, NLP is everywhere. For instance, compiling and interpreting information provided by the service engineers (age of devices, parts replaced, fault description, etc.) could be a complex task for quality engineers as the text can be full of abbreviations, spelling mistakes and can range from verbose to abrupt in content length. NLP can effectively refine such data and provide appropriate information for quality engineers.

NLP can be implemented in all those areas where AI is applicable either by simplifying communication processes or by refining and analyzing information. Neural machine translation has improved the imitation of professional translations over the years of its advancement. When applied in neural machine translation, NLP helps educate neural machine networks. This can be used by industries to translate low impact content including emails, regulatory texts, and more. Such machine translation tools speed up communication with partners while enriching other business interactions. Major growth factors of the NLP market include the increase in smart device usage, growth in the adoption of cloud-based solutions and NLP-based applications to improve customer service, as well as the increase in technological investments in the healthcare industry.

This book will provide the latest research findings, ideas, and applications in the fields of interest which fall under the scope of Natural Language Processing and their applications, Computational Linguistics, Deep NLP, Web Analysis. and Sentiments Analysis for business and industry perspective.

CHALLENGES

Natural Language Processing (NLP) allows machines to "understand" natural human language. A combination of linguistics and computer science, NLP works to transform regular spoken or written language into something that can be processed by machines. Although NLP and its sister study, Natural Language Understanding (NLU) are constantly growing in huge leaps and bounds with their ability to compute words and text, human language is incredibly complex, fluid, and inconsistent and presents serious challenges that NLP is yet to completely overcome.

NLP is a powerful tool with huge benefits, but there are still a number of Natural Language Processing limitations and problems:

1. Contextual words and phrases and homonyms
2. Synonyms
3. Irony and sarcasm
4. Ambiguity
5. Errors in text or speech
6. Colloquialisms and slang
7. Domain-specific language
8. Low-resource languages
9. Lack of research and development

1. Contextual Words and Phrases and Homonyms

The same words and phrases can have different meanings according the context of a sentence and many words – especially in English – have the exact same pronunciation but totally different meanings.

For example:

*I **ran** to the store because we **ran** out of milk.*

*Can I **run** something past you real quick?*

These are easy for humans to understand because we read the context of the sentence and we understand all of the different definitions. And, while NLP language models may have learned all of the definitions, differentiating between them in context can present problems. Homonyms – two or more words that are pronounced the same but have different definitions – can be problematic for question answering and speech-to-text applications because they aren't written in text form.

2. Synonyms

Synonyms can lead to issues similar to a contextual understanding because we use many different words to express the same idea. Furthermore, some of these words may convey exactly the same meaning, while some may be levels of complexity (small, little, tiny, minute) and different people use synonyms to denote slightly different meanings within their personal vocabulary. So, for building NLP systems, it's important to include all of a word's possible meanings and all possible synonyms. Text analysis models may still occasionally make mistakes, but the more relevant training data they receive, the better they will be able to understand synonyms.

3. Irony and Sarcasm

Irony and sarcasm present problems for machine learning models because they generally use words and phrases that, strictly by definition, may be positive or negative, but actually connote the opposite. Models can be trained with certain cues that frequently accompany ironic or sarcastic phrases, like "yeah right," "whatever," etc., and word embeddings (where words that have the same meaning have a similar representation), but it's still a tricky process.

4. Ambiguity

Ambiguity in NLP refers to sentences and phrases that potentially have two or more possible interpretations.

- **Lexical ambiguity:** a word that could be used as a verb, noun, or adjective.
- **Semantic ambiguity:** the interpretation of a sentence in context. For example: *I saw the boy on the beach with my binoculars.* This could mean that I saw a boy through my binoculars or the boy had my binoculars with him
- **Syntactic ambiguity:** In the sentence above, this is what creates the confusion of meaning. The phrase *with my binoculars* could modify the verb, "saw," or the noun, "boy."

Even for humans this sentence alone is difficult to interpret without the context of surrounding text. POS (part of speech) tagging is one NLP solution that can help solve the problem, somewhat.

5. Errors in Text and Speech

Misspelled or misused words can create problems for text analysis. Autocorrect and grammar correction applications can handle common mistakes, but don't always understand the writer's intention. With spoken language, mispronunciations, different accents, stutters, etc., can be difficult for a machine to understand. However, as language databases grow and smart assistants are trained by their individual users, these issues can be minimized.

6. Colloquialisms and Slang

Informal phrases, expressions, idioms, and culture-specific lingo present a number of problems for NLP – especially for models intended for broad use. Because as formal language, colloquialisms may have no "dictionary definition" at all, and these expressions may even have different meanings in different geographic areas. Furthermore, cultural slang is constantly morphing and expanding, so new words pop up every day. This is where training and regularly updating custom models can be helpful, although it oftentimes requires quite a lot of data.

7. Domain-Specific Language

Different businesses and industries often use very different language. An NLP processing model needed for healthcare, for example, would be very different than one used to process legal documents. These days, however, there are a number of analysis tools trained for specific fields, but extremely niche industries may need to build or train their own models.

8. Low-Resource Languages

AI machine learning NLP applications have been largely built for the most common, widely used languages. And it's downright amazing at how accurate translation systems have become. However, many languages, especially those spoken by people with less access to technology often go overlooked and under processed. For example, by some estimations, (depending on language vs. dialect) there are over 3,000 languages in Africa, alone. There simply isn't very much data on many of these languages. However, new techniques, like multilingual transformers (using Google's BERT "Bidirectional Encoder Representations from Transformers") and multilingual sentence embeddings aim to identify and leverage universal similarities that exist between languages.

9. Lack of Research and Development

Machine learning requires A LOT of data to function to its outer limits – billions of pieces of training data. The more data NLP models are trained on, the smarter they become. That said, data (and human language!) is only growing by the day, as are new machine learning techniques and custom algorithms. All of the problems above will require more research and new techniques in order to improve on them. Advanced practices like artificial neural networks and deep learning allow a multitude of NLP techniques, algorithms, and models to work progressively, much like the human mind does. As they grow and strengthen, we may have solutions to some of these challenges in the near future. SaaS text analysis platforms, like MonkeyLearn, allow users to train their own machine learning NLP models, often in just a few steps, which can greatly ease many of the NLP processing limitations above. Trained to the specific language and needs of your business, MonkeyLearn's no-code tools offer huge NLP benefits to streamline customer service processes, find out what customers are saying about your brand on social media, and close the customer feedback loop.

SOLUTIONS

The Natural Language Processing solution empower the computer to manipulate the human language and generates text, obtains meaning, and make communications easier by using voice-enabled AI and conversational intelligence technologies.

Natural Language Processing Solutions using the integration of Machine Learning as a service, Deep Learning algorithms, and Computer Vision techniques. We help your business to integrate the AI-Driven NLP Services for Building AI Chatbot, Sentimental analysis, Entity Recognition, Intent Classification, Text Categorization, Extract data from PDF, Extract information using NLP, IoT development and more. Natural Language Processing Solutions are becoming an important entity for every kind of industry like Laws, Stocks and Finance, Healthcare, E-Commerce, Marketing and Advertising, Mobile Intelligence, Manufacturing and Telecommunications, etc.

Our Natural Language Processing Solutions can serve a wide range of needs. Our AI-Driven NLP Services include Machine Learning algorithms and deep learning techniques to analyze and understand the unstructured data in order to operate effectively.

ORGANIZATION OF THE BOOK

The book is organized into 11 chapters. A brief description of each of the chapters follows:

Chapter 1 provides a comprehensive discussion on deepfakes, its generation, detection techniques, deepfake generation tools, datasets, applications and research trends. The authors of this chapter discussed that AI algorithms can generate fake digital content that appears to be realistic. The generated content can deceive the users into believing it is real and discussed various methods to avoid.

Chapter 2 indicated the major concern of Internet literacy and social transparency related to various issues of mankind. The abundance of accessibility of the Internet in much less time has led the end user to get diverted more easily and vastly. Authors indicated the limitation of research work.

In Chapter 3, theoretical analysis of the twitter dataset using social network metrics like centrality measures like closeness, Eigen value centrality measures, etc. have been discussed. Authors have used gephi method to evaluate and used 20k nodes for analysis in less than 20 minutes. This proposed work shows the credibility of the users.

Chapter 4 reviews the various deep learning techniques applied for Chemical NER and introduced the fundamental concepts of chemical named entity recognition, the textual contents of chemical documents and how these chemicals are represented in chemical literature. The chapter concludes with the strengths and weaknesses of the above methods and also the types of the chemical entities extracted.

Chapter 5 discussed about the recent advancement in formula based search engines, various formula representation styles and indexing techniques, benefits of formulas based search engine in various future applications like plagiarism detection, math recommendation system, etc. Authors also highlighted the key challenges in developing a mathematical information retrieval system that enables access and searches for mathematical formulae in existing information systems. This chapter basically designed to confirm the assumption where the development of math-enabled digital libraries essentially blends both users' needs and technological opportunities.

Chapter 6 delivers the fundamental concepts of Language processing in Python such as text and word operations, preference of Python language for Language Processing and its advantages. Authors also presented how a structured program can be written using python, Categorizing and tagging of words, how an information can be extracted from a text, Syntactic and Semantic analysis and NLP applications. Authors also concentrates some of the research applications where NLP is applied and the challenges of NLP processing in the real time area of applications..

Chapter 7 explored how NLP/NLU could bring financial solutions to the unbanked populations through innovative approaches. NLP being fundamentally less invasive than requiring direct access to a person's full contact list or social media account represents a fairer way to assess risk with a capability to reach a broader audience..

Chapter 8 presented the implementation of the Chabot application using deep learning network. The authors contend that Chatbot is an instantaneous messaging account that in a position to provide the use of immediate messaging framework with the aim of providing an efficient service.

Chapter 9 shows that the Natural Language Processing Techniques has drastically modified the way to discover and interact with data. In the recent world, the same advanced techniques are primarily used in the data analysis using NLP in Business Intelligence tools. This chapter elaborates the significance of Natural Language processing in the field of Business Intelligence.

Chapter 10 built up a design using Convolution Neural Networks (CNN) and Reinforcement Learning Technique for detecting RA from hand and wrist MRI. Authors have used 564 cases which provided a precision of 100%. As compared to the existing system, the system showed a high performance with very good results. The author contends that the model is highly recommended to detect Rheumatoid arthritis automatically, without human intervention.

Chapter 11 explores how issues like sustainability, scalability, security, privacy, efficiency, proper utilization of hardware and so on can be handled properly while synergizing artificial intelligence with blockchain technology. Author also discussed how aggregating blockchain, AI with IoT and Big Data to be use and manage the information more efficiently for any business application.

Chapter 1
Recent Trends in Deepfake Detection

Kerenalli Sudarshana
iD https://orcid.org/0000-0001-9581-6835
GITAM School of Technology, Bengaluru, India

Mylarareddy C.
GITAM School of Technology, Bengaluru, India

ABSTRACT

Almost 59% of the world's population is on the internet, and in 2020, globally, there were more than 3.81 billion individual social network users. Eighty-six percent of the internet users were fooled to spread fake news. The advanced artificial intelligence (AI) algorithms can generate fake digital content that appears to be realistic. The generated content can deceive the users into believing it is real. These fabricated contents are termed deepfakes. The common category of deepfakes is video deepfakes. The deep learning techniques, such as auto-encoders and generative adversarial network (GAN), generate near realistic digital content. The content generated poses a serious threat to the multiple dimensions of human life and civil society. This chapter provides a comprehensive discussion on deepfake generation, detection techniques, deepfake generation tools, datasets, applications, and research trends.

INTRODUCTION

As of October 2020, around 4.66 Billion folks on the Internet accounts for Fifty-nine percent of the world population. Ninety-one percent of the total users accessed the Internet through smartphones (J. Clement, 2020). A Social Network platform is a computer-enabled virtual social environment that constitutes a network of people (Dollarhide, 2020). About 3.81 Billion individuals are on any one of the social networks (Dean, 2020). These platforms enable the members to generate information and share opinions, ideas, tags, and other types of social activities online (Kietzmann et al., 2011). The cyber flocks fooled almost Eighty-six percent of Internet users to spread fake news through the social media platform or publishing media platforms. (Center for International Governance Innovation (CIGI), 2019).

DOI: 10.4018/978-1-7998-7728-8.ch001

Deep learning algorithms solve various complex problems ranging from self-driving cars, online-games, big data analytics, natural language processing, computer vision, and computer-human interaction, to quote a few. One such area is deepfake content generation. Deepfakes are digital content generated by swapping the target person's information with the original to deceive the audience (Westerlund M., 2019). A sophisticated deep learning algorithm, commonly used for dimensional reduction in the computer vision domain, is used for deepfake generation. The auto-encoders (Badrinarayanan V. et al., 2017), GANs (Yang, W. et al., 2019) are commonly used to generate more realistic digital content to distinguish by the human sensory organs. Deepfakes not only capable of content swapping but also can generate novel content (Avatarify, 2020). Some software can create real-time deepfakes, and some require just a still image or just a few seconds of an audio bit to generate the deepfake.

The first deepfake was reported in 2017, where a Hollywood actress's face was swapped with a porn actress. The most famous deepfake video, which went viral, was released in Barack Obama's 2018 video (Bloomberg, 2018). Less powered hardware requirements, low learning curves, technology access to the public are a few reasons for the voluminous deepfake traffic on the Internet. Even the source of the generated content, sometimes, is going to be anonymous. After the 2016 US presidential elections, the detection of such manipulated content attracted academics. The data obtained from the https://app.dimensions.ai (dimensions, 2021) discloses the available information on deepfakes till to date. It is as given in table 1. There are totally 62 policy documents and one clinical trail on deepfakes.

*Table 1. Research trend on deepfakes (Source:*app.dimension.ai*)*

Sl. No	Year of Publication	No. of Published Papers	No. of Datasets	No of Patents Filed	No. of grants
1	Before 2018	04	--		
2	2018	65	1		
3	2019	368	2	118	18
4	2020	1299	5		
5	2021	447[1]	8		

The objectives of the proposed chapter are to:
- ◦ Provide a concise overview of deepfake technologies.
- ◦ Describe various methods employed for generating the deepfakes.
- ◦ Describe the key methodologies used to identify deepfakes.
- ◦ Enlist the deepfake generation software tools along with their salient features.
- ◦ Explore the datasets that were used to assess the deepfake detection techniques.
- ◦ The applications and research trends in deepfake technology.

BACKGROUND

Deepfakes are artificially generated digital media using deep learning methods, wherein the features of an individual in a source content are substituted by someone else (Dirik, 2020). The standard category of deepfakes is video deepfakes. They are often circulated on social media and the Internet. The trend

Figure 1. Publication trend on deepfake techniques (Source: https://app.dimensions.ai.)

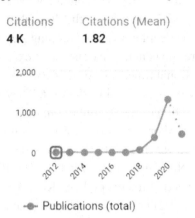

in research publications on deepfake technology according to the data is sourced from the https://app.dimensions.ai is shown in figure 1.

Detecting deepfakes has been a challenging and complex task in nature (Siarohin A. et al., 2020). Deepfake technology has both positive and negative applications (Paul K., 2020). The intention of the content creator is of utmost importance. If the intention is malicious, then the generated content is a serious threat to democracy, public harmony, financial markets, and individual safety, security, and reputation. If the intention is non-malicious, it is beneficial for health care, education, film making, and several other sectors.

Most of the existing models use face-swapping, facial enactments, lip-sync techniques for creating deepfakes. Advancements in the domain of deep learning techniques had inspired the commonly applied techniques. The first attempt was by a Reddit user, who developed FakeApp (Faceswap, 2017) tool using an auto-encoder-decoder architecture. VGGFace app was developed using the Encoder-Decoder architecture with an addition of adversarial and perceptual losses. To make consistent and realistic eye blinks, the VGGFace perceptual losses were added. This technique generated high-quality videos. To make more reliable and stable face alignments, Multi-task CNN architectures were used (Nguyen T. et al. 2020).

Deepfake detection problem is considered as a binary classification problem by many researchers (Lyu S., 2020). The deepfake detection methods are classified into two broad categories based on the *content type* such as - fake images and videos(Nguyen T. et al. 2020). *3D-based face-swapping methods* were the earlier detection attempts—machine learning-based automatic face swapping method used for detection of fake images (Zhang et al. 2017). The *bag of words* is fed into the classifiers- such as Support Vector Machines, Random forests, multi-layer perceptron (MLP), for authenticity verification. They achieved a detection accuracy of ninety-two percent. (Xuan, X. et al., 2019) A forensic algorithm developed to enhance the generalization capability.

A *hypothesis-based statistic framework* was used to detect the GAN-based deepfakes (Agarwal et al., 2019). A deep learning-based *two-phase approach* was used for deepfake image detection (Hsu. et al., 2020).

Methods used for the detection of fake videos are well understood by considering the *temporal features* across the frames or within a frame. A physiological signal, such as *frequent eye blinking*, was used (Li. Y. et al., 2018) to detect the deepfake videos. This technique provided a promising performance over state-of-the-art methods. The Intra frame and temporal inconsistencies involved in the video generation process (Guera et al., 2018) were used to detect the deepfake videos. The Spatio-temporal attributes of a video stream were used (Sabir et al., 2019) to detect the deepfake video.

The artifacts introduced during the deepfake video wrapping step (Li, Y. et al., 2019) were explored for the detection. The method requires no generation of negative examples for training the model. Which in turn saves both time and computational time. A Capsule network was proposed (Nguyen et al., 2019) to detect both forged image and video on CGI and PI data-set. They have deployed with an impressive early performance due to the introduction of the *dynamic routing protocol* and the *expectation maximization routing protocol*. These proposed protocols address the limitations of CNN.

Cells in the camera reproduce the varying voltage levels when a uniform light falls on them. The voltage variance is Photo Response Non-Uniformity (PRNU). The PRNU is a camera fingerprint. The PRNU analysis was proposed for detecting the deepfakes. (Koopman, M. et al., 2018).

Recently, Zhao et al.(Zhao et al., 2021) proposed a fine-grained classification approach for multi-attentional deepfake detection. Three basic elements of this architecture are: i.multiple spatial attention heads to direct the network's attention to various local parts; ii.textural function enhancement block to magnify subtle objects in shallow features; and iii.a cumulative low-level compositional and high-level feature vectors directed by attention maps. They further introduced a new local independence loss and an attention driven feature extraction approach to overcome the network's learning difficulties. Authors reported that their methodology outperformed current methods after thorough testing on different datasets.

Dynamic models- DPNet -for comprehensible and reliable deepfake detection was proposed by Loc. et al. It is a new human-centered strategy for detecting forgery in face pictures by employing adaptive models as visual interpretations. They built temporal logic requirements based on these dynamics on top of DPNet's prototypical architecture, ensuring the model's conformity with desirable temporal behaviours and thus providing trustworthiness for such crucial detection systems. DPNet outperformed rivals on previously unseen examples from datasets such as Google's DeepFakeDetection, DeeperForensics, and Celeb-DF, while also providing basic referential accounts of deepfake dynamics, according to extensive testing(Loc et al., 2021).

The majority of mainstream deep learning-based detection methods are not transferable or generalizable. In the work by Shahroz et al, a novel technique sought to build a simplified system for detecting various types of Deepfakes including contents generated using unknown methods (Shahroz et al., 2021). For exploring the spatial and temporal details in deepfakes, a special model training technique using Convolutional LSTM-based Residual Network (CLRNet) was used. The proposed CLRNet model demonstrated that it generalizes well toward high-quality deepfake in the wild images, achieving a detection accuracy of 93.86 percent, which is significantly outperforming current state-of-the-art security methods.

M2TR (Wang et al., 2021) was proposed with an aim of collecting subtle manipulation objects at various scales for Deepfake recognition using transformer models. A Multi-modal Multi-scale TRansformer (M2TR) detects local inconsistency at various spatial levels by using a multi-scale transformer on different size patches. To increase the detection results and the robustness of the proposed image compression process, M2TR uses a cross modality fusion module to merge frequency information with RGB features. These approaches necessitate large-scale databases for development and evaluation. Face swapping and facial reenactment techniques are used to build a high-quality SR-DF Deepfake data-set of 4,000 DeepFake videos.

The iCaps-Dfake approach was introduced(Khalil et al., 2021) to counter current methods' poor generalization. For applying a concurrent routing strategy, two feature extraction methods are combined with capsule neural networks (CapsNets): texture-dependent Local Binary Patterns (LBP) and Convolutional Neural Networks (CNN) based High-Resolution Network (HRNet). The proposed model was trained and tested on the DeepFakeDetectionChallenge-Preview (DFDC-P) dataset before being tested on Celeb-DF to see whether it could generalise. It was possible to obtain a 20.25 percent increase in the Area-Under-Curve (AUC) ranking over existing ones.

A *Convolutional neural network to the Vision Transformer architecture was applied* to detect the deepfakes, recently(Wodajo & Atnafu, 2021). In this architecture, the neural network component selects learnable characteristics. The Vision Transformer component takes these learnable characteristics as input for classifying an example using an attention process. The proposed model was trained using the DeepFake Detection Challenge Dataset (DFDC). Convolutional Vision Transformer had a 91.5 percent accuracy, a 0.91 AreaUC, and a 0.32 loss value.

DEEPFAKE GENERATION METHODS

Early in the 1990s, academic researchers and online interested groups began the work on deepfakes. It was later adopted by the industry. The first recording of Image manipulation dates back to the 19th century. During the 20th century digital revolution, more sophisticated technologies were employed in digital content manipulation-including images, videos, and audio. Following methods are commonly used to generate the deepfakes

1. Auto-Encoder Networks (AEN)
2. General Adversarial Networks (GAN)

Deepfake Generation Using Auto-Encoder Networks

Auto-encoder is an unsupervised learning method in artificial neural network technology for efficient encoding of the data. The main objective of the auto-encoder is to *acquire sufficiently enough features to represent the original data* by *reducing the dimensionality*. Also, it attempts to produce the output data from this reduced feature set which is as similar as the original input.

There are variants of the basic encoder network model, developed with the purpose of improved learning using the input features and reducing the losses. They are Regularized auto-encoders and Variational auto-encoders.

The Architecture of the Encoder Network Model

The auto-encoder, in its simple form shown in figure 2, there is a feed-forward, non-recurrent neural network. It has an input layer, an output layer, and hidden layers. Both the input and output layers have an identical number of neurons. It aids in unsupervised reconstructing the original data by reducing the dissimilarity among the original input and targets.

Figure 2. Architecture of an auto-encoder network (Source:www.wikipedia.org)

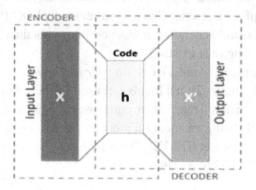

An auto-encoder has two components: the encoder transition function Φ and the decoder transition function Ψ.

Φ: *X F*

Ψ: *F X*

The auto-encoder tries to reduce the difference with respect to Φ and Ψ as in Eq 1.

$$\Phi, \Psi = \left(\left(| X - \Phi o \Psi X \right) | \right)^2 \tag{1}$$

In the basic architecture, at the time of encoding, x Σ R^d =X from the input set is mapped onto h Σ R^p =F of latent feature set, as in Eq 2, such that

$$h = \sigma(Wx + b) \tag{2}$$

Where h: latent variable, σ is an activation function, W is the weight matrix, and b is the bias error. The values for W and b are randomly initialized. Through the back propagation, these values are repetitively tuned.

During the decoding, auto-encoder maps h to the synthesized x' of the same shape as x such that as in Eq 3:

$$x' = \sigma'\left(W'h + b'\right) \tag{3}$$

Where h': latent variable, σ' is an activation function, W' is the weight matrix and b' is the bias error. These values may be different from their corresponding encoder counterparts.

The auto-encoders are trained such that the reconstruction error or loss is minimized(refer Eq 4).

$$L\left(x - x'\right) = \|x - x'\| = \left\| x - \sigma'\left(W'\sigma\left(Wx + b\right)\right) + b' \right\|^2 \tag{4}$$

Variations of Auto-encoders

There are several variations of auto-encoders that have a higher capability to

1. Capture useful information from the input set
2. Learn the richer representation of the input set

They are classified into two types:

1. *Regularized auto-encoders*: With the aim of reducing the sensitivity of the auto-encoder, the normalization or regularization is carried out. Three common types are:
   a. *Sparse auto-encoder*: They possess more number concealed units than inputs constrained that only a few are allowed to be active to improve the classification performance.
   b. *Denoising auto-encoders*: By changing criteria for the reconstruction, this kind of encoders aims to improve the representation.
   c. *Contractive auto-encoder*: An explicit regularizer is added to the objective function, which makes the learning model be more robust to minor disparities of input data.
2. *Variational auto-encoder (VAE)*: Variational auto-encoders (VAEs) belong to the category of generative models. These models assume that the distribution of the latent variables is strongly related to the input representation. To learn the latent representation, a variational approach is used by variational auto-encoder. When compared to the traditional regularized auto-encoders, variational auto-encoders map the distribution of the training data and the latent vector very closely.

Deepfake Creation Model Using Two Encoder-Decoder Pairs

Reddit users first attempted to create the deepfakes using the pairing of encoder-decoder architecture. The architecture (Nguyen T. et al., 2020) has encoder and decoder networks, as shown in figures 3 and 4. The latent face image features such as- eyes, nose, mouth, head positions- are extracted by the encoder network. The face images are recreated by the decoder network. The single shared encoder component is used to capture the common set of face landscapes from both source and target images. The proposed tactic enabled the shared encoder to discover and acquire the correspondence among two image sets.

Figure 3. Encoder-decoder pair for image reconstruction

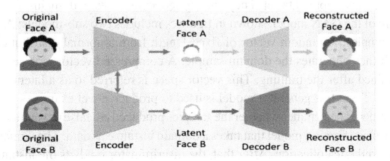

Figure 4. Two encoder-decoder pairs model for deepfake creation

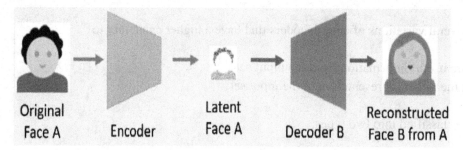

Original Face A   Encoder   Latent Face A   Decoder B   Reconstructed Face B from A

To carry out the face exchange between the original image and target image, two encoder-decoder pairs are used. Both the pairs use the shared encoder network. Figure 3 displays a model for the deepfake creation using two pairs of encoders and decoders. In this method, B's decoder is coupled with A's face feature set.

Advantages of Deep Encoders and Decoders

Deep encoders and decoders are better than single-layer encoder-decoders for the following reasons:

1. The computational cost of representing certain functions can be minimized exponentially by using depth of learning.
2. The amount of training data used to learn can be minimized by an order of magnitude.
3. Better approximations may be achieved with deep auto-encoders rather than shallow or linear auto-encoders.

Generative Adversarial Networks (GANs)

Ian Goodfellow first described the "Generative Adversarial Networks (GAN)" architecture in 2014 (Goodfellow I. et al. 2014). The more stabilized model and standardized approach were formalized by Alec Radford as deep convolutional generative adversarial networks (DCGAN) (Radford A. et al., 2015).

Generative Adversarial Networks (GANs) is a generative model that uses the deep learning method. Generative modeling is an unsupervised machine learning task in which the input data patterns are automatically recognized and learned to synthesize the novel output instances that could have been obtained from the original input data set. They are applied across several domains of machine learning.

The architecture of the GAN model, shown in figure 5, includes two sub-models: A *generator* model for creating new samples. A random vector of fixed-length from a normal distribution is input to the generator model. It then generates the domain sample. A compressed vector representation of the data distribution is obtained after the training. This vector space is referred to as a latent space that has the concealed variables. Then, this generator model is used to produce novel examples.

A discriminator model determines whether the samples produced are false or genuine. The discriminator model is a basic classification model that takes a domain instance as data. The domain's input may be from the actual or synthetic collection. After that, the discriminator predicts the instance's binary class label—fake or true. The discriminator model is then discarded once the training process is complete. In certain cases, the generator can also be used for discrimination since it efficiently derived features from the sample, which can then be used for discrimination. Using the same or similar input data, all of the feature extraction layers or some of them can be used in transfer learning applications.

Figure 5. Architecture of the GAN model

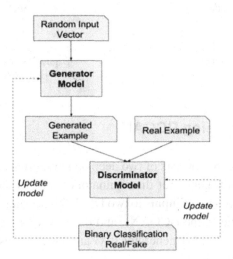

GANs: Two-Player Game

Simultaneous training of the generator and discriminator models is performed. The discriminator takes input samples from both the real and generator sets and categorises them as false or actual. This discrepancy is used to tune the discriminator in subsequent iterations, resulting in better results for distinguishing between true and false instances. Simultaneously, the generator is restructured by fine-tuning the relative parameters in order to produce samples that might fool the discriminator. In a zero-sum game (Brownlee, 2019), the two models battle with each other before the discriminator is deceived by the generator, i.e.,the instances are fabricated so that they resemble the inputs from the original image set as closely as possible.

Conditional GAN's

Additional criteria may be added to the GAN architecture to produce samples from a specific class of domain. The Conditional GANs was used to address problems such as text-to-image conversion and image-to-image translation (Mirza M et al. 2014). When using conditional GANs for image-to-image conversion, such as converting day to night, the discriminator is fed examples of actual and created night-time images, as well as (conditioned on) real daytime photos. A random vector from the latent space, as well as (conditioned on) actual daytime images, are fed into the generator. Any additional information, such as class label-{male, female} is fed into the generative model for training in order to produce new examples from the input domain. (See Figure 6.) The input is a vector. Similarly, the discriminator is conditioned by the inclusion of additional data.

Figure 6. Architecture of conditional GANs

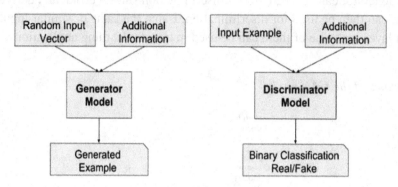

Generation of Deepfakes using DCGAN

A Cycle-GAN (Shen T. et al., 2018) consists of two deep convolutional generative adversarial networks (DCGAN)s having two pairs of the generator-discriminator couple, as shown in Figure 6. Two different sets of pictures, from X and Y, are sent as inputs to two DCGANs, during the training phase. An example $\{x| x \Sigma X\}$ is sent as input to one of the DCGANs, and the fake y' is generated, which is analogous to an example of domain Y. This GAN G1 generator is G and G(x) represents the samples produced by G(Eq.5). For G, the Y is the target domain.

$$G(x): GY \tag{5}$$

Similarly, for GAN G2, an example $\{y| y \Sigma Y\}$ sent as input, and the fake x' is generated, which is analogous to an example of domain X. The generator, F, generates the sample for G2 and is denoted as F(y). For G2, the target domain is X(Eq.6). The GAN G1 discriminator with generator G is denoted as D_Y, and the discriminator of the GAN G2 is denoted as D_X.

$$F(y): FX \tag{6}$$

Algorithm 1: Algorithm to train a cycle-GAN

```
Step 1:  learnRate ← learnRateinit
Step 2:  for e = 0 → E - 1 do
Step 3:      for i = 0 → N - 1 do
Step 4:          Calculate LG// calculate and back propagate LG
Step 5:          Back-propagate LG
Step 6:          Calculate LDX// calculate and back propagate LDX
Step 7:          Back-propagate LDX
Step 8:          Calculate LDY// calculate and back propagate LDY
Step 9:          Back-propagate LDY
Step 10:     end for
Step 11:     if e ≥ E0, then
```

```
Step 12:      learnRate ← learnRateinit *(1 - (e -E0)/ (E - E0))
Step 13:      end if
Step 14: end for
```

E represent the number of training epochs,

N represent the number of training mages, and

learnRateinit represents the initial learning rate, respectively.

During the training period of each epoch, the learning rate will start decreasing linearly until it equals zero in the last epoch.

Applications of GANs

The GANs are able to generate

1.   Realistic pictures that are visually indistinguishable by the naked eyes.
2.   Input images of high-resolution types.
3.   New and artistic images, sketches, painting, and translate pictures among the several domains.

Figure 7. Cycle-GAN architecture

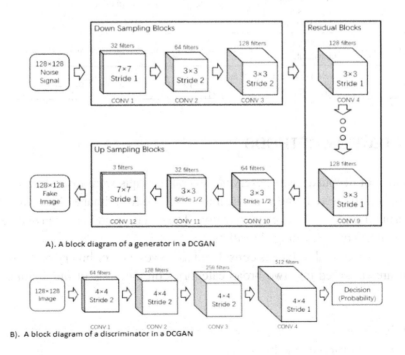

Summary of Notable Deepfake Software Tools

Popular deepfake software tools, features, and their respective links are given in table 2(Nguyen T. et al., 2020).

Table 2. Popular software tools for the creation of deepfakes

Sl#	Tool Name	Features	Links
1.	Faceswap	1. It uses two pairs of encoder-decoder. 2. Encoder Parameters are shared	https://github.com/deepfakes/faceswap
2.	Faceswap-GAN	1. To an auto-encoder architecture, Adversarial loss and perceptual loss are added.	https://github.com/shaoanlu/faceswap-GAN
3.	Few-Shot Face Translation GAN	1. To extract latent embedding pre-trained face recognition model is used.	https://github.com/shaoanlu/fewshot-face-translation-GAN
4.	DeepFaceLab	1. Supports several new models are 2. supports multiple face extraction modes	https://github.com/iperov/DeepFaceLab -
5.	DFaker	1. Face reconstructed using DSSIM loss function. 2. The keras-based library is used for Implementation.	https://github.com/dfaker/df -
6.	deepfakes_tf	1. Tensorflow based Implementation.	https://github.com/StromWine/deepfakes_tf
7.	Deepfakes web	1. Web-based commercial face-swapping application	https://deepfakesweb.com/ Commercial

DEEPFAKE DETECTION METHODS

As the potential threat of deepfakes was observed, several attempts were made towards their effective detection. The initial efforts were founded on attributes derived from image objects and the discrepancies introduced during the course of fake video fusion. The recent trend in deepfake detection includes automated detection using deep learning algorithms.

Detection of deepfakes as real or fake is considered as a two-class or binary problem. The deepfake detection methods are classified into two broad categories on the basis of the features that are used. They are:

1. Detection of *fake images*
    a) *3D-based face-swapping* methods.
    b) *Automatic face-swapping* methods
2. Detection of *fake videos*
    a) Temporal features across the frames

    b)   Visual artifacts within a frame
        i.   Shallow classifier
        ii.   Deep Classifier

Detection of Fake Images

In this section following fake image detection techniques are considered for discussion. They are

1.   *Automatic Face Swapping* method,
2.   Common Fake Feature Network (CFFN) method.

Automatic Face Swapping Method

Primarily proposed methods were aimed at confidentiality preserving and entertainment. In these techniques, the visual information from images is identified as key points, which are represented by the descriptor for capturing the local information. A clustering algorithm is applied to all the descriptors. The centroids of the cluster are composed as a codebook. Using these codebooks, every image could be compactly represented. This new feature is then fed into the linear or nonlinear machine-learning algorithm to predict genuineness.

     The pictorial representation of this approach is given in figure 7. The procedure for face swapping is given below:

1.   Consider the original image (a).
2.   Select the target image to be replaced(b);
3.   Extract the Landmarks of (a);
4.   Extract the Landmarks of (b);
5.   The aligned face of (b);
6.   The face region to be cropped from (e);
7.   A smoothed mask;
8.   Swapping result.

Figure 8. The procedure for face swapping using 3D features

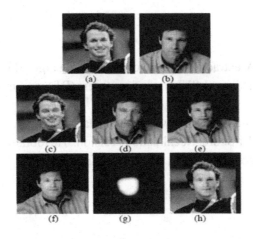

1. *Face Swapping*: Four steps are carried out during face-swapping. They are
    a. *Facial landmarks determination:* From each face, 83 landmarks are extracted. The area to be replaced is represented as the outer contour of the face.
    b. *Align:* Based on the thin-plate spline model, the two faces are aligned.
    c. *Color correction.* A smooth Gaussian filter is applied on the mask to generate realistic faces with identical skin-tone and lighting amid the two.
    d. *Blend*: Using the smoothed mask, blend the second face to the first one.
2. *Speed Up Robust Features (SURF) Detector:* For simplifying the learning process, feature vector SURF is used. The local descriptors are extracted either at pre-defined grids or by considering the interest points using Gaussian Smoothing.
3. *Bag of Words (BoW):* To represent an image in a compact and effective way, the BoW model is used. Using the codebook generation or the histogram representation, the bag of words model is generated. By applying the k-means approach, all SURF descriptors are selected to generate the codebook from the training data. To avoid the bias, the same quantity of face images are swapped between the fake and original image sets. It is illustrated in figure 8.

Let C be the set of clusters, X be the set of descriptors. The 'N' cluster centers are found by minimizing the 2D distance between the center and the rest of the points of the cluster. These N visual points are composed into a codebook. Then these N visual words are encoded into each query image.

Figure 9. The procedure for face swapping using 3D features

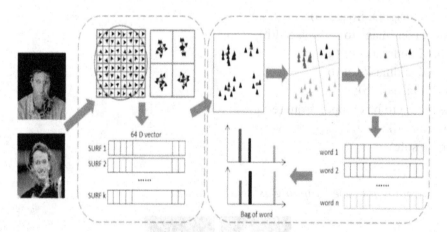

3. *Classifier:* After the BoW extraction, the machine learning algorithm is used for training - such as linear support vector machines (LSVM), random forest (RF), and multi-layer perceptron (MLP).

The performance of the trained classifier was evaluated against the Test set. The metrics used for the measurement were Accuracy, F1 Score, Recall, and Precision. The obtained Receiver Operator Characteristic (ROC) curve for the above classifiers is shown in figure 9.

Figure 10. Receiver Operator Characteristic (ROC) curve for various classifiers

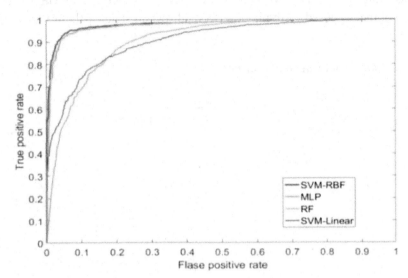

An Automated Two-Step Process for Detection of Face Manipulation: CFFN Method

An automated two-step- Feature extraction and classification- deep learning method for deepfakes image detection (Hsu, C. et al., 2020) is described below. The Siamese network architecture *common fake feature network (CFFN)* is used to extract the features. The CFFN includes several dense units. To increase the representativeness of the fake images, different numbers of dense blocks are included in each dense unit. Using the CFFN learning process, pairwise discriminative data are extracted between real and fake images. This constitutes the input for the second phase. To classify the given data, a small CNN is concatenated to the last convolutional layer of CFFN. The architecture is as shown in figure 10.

Figure 11. Architecture of CFFN Method

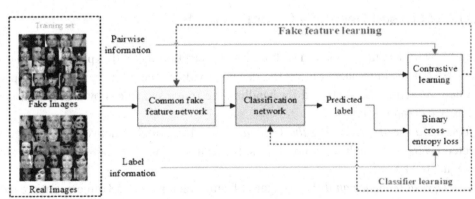

The pairwise learning approach allows the detection of GAN-generated fake images, too. The precision and recall rate of the proposed method outperformed several state-of-the-art techniques.

Figure 12. RoC curve for various deep classifiers

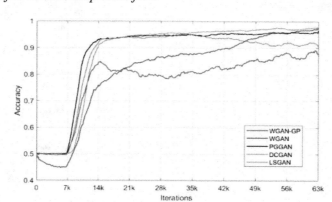

VIDEO DEEPFAKE DETECTION

Detection of deep videos is more challenging than the image since:

1.   The video compression results in the degraded frame data.
2.   The temporal features of the video differ from frame to frame.

In this section, two different video deepfake detection methods are discussed. They are:

1.   *Convolutional Neural Network (CNN) and Long short-term memory (LSTM)* method, which addresses the *temporal and intra-frame inconsistencies.*
2.   Deep classifier-based *Capsule network* that uses visual artifacts within video frame.

CNN and LSTM Based Deepfake Detection Method

The CNN and LSTM deepfake (Guera, D, et al., 2018) detection method exploit the intra-frame and temporal inconsistencies introduced during the deepfake video generation by the FakeApp tool. The proposed system, in figure 12, is created for handling the frame sequences by a convolutional LSTM scheme. It has two components:

Frame features are extracted using the CNN network: InceptionV3 network is adopted with the fully-connected layer. After the last pooling layers, the feature vectors of 2048-dimensions are used as an input to sequential LSTM.

LSTM for temporal sequence analysis: ImageNet feature vectors of 2048 dimensions are fed into the LSTM model during the training phase. With a dropout rate of 0.5, 512 fully connected layers are executed. The softmax layer is used to predict the authenticity of the frames by calculating their probabilities.

Given an image sequence, the convolutional LSTM is employed to produce a temporal sequence descriptor for image manipulation of the shot frame. For end-to-end learning, integration of fully-connected layers is used to map the high-dimensional LSTM descriptor to a final detection probability. This shallow network consists of two fully-connected layers and one dropout layer to minimize training over-fitting. The proposed model (Guera et al., 2018) outperformed the existing methods, i.e., a two seconds video, having 40 frames which were sampled at 24fps, accurately predicted- as fake or real- by the system with an accuracy of ninety-seven percent.

Figure 13. Architecture for convolutional LSTM scheme

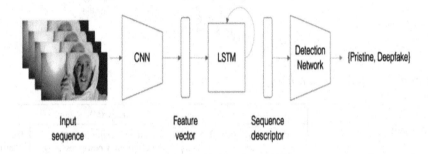

Deepfake Detection Using Visual Artifacts within a Video Frame: Capsule Network

The drawbacks of convolution neural networks for inverse graphics operations were addressed in 2011 (Hinton et al., 2011), paving the foundations for a more robust "capsule" architecture. Complex nature of capsule networks, however, could not be successfully implemented due to a lack of a suitable algorithm and the limitations of computer hardware at the time. As a result of the dynamic routing algorithm and the expectation maximization routing algorithm, capsule networks have been deployed with excellent results as a result of convolution neural networks, which are simple to design and train.

The Capsule Network (Nguyen T. et al., 2020) method finds the distinguishing visual features within single video frames. In the Capsule network method, statistical pooling is used to detect content manipulation. The capsule network model, shown in figure 13, is capable of detecting both video and image tampering.

Firstly, the face regions are detected and scaled to 128x128 size. They are then fed into the VGG-19 network to retrieve the latent features. The retrieved features are fed into the capsule network. It consists of five capsules: three primary and two output for fake and real classes. The Capsule network then detects the class of the video sample, either fake or real.

On the FaceForensics dataset, Deepfake dataset(Darius et al., 2018), Computer Generated Images (CGI), and Photographic Images (PI) datasets(Rahmouni et al., 2017), the accuracy of state-of-the-art facial reenactment(Darius et al., 2018), face swapping recognition(Darius et al., 2018) and generated image techniques(Nguyen, et al., 2018) is shown in the table below. According to the results, capsule forensics outpaced both content types - images and video.

Figure 14. Capsule network architecture

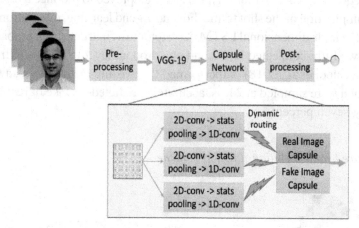

Table 3. Performance of capsule vs. others

Method	Accuracy (%)		
	Face swapping video detection	Facial reenactment detection(easy compression)	Discriminating CGI and PI.(full size)
Meso-4(Darius et al., 2018)	96.90	95.30	--
MesoInception-4(Darius et al., 2018)	98.40	95.30	--
Capsule-Forensics-Noise	**99.23**	**96.00**	**100**
Nguyen (Nguyen, et al., 2018)	--	--	99.72

AUDIO DEEPFAKE DETECTION

The biometric data- such as speech rate, voice frequency, amplitude, duration, and spectrum distribution- were used by traditional methods for detecting the spoofing audio. Currently, deep learning algorithms are applied to audio spoofing detection.

Figure 15. Architecture of self-supervised spoofing audio detection

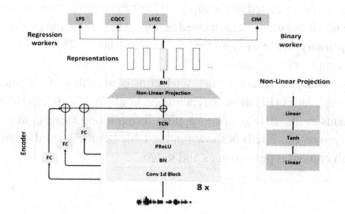

A self-supervised spoofing audio detection (SSAD) scheme is a deep learning-based algorithm used for audio spoofing detection. SSAD scheme (Jiang Z., 2020), as shown in figure 14, consists of a shared encoder and two workers (regression and binary) for meaningful and robust representation of the sample.

SSAD Encoder: The encoder consists of 3 types of small feed-forward neural networks- 8 convolutional blocks, a temporal convolutional network (TCN) layer, and a nonlinear projection layer. The eight convolutional blocks generate the waveform chunks from the raw input. Every block has one-dimensional convolution (Conv1d), followed by batch normalization (BN) and a multi-parametric rectified linear unit (PReLU) activation function. For improving gradient flows, a convolution sliding window with a 10ms shift is set. Also, the intermediate convolution layers *skipconn* are introduced to transfer different levels of abstractions to the final representations.

Workers: The front-end model output representation is fed into the Workers for regression or discrimination tasks. They are solved as self-supervised tasks by workers. The small feed-forward network workers' average error is then fed back to the encoder that tunes itself to discover better high-level representations with limited capacity. For spoof, audio detection following self-supervised tasks is used.

1. *Regression Tasks:* The *Libros* or a script used to predict the target features extracted. The objective of training the workers is to minimize the mean squared error (MSE) among the target and the network predictions. The regression workers considered in work were Log power spectrum (LPS), Log-frequency cepstral coefficients (LFCC), and Constant Q cepstral coefficients (CQCC).
2. *Binary Task:* For the controversial learning of high-level representations, a binary function framework is used. From the original random sample encoder d (·), extract the S_a and S_r representations. The S_f representation is extracted from a random speech of the other type. Later, the loss due to cross-entropy among the S_r, S_f, and S_a is computed to reduce the difference among the analogous speeches and maximize the dissimilarity among the two heterogeneous speeches.

Training SSAD: At the beginning, the workers' learning rate is set to 0.5×10^{-3} msec. Depending on a polynomial scheduler, it gradually reduces. To adjust the parameters, an average loss of all workers is fed back to the encoder. To get high transferability, the SSAD scheme is combined with different spoofing audio detection classifiers, as shown in Table 4.

Table 4. Equal Error Rate (EER (%)) for various spoofing detection methods on the ASV spoof 2019 data set

Method	Baseline	SENet12		LCNN-Small		LCNN-Big	
	Eval	Dev	Eval	Dev	Eval	Dev	Eval
LPS	-	0.04	9.27	0.09	9.76	0.12	6.82
LFCC	8.09	1.73	8.45				
CQCC	9.57	8.01	15.14				
SSAD	-	0.47	**6.55**	0.86	**7.16**	0.78	**5.31**

DATASETS FOR DEEPFAKE DETECTION

The deepfakes detection (DFD) (Dolhansky B. et al., 2020) datasets are commonly used as input for deepfake detection methods. They are helpful in evaluating performance and efficacy of the detection methods. They are categorized into three generations.

1.   First generation datasets (DFTIMIT, UADFV, FaceForensics++ DF)
2.   The second generation (Google DFD, CelebDF and the DFDC Preview Dataset).
3.   Third Generation datasets (DFDC, and DeeperForensics-1.0 (DF-1.0))

First-generation data sets: Characteristics of this generation datasets are:

1.   They typically have less visual content.
2.   They do not generally represent the content or contractual rights of the person's consent. Most of them are sourced from youtube.
3.   Models trained on these datasets typically fail to generalize the real Deepfake videos due to the small scale.
4.   Data Set Examples include: DFTIMIT, UADFV, FaceForensics++ DF.

Second generation: Characteristics of this generation datasets are:

1.   They generally cover between 1 and 10 thousand videos and 1 and 10 million frames,
2.   They have better perceptual quality videos versus the first-generation videos.
3.   They include the contents with use restrictions from consenting members.
4.   They do not contain a scalable amount of video content for generalizing the Deepfake detection.
5.   Data Set Examples include Google DFD, CelebDF, and the DFDC Preview Dataset.

Third generation: Characteristics of this generation datasets are:

1.   They represent the most recently added deepfakes datasets with higher resolutions and generated data.
2.   They cover tens of thousands of videos and tens of millions of frames.
3.   The trend is continuing in both datasets by the incentive paid actors.
4.   Examples include DeeperForensics-1.0 and the DFDC Dataset,

   Table 5 enlists the summary of the different data sets including right issues, agreed number of subjects, perturbations and benchmarks. Table 6 provides the more information on the data source(Dolhansky B. et al., 2020).

APPLICATIONS OF DEEPFAKES

Deepfake technology must be used with caution as it has both positive and negative use cases. It depends on the author's desire to use the technology.

Table 5. Quantitative comparison of various deepfake datasets

Data Set	Unclear Right	Agreeing subjects	Total Subjects	methods	No. of perturb.	No. of Benchmarks
DFTIMIT	No	0	43	2	-	4
FF++ DF	No	0	?	4	2	19
G-DFD	Yes	28	28	5	-	-
Celeb-DF	No	0	59	1	-	-
DF 1.0	No	100	100	1	7	5
DFDC	Yes	960	960	8	19	2116

Table 6. Deepfake data-set sources

Data Set	Data-set Sources	Unique Fake Videos	Total videos
DFTIMIT	https://www.idiap.ch/en/dataset/deepfaketimit	640	960
FF++ DF	https://github.com/ondyari/FaceForensics	4000	5000
G-DFD	https://ai.googleblog.com/2019/09/contributing-data-to-deepfake-detection.html	3000	3000
Celeb-DF	https://github.com/danmohaha/celeb-deepfakeforensics	5639	6229
DF 1.0	https://github.com/EndlessSora/DeeperForensics-1.0	1000	60000
DFDC	https://paperswithcode.com/dataset/dfdc	104500	128154

Positive Applications of Deepfakes

The deepfake technology has a range of positive applications in the realm of broadcasting, entertainment, accessibility, education, film making, criminal forensics, and artistic expression.

1. By applying the capabilities of deepfake technology advancements to edit and change video transcripts, massive amounts of money and time can be saved by the studios without reshooting. David Beckham's video was created to launch a petition to end malaria (Malaria Must Die, 2019).
2. Deepfakes can revolutionize individuals as an alternative to the costly VFX technology (Files I., Nov 2020) for generating high-quality videos.
3. Deepfake technology presents a dream solution for limited-budget small retailers for creating their own custom model. (Baron K., 2019)
4. The educator can use the deepfake technology to conduct training and classes in an innovative manner that engages the engaging trainee more than the traditional visual and media presentation. Chris Pidcock's project on "JFK Unsilenced project" [2]. (Kalmykov M., Nov 2019)
5. Without having the actual patient disease data, medical researchers could use the artificial data generated from deepfake technology for treatment (Jaiman A, 2020).
6. By creating *virtual trial rooms*, E-commerce industry retailers can offer real shopping experiences for online consumers (Jaiman A, 2020).
7. Deepfake technology-based AI tools can bring accessible solutions to all. Example: Microsoft's Seeing.ai and Google's Lookout and Canetroller applications (Jaiman A, 2020).

8. Deepfakes will take influencer marketing to another level. For example, a deepfake technology (Nilesh C., 2020) used by the Indian politician to reach out to multi-lingual voters during recent elections[3].
9. By reconstructing the crime scene, virtually more investigative insights could be obtained (Schwartz M., 2018)
10. Deepfakes are used to augment and improve the resolution of low-resolution images (Berthelot D. et al., 2020).

Harmful Uses of Deepfake Technology

The deepfakes have the power of driving the digital media domain that causes severe societal effects. They are listed as below:

1. Voice Phishing for identity theft: using AI deepfakes to trick individuals or companies into sending them money.
2. Damage to Individuals or Organizations:
    a. Exploitation: identity theft (Statt N. 2019), personal abuse (Mosley T., 2019), etc.
    b. Sabotage: Revenge pornography, reputational sabotage (Adrain J., et al. 2018) and psychological harm, etc.
3. Damage to Society (Danielle K, 2019).
    a. Misrepresentation of Democratic Dialog:
    b. Influence during the Elections
    c. Eroding faith in organizations
    d. Intensifying communal separations
    e. Destabilizing the community safety
    f. Diplomacy discouragement
    g. Threatening the national security
    h. Damaging the trust in Press

Responses from Social Media Platforms and Governments

Most of the fake news, including fake images, videos, and audio, are spread on the Internet, especially on social networks, more rapidly than traditional media. They should alarm the victims as soon as they find such content on their premises. But, to date, no such technology exists. To encounter the adverse effects of deepfakes technology, Social Media Platforms, Internet Forums, and Governments are responding in a progressive way. In this section, the responses from the various stakeholders are discussed.

Responses from Online Social Media Platforms

Social media platforms have to play a more crucial role in combating the detection and spread of deepfakes. Facebook, Twitter, Instagram, and other social media platforms need to collaborate to safeguard the right of every individual using their platforms. In that direction following actions were carried out (Paul K., 2020)

1. Twitter has created a deepfakes policy that labels and warns about fabricated data but does not always remove it.
2. Google said that it would remove any content that was technically manipulated or doctored.
3. TikTok issued a widespread ban on deceptive material.
4. Facebook clarified that media created by AI would be removed from their premise and that non-AI-generated content would be labeled as false.

Responses from the Governments

The digital divide among the citizens of different countries in the global scenario needed to be considered for responding to the issues of the deepfakes. In this respect, several governments have initiated their role in penalizing, prosecuting criminals under current cyber security laws. Some of the specific responses are listed below.

1. The Malicious Deepfake Prohibition Act was presented to the US Senate in 2018.
2. Deepfakes Accountability Act was introduced in the US House of Representatives in 2019.
3. In 2019 November, China stated its policy on Deepfakes on the respective website.
4. The United Kingdom, allowed to prosecute the deepfake content producers for harassment.
5. Security Establishment of Canada said to initiate appropriate action against anyone involved in the deepfake related crimes.

DEEPFAKES AND RESEARCH TRENDS

The phrase "Seeing is believing" in the digital era is hard to trust as it is difficult to even for the experts to distinguish between the real and forged content on the Internet. Most of the current research work on the deepfakes emphasize the limitations of the deepfake generation technologies. But, the gap between the deepfake generation and detection is broadening. In this tug-of-war, the researchers need to focus on the following aspects of deepfakes.

1. There is a need for more robust, scalable, and generalized deepfake detection models.
2. Current targets of the deepfakes are humans, but in the near future, the targets could be AI-enabled physical systems- such as self-driving cars—the design issues of such systems needed to be studied in detail.
3. Most of the detection models are unexplainable, and there is a need for explainable detection models for cyber forensics investigation.
4. Integration of the detection and filtering capabilities towards the social media platform end.
5. Encouraging the development of standard policies and adherence to them by companies, media houses, publishing houses, and governments to deal the deepfakes.
6. Watermarking or block chain based strategies integrating into generating tools, or platforms to trace the originality of the content.
7. A study on digital literacy campaigns to individual members of the platform could mitigate the spread of deepfakes.

8.   A study on understanding the intent of the deepfake creator and spreader could provide psychological insights in combating the fake information.

CONCLUSION

Almost fifty-nine percent of the world population is exposed to the Internet or online social media platforms. They virtually share the information, likes, tags, opinions, and so on. The deepfakes are the artificially generated digital contents both in audio and visual forms. Specifically, advanced deep learning methods such as deep encoders and generative networks are used to generate them. As soon as the threats of the deepfakes on the society and individual were observed, attempts were made to detect the deepfakes. Most of the existing methods use the inconsistencies introduced during the content generation as investigation material. The detailed and large quantity of realistic datasets is being progressed due to the contribution of the research community. As with any other technology, the deepfakes come with a bunch of positive applications for the well-being of humankind. The harmful applications of the deepfakes have the potential of causing the threat at both individual and community levels. The Internet forums, social media platforms, and governments are taking the necessary action to curb the harmful effects of the deepfakes. Digital literacy to social media and Internet users can play a major role to thwart the spread of fake content. Future research should aim towards the explainable nature of the detection strategies.

REFERENCES

Agarwal, S., & Varshney, L. R. (2019). *Limits of deepfake detection: A robust estimation viewpoint.* arXiv preprint: arXiv:1905.03493

Avatarify: Avatars for Zoom Skype and Other Video-Conferencing Apps. (2020). Available at: https://github.com/alievk/avatarify

Badrinarayanan, V., Kendall, A., & Cipolla, R. (2017). SegNet: A deep convolutional encoder-decoder architecture for image segmentation. *IEEE Transactions on Pattern Analysis and Machine Intelligence, 39*(12), 2481–2495. doi:10.1109/TPAMI.2016.2644615 PMID:28060704

Baron, K. (2019). *Digital Doubles: The Deepfake Tech Nourishing new wave Retail.* https://www.forbes.com/sites/katiebaron/2019/07/29/digital-doubles-the-deepfake-tech-nourishing-new-wave-retail/?sh=1e1f74654cc7

Berthelot, D., Milanfar, P., & Goodfellow, I. (2020). *Creating High Resolution Images with a Latent Adversarial Generator.* arXiv preprint:arXiv:2003.02365v1.

Bloomberg. (2018). *How faking videos became easy and why that's so scary.* https://fortune.com/2018/09/11/deep-fakes-obama-video/

Brownlee, J. (2019). *A Gentle Introduction to Generative Adversarial Networks (GANs).* https://machinelearningmastery.com/what-are-generative-adversarial-networks-gans/

Centre for International Governance Innovation (CIGI). (2019). *86 percent of internet users admit being duped by fake news: survey.* https://phys.org/news/2019-06-percent-internet-users-duped-fake.html

Christopher, N. (2020). *We've Just Seen the First Use of Deepfakes in an Indian Election Campaign.* https://www.vice.com/en/article/jgedjb/the-first-use-of-deepfakes-in-indian-election-by-bjp

Clement, J. (2020). *Global digital population as of October 2020.* https://www.statista.com/statistics/617136/digital-population worldwide/#:~:text=Almost%204.66%20billion%20people%20 were,percent%20of%20the%20global%20population

Darius, A., Vincent, N., Junichi, Y., & Isao, E. (2018). *MesoNet: a Compact Facial Video Forgery Detection Network.* IEEE. doi:10.1109/WIFS.2018.8630761

Dean, B. (2020). *Social Network Usage & Growth Statistics: How Many People Use Social Media in 2020.* https://backlinko.com/social-media-users#how-many-people-use-social-media

Citron & Chesney. (2019). Deep Fakes: A Looming Challenge for Privacy, Democracy, Democracy, and National Security. *California Law Review, 107,* 1753.

Dimensions. (2021). https://app.dimensions.ai/discover/data_set?search_mode=content&search_ text=deepfakes&search_type=kws&search_field=full_search

Dirik. (2020). *Why it's time to change the conversation around synthetic media.* https://venturebeat.com/2020/08/12/why-its-time-to-change-the-conversation-around-synthetic-media

Dolhansky, B., Bitton, J., Ben Pflaum, J. L., Howes, R., Wang, M., & Ferrer, C. C. (2020). *The deepfakes Detection Challenge (DFDC) Dataset.* arXiv preprint: arXiv:2006.07397v4.

Dollarhide. (2020). *Social Media Definition.* https://www.investopedia.com/terms/s/social-media.asp

Faceswap: Deepfakes software for all. (2017). https://github.com/deepfakes/faceswap

Files, I. (2020). *deep fakes: part-1 A-creative-perspective.* https://www.vfxvoice.com/deep-fakes-part-1-a-creative-perspective/

Goodfellow, I., Pouget-Abadie, J., Mirza, M., Xu, B., Warde-Farley, D., Ozair, S., Courville, A., & Bengio, Y. (2014). *Generative Adversarial Nets.* arXiv preprint:arXiv:1406.2661v1.

Guera, D., & Delp, E. J. (2018, Nov). Deepfake video detection using recurrent neural networks. In *15th IEEE International Conference on Advanced Video and Signal Based Surveillance (AVSS), Auckland, New Zealand* (pp. 1-6). IEEE. 10.1109/AVSS.2018.8639163

Hinton, G. E., Krizhevsky, A., & Wang, A. S. D. (2011). *Transforming auto-encoders* (Vol. 6791). Springer. doi:10.1007/978-3-642-21735-7_6

Hsu, C. C., Zhuang, Y. X., & Lee, C. Y. (2020). Deep fake image detection based on pairwise learning. *Applied Sciences (Basel, Switzerland), 10*(1), 370. doi:10.3390/app10010370

Jaiman, A. (2020). *Positive Use Cases of Deepfakes.* https://towardsdatascience.com/positive-use-cases-of-deepfakes-49f510056387

Jiang, Z., Zhu, H., Peng, L., Ding, W., & Ren, Y. (2020, October). Self-Supervised Spoofing Audio Detection Scheme. *Proc. Interspeech, 4223-4227*, 4223–4227. Advance online publication. doi:10.21437/Interspeech.2020-1760

Kalmykov, M. (2019). *Positive Applications for Deepfake Technology*. https://hackernoon.com/the-light-side-of-deepfakes-how-the-technology-can-be-used-for-good-4hr32pp

Khalil, S. S., Youssef, S. M., & Saleh, S. N. (2021). iCaps-Dfake: An Integrated Capsule-Based Model for Deepfake Image and Video Detection. *Future Internet, 13*(4), 93. doi:10.3390/fi13040093

Kietzmann, J. H., Hermkens, K., McCarthy, I. P., & Silvestre, B. S. (2011). Social media? Get serious! Understanding the functional building blocks of social media. *Business Horizons, 54*(3), 241–251. doi:10.1016/j.bushor.2011.01.005

Koopman, M., Rodriguez, A. M., & Geradts, Z. (2018, August). Detection of deepfake video manipulation. In *The 20th Irish Machine Vision and Image Processing Conference (IMVIP)*. Ulster University.

Li, Y., & Lyu, S. (2019). Exposing deepfake videos by detecting face warping artifacts. *Proceedings of the IEEE Conference on Computer Vision and Pattern Recognition Workshops*, 46-52.

Loc, T., Michael, T., Sirisha, R., & Yan, L. (2021). Interpretable and Trustworthy Deepfake Detection via Dynamic Prototypes. *Proceedings of the IEEE/CVF Winter Conference on Applications of Computer Vision (WACV), 1*(1), 1973-1983. https://openaccess.thecvf.com/content/WACV2021/papers/Trinh_Interpretable_and_Trustworthy_Deepfake_Detection_via_Dynamic_Prototypes_WACV_2021_paper.pdf

Lyu, S. (2020). Deepfake Detection: Current Challenges and Next Steps. *IEEE International Conference on Multimedia & Expo Workshops (ICMEW)*, 1-6. 10.1109/ICMEW46912.2020.9105991

Malaria Must Die. (2019). *David Beckham speaks nine languages to launch Malaria Must Die Voice Petition*. https://youtu.be/QiiSAvKJIHo

Mirza, M., & Osindero, S. (2014). *Conditional Generative Adversarial Nets*. arXiv preprint: arXiv:1411.1784v1.

Mosley, T. (2019). *Perfect Deepfake Tech Could Arrive Sooner Than Expected*. https://www.wbur.org/hereandnow/2019/10/02/deepfake-technology

Nguyen, H. H., Tieu, N.-D. T., Nguyen-Son, H.-Q., Junichi Yamagishi, V. N., & Echizen, I. (2018). Modular convolutional neural network for discriminating between computer-generated images and photographic images. *Proceedings of the 13th International Conference on Availability, Reliability and Security, 1*(1), 10. 10.1145/3230833.3230863

Nguyen, H. H., Yamagishi, J., & Echizen, I. (2019, May). Capsuleforensics: Using capsule networks to detect forged images and videos. *2019 IEEE International Conference on Acoustics, Speech and Signal Processing (ICASSP)*, 2307-2311. 10.1109/ICASSP.2019.8682602

Nguyen, Nguyen, Nguyen, Nguyen, & Nahavandi. (2020). *Deep Learning for Deepfakes Creation and Detection: A Survey*. arXiv preprint: arXiv:1909.11573v2.

Paul, K. (2020). *Twitter to label deepfakes and other deceptive media*. https://www.reuters.com/article/us-twitter-security-idUSKBN1ZY2OV

Radford, A., Metz, L., & Chintala, S. (2015). *Unsupervised representation learning with deep convolutional generative adversarial networks*. arXiv preprint:arXiv:1511.06434

Rahmouni, N., Nozick, V., Yamagishi, J., & Echizen, I. (2017). Distinguishing computer graphics from natural images using convolution neural networks. *2017 IEEE Workshop on Information Forensics and Security (WIFS)*, *1*(1), 1-6. 10.1109/WIFS.2017.8267647

Sabir, E., Cheng, J., Jaiswal, A., Abd Almageed, W., Masi, I., & Natarajan, P. (2019). *Recurrent convolutional strategies for face manipulation detection in videos*. arXiv preprint: arXiv:1905.00582v3.

Schwartz, M. (2018). *Who Killed the Kiev Protesters? A 3-D Model Holds the Clues*. https://www.nytimes.com/2018/05/30/magazine/ukraine-protest-video.html

Scott, A. J., & Gavin, J. (2018, April 11). Revenge pornography: The influence of perpetrator-victim sex, observer sex, and observer sexting experience on perceptions of seriousness and responsibility. *Journal of Criminal Psychology*, *8*(2), 162–182. doi:10.1108/JCP-05-2017-0024

Shahroz, T., Sangyup, L., & Simon, W. S. (2021). *One Detector to Rule Them All: Towards a General Deepfake Attack Detection Framework*. arXiv e-prints. https://ui.adsabs.harvard.edu/abs/2021arXiv210500187T

Shen, T., Liu, R., Bai, J., & Li, Z. (2018). *"Deep fakes" using Generative Adversarial Networks (GAN)*. http://noiselab.ucsd.edu/ECE228_2018/Reports/Report16.pdf

Siarohin, A., Lathuilière, S., Tulyakov, S., Ricci, E., & Sebe, N. (2020). *First Order Motion Model for Image Animation*. arXiv preprint: arXiv:2003.00196.

Statt, N. (2019). *Thieves are now using AI deepfakes to trick companies into sending them money*. https://www.theverge.com/2019/9/5/20851248/deepfakes-ai-fake-audio-phone-calls-thieves-trick-companies-stealing-money

Wang, J., Wu, Z., Chen, J., & Jian, G. Y. (2021). *M2TR: Multi-modal Multi-scale Transformers for Deepfake Detection*. CoRR, abs/2104.09770. https://arxiv.org/abs/2104.09770

Westerlund, M. (2019). The Emergence of Deepfake Technology: A Review. *Technology Innovation Management Review*, *9*(11), 39–52. doi:10.22215/timreview/1282

Wodajo, D., & Atnafu, S. (2021). *Deepfake Video Detection Using Convolutional Vision Transformer* (Vol. abs/2102.11126). CoRR. https://arxiv.org/abs/2102.11126

Xuan, X., Peng, B., Dong, J., & Wang, W. (2019). *On the generalization of GAN image forensics*. arXiv preprint: arXiv:1902.11153. doi:10.1007/978-3-030-31456-9_15

Yang, W., Hui, C., Chen, Z., Xue, J. H., & Liao, Q. (2019). FV-GAN: Finger vein representation using generative adversarial networks. *IEEE Transactions on Information Forensics and Security*, *14*(9), 2512–2524. doi:10.1109/TIFS.2019.2902819

Zhang, Y., Zheng, L., & Thing, V. L. (2017). Automated faceswapping and its detection. *2017 2nd IEEE International Conference on Signal and Image Processing*. 10.1109/SIPROCESS.2017.8124497

Zhao, H., Zhou, W., Chen, D., Wei, T., Zhang, W., & Yu, N. (2021). *Multi-attentional Deepfake Detection.* CoRR, abs/2103.02406(1). https://arxiv.org/abs/2103.02406

KEY TERMS AND DEFINITIONS

Artificial Intelligence: Artificial intelligence (AI) is the intelligence displayed by machines, unlike the natural intelligence displayed by humans and animals.

Auto Encoders: It is a set of recurrent neural network units. Each component automatically receives an element of the input sequence, collects, and propagates information.

Cyber Forensics: This is a sub-domain of forensic science, which tries to detect and investigate digital information used in solving cybercrimes.

Deep Learning: It is an artificial intelligence (AI) technique for decision making by mimicking the human brain function for pattern discovery and data processing.

Deepfakes: Deepfakes are artificial media in which an individual in a source picture or video is substituted by someone else by using the deep learning methods.

Fake News: It is a false or misleading news presented to deceive the recipient.

Generative Adversarial Networks (GAN): They are the generative models using unsupervised learning task to automatically discover and learn patterns in input data to generate or output new examples that look like original.

Multimedia Content: It is an information containing more than one form of data including- text, audio, image, animation, or video- in a single presentation.

Voice Phishing: A telephone-based phishing attack to access the personal or financial data using social engineering.

ENDNOTES

[1]   Information obtained from app.dimensions.ai as on 11th May 2021.

[2]   https://youtu.be/wZF59wIIBLI of JF Kennedy Speech.

[3]   https://youtu.be/88GUbuL89bQ.

Chapter 2
Text Mining Using Twitter Data

Falak Bhardwaj
Manav Rachna International Institute of Research and Studies, India

Pulkit Arora
Manav Rachna International Institute of Research and Studies, India

Gaurav Agrawal
Manav Rachna International Institute of Research and Studies, India

ABSTRACT

The microblogging social networking service Twitter has been abuzz around the globe in the last decade. A number of allegations as well as exculpation of different types are being held against it. The list of pros and cons of social networks is huge. India on one hand had an abundance of internet access in last half of the decade. The growth of social media and its influence on people have affected the society in both good as well as in bad way. The following research was done in the month of September and October. The research was carried out on 13 lakh tweets approximately, collected over the course of a month from September to October providing insights about the different attributes of general tweets available on Twitter API for analysis. Insights include the hashtags, account mentions, sentiment, polarity, subject, and object of a tweet. The topics like Rhea Chakraborty and Sushant Singh Rajput, PM Narendra Modi's Birthday, IPL 2020 overshadowed the topics like COVID-19 and women's security.

INTRODUCTION

Twitter is a social networking service used for microblogging by more than 321 million active users with monetizable active accounts, worldwide. United States having the most, 68.7 million users and India being the third highest number of users at 18.9 million active accounts. Since its launch in 2006, twitter has been the source of information as well as misinformation. A large part of the microblogging service is used for news and announcements while in recent times a larger part of it is used to spread misinformation, fake news and to run a particular propaganda. Hence, it has affected major sectors like economy and politics, globally. In India, since the introduction of certain telecom providers in 2016,

DOI: 10.4018/978-1-7998-7728-8.ch002

the internet accessibility doubled up, which led to the exposure of the public to the internet. The sudden change and the digitalization escaped internet literacy. The abundant accessibility of the internet provided the end user with all types of information and data. Government bodies use twitter to provide important updates related to anything and everything while different bodies use it to provide users with different services. Celebrities and personalities use it to interact with their people. The significant use of the microblogging service is, it lets users share their views related to any social, economic, political or any other demographic topic with other people. The rapid increase in the usage of social networking websites provides an insight into many research challenges related to data mining and gained knowledge. Traditionally, the internet was comprehended as an information corpus, where users are passive. Social networking sites paved the way where users can create, publish and share intellectual contents online. It enhances the community strength and reach as people interact over a particular view related to a particular topic. It may lead to agreement or disagreement; in any case it ends up in interaction among people. As certain as it is that it leads to agreement and community strength, disagreement leads to riots and political imbalance. The internet literacy rate is almost proportional to the rate of increase of internet users in India. Social media has affected the youth as well as the elder generation of this time. The unemployment rate has led the youth to spend more time on social media. The hate speech content gets shared widely so easily due to a sole reason of communalism and fake news. The content once shared on social media cannot be retrieved back as the reach of such content is so wide and fast. In India, in recent times, there are more than 100 cases of riots and mob lynching registered due to social media and fake reports being generated over them. While the misinformation led to riots on ground level, the news media was involved in some cases. The misleading facts and the act of misleading is creating havoc among the people who are consumers of such media content. In the months of September and October the COVID-19 cases surged and the need to look over the situation was high. But, the topics of the conversation around the media do not look even around healthcare. Among social media, Twitter recently attracted researchers due to its sudden growth. The objective of sentiment analysis is to identify and extract sentiments from user-generated content. There has been a progressive shift in the area from review websites to micro blogs. Twitter sentiment analysis in itself is challenging due to its unique features such as the length of the tweet which is limited to 240 characters. Hence, the research was carried out using the Twitter API to extract real-time data available for free access for analysis at academic level. Then, the extracted data was analyzed and only the required fields and attributes were saved and later analyzed based on the attributes and requirements. This chapter focuses on the short sentences and entity level sentiment analysis and classifies the streamed tweets into positive, neutral and negative tweets using standard classifier. There are many challenges in Sentiment Analysis. Firstly, an opinion word which is considered to be positive in one state may be considered negative in a different situation. Second one, people may not always express opinions in a similar manner, e.g.: "the picture was a great one" differs completely from "the picture was not so great". The Opinions of people may be contradictory in their statements. It is more difficult for a machine to analyze. Most of the time people find it difficult to understand what others mean within a short sentence of text because it lacks context. Sentiment analysis is done on three levels:

1. Document Level: Analysis is done on the whole document and then expresses whether the document has positive or negative sentiment.
2. Sentence level: It is related to finding sentiment polarity from short sentences. Sentence level is merely close to subjectivity classification.

3.   Entity /Aspect Level sentiment analysis performs augmented analysis.

The aim is to find sentiment on entities or aspects. E.g.: consider the statement "My Samsung S5 phone's picture quality is good but its phone storage capacity is low". Samsung camera and the quality of display has positive sentiment but phone's storage memory sentiment is negative.

SENTIMENT ANALYSIS ON TWITTER

Over the past few years, an interesting and popular research area emerging lately is sentiment analysis. The opinions that are held by any numbers of individuals are reviewed and analyzed using sentiment analysis. These reviews can be related to an event, brand, person or product. Earlier, magazines, newspapers and other sources were used to express people's views. However, with the advancement in technology the people have begun to express their feelings on different social networking and microblogging sites. In a productive manner, the opinions of individuals have been extracted, studied and then evaluated by researchers. Twitter has gained the highest popularity in comparison to all other microblogging platforms in the past few years. It can be considered as a valid indicator for the sentiments of people. Different ways have been developed by several media organizations to mine the twitter information

- Conduct training, testing and analysis, the tweets are collected using API.
- Topics: On any imaginable topic the messages are posted by the Twitter users. This is different from other microblogging sites in which only a particular topic and purpose is discussed.
- Real time: Since the blogs are longer and a huge amount of time needs to be invested, these blogs are updated at longer time intervals.

Sentiment analysis research has focused on microblogs, in particular on Twitter. Because Twitter is short text (240 characters), the term occurrence is insufficient to classify the tweet polarity (positive/negative/neutral). Therefore, the clues are extended by considering tweet contexts and Twitter writing style. classification of tweet polarities by focusing on the syntactic relationships to the target query. However, the Twitter parsing accuracy is not very high and extended sentiment expressions based on the term co-occurrence in a specific domain with the seed sentiment expressions. Here, we also extended sentiment Twitter-oriented clues including hashtags.

DATA EXTRACTION

Data extraction is the process of retrieving data from data sources for further data processing or storage. Data extraction is perhaps the most important part of the Extract/Translate/Load (ETL) process because it inherently includes the decision making on which data is most valuable for achieving the goal driving the overall ETL. (Figure 1)

Figure 1. Data extraction

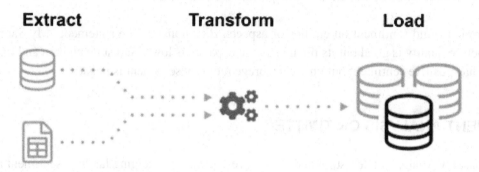

TYPES OF DATA EXTRACTIONS

Extraction jobs may be scheduled, or analysts may extract data on demand as dictated by business needs and analysis goals. Data can be extracted in three primary ways:

1.   Update Notification

The easiest way to extract data from a source system is to have that system issue a notification when a record has been changed. Most databases provide a mechanism for this so that they can support database replication (change data capture or binary logs), and many SaaS applications provide webhooks, which offer conceptually similar functionality.

2.   Incremental Extraction

Some data sources are unable to provide notification that an update has occurred, but they are able to identify which records have been modified and provide an extract of those records. During subsequent ETL steps, the data extraction code needs to identify and propagate changes. One drawback of incremental extraction is that it may not be able to detect deleted records in source data, because there's no way to see a record that's no longer there.

3.   Full Extraction

The first time you replicate any source you have to do a full extraction, and some data sources have no way to identify data that has been changed, so reloading a whole table may be the only way to get data from that source. Because full extraction involves high data transfer volumes, which can put a load on the network, it's not the best option if you can avoid it.

API-Specific Extraction

The extraction process for SaaS products relies on each platform's application programming interface (API) (Figure 2). Working with APIs can be challenging:

1.   APIs are different for every application.
2.   Many APIs are not well documented. Even APIs from reputable, developer-friendly companies sometimes have poor documentation.
3.   APIs change over time. For example, Facebook's "move fast and break things" approach means the company frequently updates its reporting APIs and Facebook doesn't always notify API users in advance. (PPC Hero, n.d.)

Figure 2. API Approach for data extraction

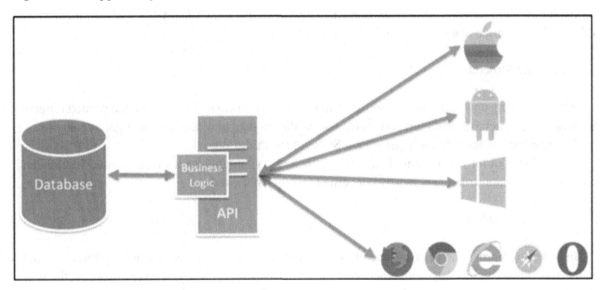

DATA CLEANING

Data cleaning means the process of identifying incorrect, incomplete, inaccurate, irrelevant or missing parts of data and their subsequent modification, replacement or deletion as required. Data cleaning is considered an essential element of basic data science. This data is usually not necessary or useful for data analysis because it can hinder the process or provide inaccurate results. There are several methods of cleaning up data, depending on how they are stored along with the answers you are looking for. Data cleansing is not just about deleting information to make room for new data, but rather about finding a way to maximize the accuracy of a dataset without necessarily deleting information.

Data Cleaning Methods

1.   Removal of Unwanted Observations

Since one of the primary goals of data cleansing is to ensure that the dataset is free of unwanted observations, this is categorized as the first step in data cleansing. Unwanted observations in a dataset are of 2 types, namely; the duplicates and irrelevances.

2.   Duplicate Observations

A data is said to be a duplicate if it is repeated in a dataset, with it having more than one occurrence. This usually arises when the dataset is created as a result of combining data from two or more sources. This can also occur in some other cases, including when a respondent makes more than one submission to a survey or error during data entry.

3.   Irrelevant Observations

Irrelevant observations are those that don't actually fit the specific problem that you're trying to solve. Like having the price when you are only dealing with quantity.

4.   Fix Data Structure

After removing unwanted observations, the next thing to do is to make sure that the wanted observations are well-structured. Structural errors may occur during data transfer due to a slight human mistake or incompetency of the data entry personnel. Some of the things one
should look out for when fixing data structure include; typographical errors, grammatical blunders, and so on. The data structure is mostly concerned with categorical data.

5.   Filter-Out Outliers

In order to improve the performance of your model, you should remove outliers. Outliers are data points that differ significantly from other observations in a data set. Outliers are very tricky, in the sense that they are of the same type with other observations, making them look wanted but hugely different from the others. Outliers may give more insight into your model the way the other observations can't. Hence, you should be careful when removing outliers from your data.

6.   Handle Missing Data

You may end up with missing values in your data due to errors during data collection or non response-bias from respondents. You can avoid this by adding data validation to your survey.
There are 2 common ways of handling missing data, which are;
entirely removing the observations from the data set and imputing a new value based on other observations.

7.   Drop Missing Values

By dropping missing values, you drop information that may assist you in making better conclusions on the subject of study. It may deny you the opportunity of benefiting from the possible insights that can be gotten from the fact that a particular value is missing.

8.   Impute Missing Values

If data is missing, you should always indicate it in your dataset. You can indicate missing values by simply creating a Missing category if the data is categorical, or flagging and filling with 0 if it is numerical. The whole process can be analyzed in Figure 3. (AiB Book, n.d.)

Figure 3. Data cleaning cycle

Data Transformation

Data transformation is the process of changing data from one particular format or arrangement to another one. Every social media generates a good amount of data on a daily basis, but the same is not useful until it is transformed into a specific and easy-to-read format. With data transformation, you can make different pieces of data compatible with one another, move them to another system, and join with other data to drive meaningful insights and for further analysis.

Quality Assessment

Data quality assessment is the process of scientific and statistical evaluation of data to determine whether they meet the required quality for projects or business processes and whether they are of the right type and quantity to actually support their intended use. In order to maintain the quality standard of the selected studies a careful consideration had been affirmed by taking the novelty of the technique proposed and the technical content (data set and evaluation methods used). The quality check had already been ensured as we had only considered selective high quality, high impact journals from reputed digital libraries.

LITERATURE SURVEY

Twitter data is a popular choice for text analysis tasks because of the limited number of characters allowed and the global use of Twitter to express opinions on different issues among people of all ages, races, cultures, genders, etc. In this chapter, we analyzed a Twitter network for sentiment detection and analysis. We detected the sentiments from tweets and their replies and formed an emotion network based on texts posted by users. From the emotion network, we detected influential people for both positive and negative emotions. Afterwards, we showed how influential people in an emotion network contribute to changes in emotion in the overall network. Finally, we computed a trust network based on emotion similarities and influences by generating recommendations. For example a sample tweet and various types of replies to the tweet. The author of the tweet expressed his surprise on an issue and some people replied agreeing to it like the second and third replies. Some people disagreed with the tweet and showed disgust or anger like the fourth reply. Some replies like t tried to answer to the tweet with logic and some other replies expressed no particular emotions at all. As no existing twitter datasets were found consisting of both tweets and their replies, we collected text from tweets and replies on specific recent topics to create our customized dataset. We collected both text-based and user-based data for our dataset. After passing them through a few preprocessing and cleaning phases, we generated a structured dataset. We annotated our text according to their emotions and sentiments. The annotated datasets were then used for emotions and sentiments using the textblob library in python. Text-based parameters were then merged with user-based parameters to detect influential users of emotion and sentiment networks. Researchers have been using the Twitter network for various calculations and analysis for a long time. Emotions and sentiments of tweets, influential user detection (using retweets, posts, favorites, etc.), recommendation generation (based on Twitter posts) and user influence have been experimented by different researchers who have applied various methods. In this paper, we introduced some new ideas and incorporated them with existing ones. Inclusion of replies to tweets and reply-based parameters are the major novelties of this paper. We have included emotion and sentiment expressed in replies and also considered the agreement score (i.e., if the reply agreed with the original tweet or not), sentiment score (i.e., if the reply sentiment was same as the original tweet sentiment or not) and emotion score (i.e., if the reply emotion was similar to the original tweet emotion or not).

Although the research is totally a different approach from presently available research, there are some literatures that influenced the following search. (Sharma & Moh, 2016) predicted the results of 2016 general state elections by collecting approximately 42k tweets, all in Hindi language and used several machine learning algorithms like Naïve Bayes and SVM for prediction by calculating the sentiment of the tweets by the users. All other researchers tend to follow a particular hashtag or a person and account or a particular topic. This research analyzes the general data on a daily basis to observe the different topics, people or hashtags being trending for the period of one month.

PROCESS

The process flow of the research is stated directly in Figure 4.

The research was initially divided into 5 processes:

Figure 4. The process flow of the research

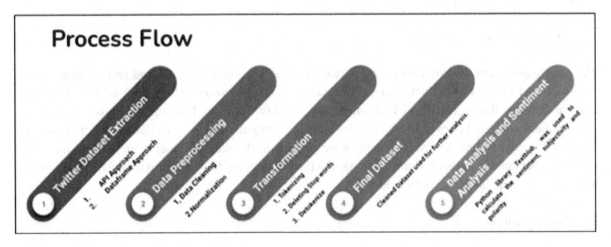

Twitter Dataset Extraction

1. API Approach

Initially, the data was stored in the Twitter database. In order to access the certain database and data, Twitter API was used which connects our machine to the database directly through a certain access token and key. (Figure 5).

Figure 5. Code for Twitter authorization

```
auth = tweepy.auth.OAuthHandler(
auth.set_access_token()
api = tweepy.API(auth, wait_on_rate_limit=

places = api.geo_search(query="india", granularity="country")
place_id = places[0].id
```

2. Data Frame Approach

Once the connection is established between the machine and the database, the statements in Figure 6, tend to save the requested then received data from the database in the .csv file (comma separated file).

Figure 6. Dataframe building

```
csvFile = open('twitterdatabase.csv', 'a', encoding='utf-8', newline='')

for tweet in tweepy.Cursor(api.search, q='corona', lang = 'en', since='2020-10-01', until='2020-10-07', count = 1
    data = tweet.json
    if 'retweeted_status' not in data.text:
        row = [tweet.id_str, tweet.created_at, tweet.source, tweet.text, tweet.user.screen_name, tweet.lang, tweet.favorite_count, t
        csvWriter.writerow(row)
        print(tweet.created_at, tweet.text)
```

Data Preprocessing

1.   Data Cleaning

The data requirement was high for a long period of time. Real-time was accessed and extracted using the Twitter API library of Python, tweepy (Roesslein, 2020). The initial extraction was carried out on a daily basis to get data in real-time. The dataset contained tweets from different locations of India. The initial dataset consisted of over 15 lakh entries including irregular and missing data, most of them were retweets. Certain tweets of advertisements were present in the dataset which were then removed by observing the authors of them. Upon cleaning, the final dataset contained approximately 13 lakh tweets with each attribute having a certain value.

2.   Normalization

The data collected was then normalized due to presence of multiple or missing values to reduce the error in the result and analysis.

Transformation

For analytical purposes, it is required to extract information from each and every tweet as per the requirements. Initially, the text of a tweet extracted consisted of different attributes as well as unnecessary elements. The useful attributes in a tweet for this research were mentions, favorite count, hashtags, date and time of the tweet, the original author, length of the tweet. Favorite count, date and time, author, were recorded directly during extraction and other attributes were extracted using python library ttp. Regular Expression library, re, was used to clean the original text of a tweet in order to get the clean text out of it. Natural Language Processing Kit (NLTK), was used to clean the text of a tweet by removing punctuations, stop words and tokenization for the purpose of further analysis. Python library Textblob, was used to calculate the sentiment, subjectivity and polarity of a tweet text that was tokenized using NLTK.

1.   **Tokenizing:** Tokenizing refers to the breaking up of a string or a sentence or a sequence of string into parts of words, lines or sentences and converting them into an array as per the requirements.
2.   **Stop Words:** Stop words can be defined as the words that need to be filtered out before the Natural Language Processing as they do not add such meaning to a sentence. They can be filtered out using the inbuilt set of stop words in the NLTK-Toolkit.
3.   **Detokenize:** Detokenize is converting the tokenized array of words into a sentence after removing Stop words and other irregularities from the sentence.

INITIAL DATASET

Figure 7, shows a sample dataset of a week's data extraction containing some basic attributes like id, created_at, source, original_text, author, favorite_count, place. The analysis ahead and the results are based on the same data for next three weeks also, summing up to 13 lakh data values approximately.

- ***id***, contains a unique id that the tweet is stored with in the twitter database.
- ***original_text*** contains the raw text about a tweet, including a link that redirects to the tweet. It includes the next line operator and tab spacing operator.
- The extent of ***created_at*** timestamp is till the seconds.

A detailed definition of all the attributes can be found in the section followed.

Figure 7. Sample dataset

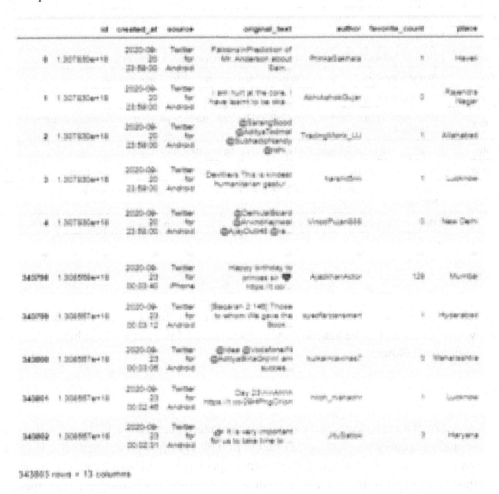

DATASET INFORMATION

The data hence prepared consists of average 41k entries per day from the first hour to the last hour of the day. Table 1 describes the different attributes and their definitions.

Table 1. Attribute definition

Attribute	Definition
id	Unique id of tweet in the Twitter database at backend
created_at	The timestamp of the tweet in the database
date	Date of the tweet, extracted from the previous attribute
source	Source of the tweet
original_text	Original tweet in the database
author	Original author of the tweet
favorite_count	Favorite Count at the time of extraction
place	Location of the tweet
hashtags	Hashtags included in the tweet, extracted from the 'original_text' upon analysis
mentions	Accounts mentioned in the tweet, extracted from the 'original_text' upon analysis
tweet_length	Length of the tweet, calculated for general understanding
clean_text	Clean tweet, upon extraction of mentions and hashtags, the remaining text was stored for sentiment and polarity calculation
polarity	Polarity of the tweet. Integers number indicating the sentimental value.
subjectivity	Subjectivity of the tweet. Integer number indicating the extent of subjectivity in the tweet
sentiment	Sentiment of the tweet. Derived attribute from 'Polarity' labelling the values according to Negative, Positive or Neutral
hour	The hour/time of the tweet, irrespective of the date, extracted from 'created_at' to analyze the traffic per hour.

ANALYSIS

We tried to cover almost every trending topic on twitter at that time in India. Certain attributes and techniques were considered for the analysis and transparency of the output with better interpretation. Following are defined below:

Hashtag

A hashtag is a word that is precedented with a hash (#) character, (i.e. '#funny'). These words are indexed separately and users can query the platform in order to find tweets with specific hashtags. Hashtags have evolved to a social phenomenon and their use has been adopted by several online and non-online media as a simple method to signify, idealize and conceptualize a single word (or phrase) in a short message. The general action of assigning hashtags to events, places or people has been described as 'social tagging', and is a vital part of Twitter and of microblogging in general. Metrics that are applied in hashtags are frequency, specificity, consistency and stability. Frequency measures the number of users and messages that contain it. Specificity measures the semantic relationship between the hashtag as a word and the context for which is used for. Consistency is the level of the hashtag's spread over different communities, as a referrer to a specific concept. Finally, stability is how the hashtag maintains both its frequency and its thematic content over time.

Mentions

A mention is a Tweet that contains another person's username anywhere in the body of the Tweet. We collect these messages, as well as all your replies, in your Notifications tab. If you include multiple usernames in your Tweet, all of those people will see your Tweet in their Notifications tab. Visiting another account's profile page on Twitter will not display Tweets that mention them. However, you can search Twitter for Tweets mentioning their username (Twitter, n.d.).

Likes

Likes are represented by a small heart and are used to show appreciation for a Tweet. You can view the Tweets you've liked from your profile page by clicking into the Likes tab. (Twitter, n.d.)

WordCloud

Word clouds or tag clouds are graphical representations of word frequency that give greater prominence to words that appear more frequently in a source text. The larger the word in the visual the more common the word was in the document(s). This type of visualization can assist evaluators with exploratory textual analysis by identifying words that frequently appear in a set of interviews, documents, or other text. It can also be used for communicating the most salient points or themes in the reporting stage. (Better Evaluation, n.d.)

Heatmap

Plot rectangular data as a color-encoded matrix. This is an Axes-level function and will draw the heatmap into the currently-active Axes if none is provided to the ax argument. Part of this Axes space will be taken and used to plot a colormap, unless cbar is False or a separate Axes is provided to cbar_ax. (seaborn.pydata, n.d.)

Bar Graph

The bars are positioned at x with the given alignment. Their dimensions are given by height and width. The vertical baseline is bottom (default 0). Many parameters can take either a single value applying to all bars or a sequence of values, one for each bar. (Matplotlib, n.d.)

Pie Chart

Make a pie chart of array x. The fractional area of each wedge is given by x/sum(x). If sum(x) < 1, then the values of x give the fractional area directly and the array will not be normalized. The resulting pie will have an empty wedge of size 1 - sum(x). The wedges are plotted counterclockwise, by default starting from the x-axis. (Matplotlib.pyplot.pie, n.d.)

Sentiment

The sentiment property returns a named tuple of the form Sentiment (polarity, subjectivity). The polarity score is a float within the range [-1.0, 1.0]. The subjectivity is a float within the range [0.0, 1.0] where 0.0 is very objective and 1.0 is very subjective. (Textblob.readthedoc, n.d.)

RESULT

Dataset

The final dataset associated with the research can be seen in Figure 8, the computed columns include polarity, subjectivity, sentiment, tweet_length, majorly. The other attributes are mainly derived attributes i.e., it is they are being derived through initially present attributes.

Figure 8. Result dataframe for polarity, subjectivity and sentiment

l_text	author	favorite_count	place	Date	Hashtags	Mentions	clean_text	state	tweet_length	polarity	subjectivity	Sentiment
sence t your ork	Yeshjan	0	Idea Nagendra Block	18-09-2020	[]	[TRAI]	This bad network speed amp say Airtel provides ...	idea nagendra block	138	0.150000	0.483333	Positive
UIDAI nment flow	Pratham96997780	0	10 Square Mall	14-09-2020	[]	[UIDAI]	No Government SOIF followed ASK SQUARE MALL CHE	10 square mall	140	-0.016667	0.066667	Negative
ppy to e that s an	BighneshaS	1	12 (O) Battalion N.C.C	18-09-2020	[happy]	[]	I happy announce justspendthoughts secret ink pu...	12 (o) battalion n.c.c.	124	0.200000	0.850000	Positive
ip the eople	Dilkhus44338898	1	17 Degrees	12-09-2020	[]	[]	Always help helpless people	17 degrees	32	0.000000	0.000000	Neutral
thood ories ps/...	Dilkhus44338898	1	17 Degrees	12-09-2020	[]	[]	First time childhood friends memories	17 degrees	62	0.250000	0.333333	Positive
thung n and Why?	srsingh1503	0	भारत Republic of India	13-09-2020	[]	[bhagwadharihung]	Warned sent back Why	Delhi	48	0.000000	0.000000	Neutral
Jvedi lease n it	srsingh1503	1	भारत Republic of India	15-09-2020	[]	[saurabhJvedi, Uppolice]	please assault fashion please stand hope u ore	Delhi	140	0.000000	0.125000	Neutral
thana layed victi	srsingh1503	0	भारत Republic of India	18-09-2020	[]	[punaruthana]	Instantly played card	Delhi	56	0.000000	0.666667	Neutral
story new odran	vikramanand1	0	पंजाब	13-09-2020	[]	[]	Ultimate double story new kothi Modren kitchen	Punjab	138	0.045455	0.484848	Positive
ws for years hild	Ranveer56582296	0	पंजाब	12-09-2020	[]	[]	Very bad news humanity years old child killed	Punjab	70	-0.335667	0.366666	Negative

Sentiment

The approach of the whole tweet sums up to the pie chart in Figure 9 . It suggests that the sentiment of a huge number of tweets is Neutral. A comparative number of tweets had Positive sentiment while a slightly low number of tweets were of negative sentiment. The 'Neutral' sentiment includes tweets with polarity 0.0 which can be a case of non-interpretability.

Figure 9. Sentiment distribution

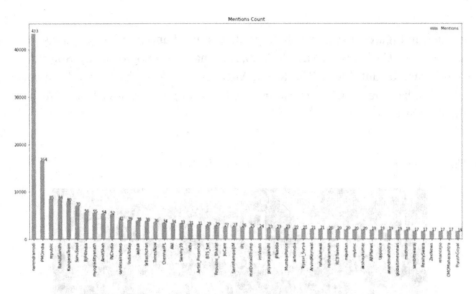

Mentions

The graph in Figure 10 shows the top 50 accounts with the highest number of mentions in the complete dataset. The personal account and the official PMO account of PM Narendra Modi is the highest-mentioned account in the month of September and October followed by the official twitter account of media house, republic and Congress Chief, RahulGandhi. Further, Bollywood actress Kangana Ranaut's account, KanganaTeam, Bollywood Actor Sonu Sood and Indian Political Party BJP's official twitter handle were mentioned.

Figure 10. Mentions (The count label in the graph is in 100s.)

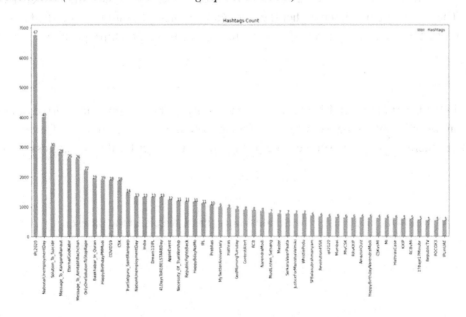

Hashtags

The hashtag graph in Figure 11 displays the top 50 most used and trending hashtags in the month of September and October. Hashtags such as IPL2020, NationalUnemploymentDay, Solution_To_Suicide, Message_To_KanganaRanaut, EternalGodKabir, Message_To_AmitabhBachan have counts of above 6k individually. The hashtag for COVID can be seen on 10th position after HappyBirthdayModi with 1.8k approximately mentions.

Figure 11. Hashtags (The count label in the graph is in 100s.)

Wordcloud

The following Word Cloud in Figure 12 contains the words with size according to their frequency in the dataset. The bigger the word, the higher the frequency. Hence, the output suggests that the birthday wish, 'Happy Birthday' and the 'Prime Minister' are the words with high frequency.

Sources

The following Pie Chart in Figure 13 shows that the majority of the users use an android device to tweet their views on this microblogging website with iPhone to be the second in the list of sources. Some users tend to use other mediums and sources like Instagram and Twitter for iPad to express their opinions.

Authors

As in Figure 14, following users have the greatest number of tweets in the dataset.

Figure 12. Word cloud   *Figure 13. Sources of tweets*

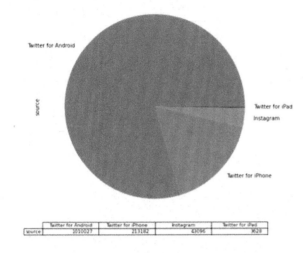

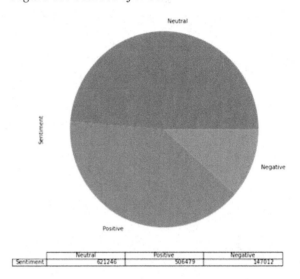

source	Twitter for Android	Twitter for iPhone	Instagram	Twitter for iPad
	1010027	213182	43096	3628

Sentiment	Neutral	Positive	Negative
	621246	506479	147012

Figure 14. Authors. (The count label in the graph is in 100s.)

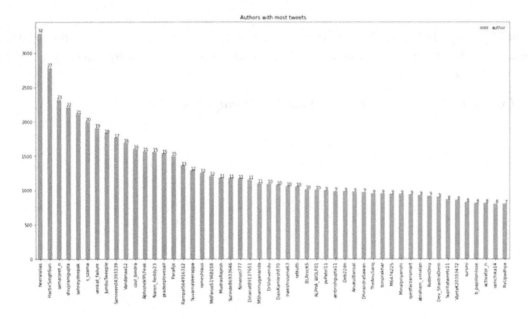

Traffic

The following Graph Figure 15 tends to provide us with the insight of the traffic per hour, i.e., the hour of the time at which the greatest number of tweets had occurred in the dataset. Clearly, the greatest number of tweets occurred between 5 AM - 7 AM and 3 PM - 6 PM.

Figure 15. Tweet traffic. (The count label in the graph is in 100s.)

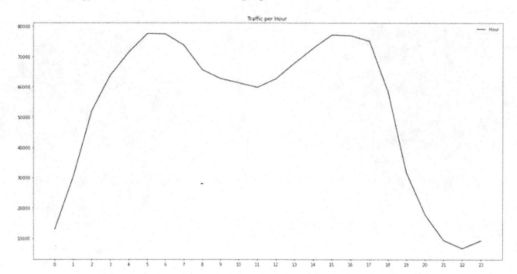

Places

The following graph in Figure 16 shows the cities and states with the most tweets. Delhi and Mumbai combined have the greatest number of active Twitter users in India followed by other cities and states.

Figure 16. Tweet location count. (The count label in the graph is in 100s.)

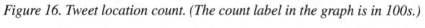

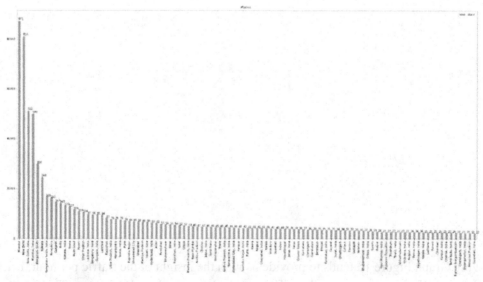

Heatmap

The following heatmap (Figure 17) displays the tweet count state-wise in heatmap format. The graph concludes that National Capital Delhi and Maharashtra city Mumbai has the highest active users as well as reach while Jammu and Kashmir (J&K) have the least number of users active.

Figure 17. Heatmap. (The count label in the graph is in the 10000s.)

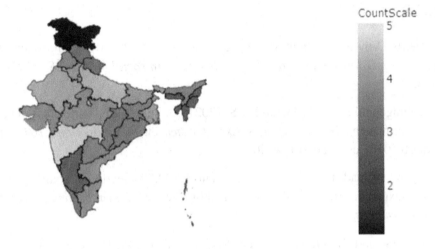

CONCLUSION

Microblogging social networking service Twitter has been a buzz around the globe in the last decade. A number of allegations as well as exculpation of different types are being held against it. The list of pros and cons of social networks is huge. India on one hand had an abundance of internet access in the last half of the decade. The growth of social media and its influence on people have affected society in both good as well as in bad ways. The following research was done in the months of September and October. The research was carried out on 13 lakh tweets approximately, collected over the course of a month from September to October providing insights about the different attributes of general tweets available on Twitter API for analysis. Insights includes the Hashtags, Account Mentions, Sentiment, Polarity, Subject and Object of a tweet using Python libraries.

The research indicated the major concern of Internet literacy and social transparency related to various issues of mankind. The abundance of accessibility of the Internet in much less time has led the end user to get diverted more easily and vastly. The topics being discussed are important but the topics not discussed are much more important. General topics of discussion in India as per the analysis includes politics, Bollywood, technology, advertisement. Social media does not buzz around the important topics instead diverts from real-life problems. Topics like: Sushant Singh Rajput and Rhea Chakraborty, IPL, Bans, Drugs can be seen transparently through hashtags and mentions. The internet has become a warzone. Communities and agendas try to force their belief on people hence results in spread of fake news. The stand they tend to take is broken in itself.

FUTURE ENHANCEMENT

One of the major limitations of this research is the availability of labelled data. The amount of data is sufficient for further development of models for real-time usage. The Subject and the Object can be analyzed and sentiment can be calculated using Machine Learning or Deep Learning techniques. The labels can be used to train many different models. Hate speech can be detected among the dataset available.

REFERENCES

Agarwal, A., Xie, B., Vovsha, I., Rambow, O., & Passonneau, R. J. (2011, June). Sentiment analysis of twitter data. In *Proceedings of the workshop on language in social media (LSM 2011)* (pp. 30-38). Academic Press.

Antonakaki, D., Fragopoulou, P., & Ioannidis, S. (2021). A survey of Twitter research: Data model, graph structure, sentiment analysis and attacks. *Expert Systems with Applications, 164*. Advance online publication. doi:10.1016/j.eswa.2020.114006

Asif, M., Ishtiaq, A., Ahmad, H., Aljuaid, H., & Shah, J. (2020). Sentiment analysis of extremism in social media from textual information. Telematics and Informatics. *Journal Telematics and Informatics, Telematics and Informatics, 48*.

Azzouza, N., Akli-Astouati, K., Oussalah, A., & Bachir, S. A. (2017, June). A real-time Twitter sentiment analysis using an unsupervised method. In *Proceedings of the 7th International Conference on Web Intelligence, Mining and Semantics* (pp. 1-10). Academic Press.

Kanakaraj, M., & Guddeti, R. M. R. (2015, February). Performance analysis of Ensemble methods on Twitter sentiment analysis using NLP techniques. In *Proceedings of the 2015 IEEE 9th International Conference on Semantic Computing (IEEE ICSC 2015)* (pp. 169-170). IEEE.

Kanakaraj, M., & Guddeti, R. M. R. (2015, February). Performance analysis of Ensemble methods on Twitter sentiment analysis using NLP techniques. In *Proceedings of the 2015 IEEE 9th International Conference on Semantic Computing (IEEE ICSC 2015)* (pp. 169-170). IEEE.

Kumar, A., & Jaiswal, A. (2019). Systematic literature review of sentiment analysis on Twitter using soft computing techniques. *Concurrency and Computation, 32*(1), e5107.

Kumar, N. (2017, December). Sentiment Analysis of Twitter Messages: Demonetization a Use Case. In *2017 2nd International Conference on Computational Systems and Information Technology for Sustainable Solution (CSITSS)* (pp. 1-5). IEEE.

Li, J., Song, Y., Wei, Z., & Wong, K. F. (2018). (2018, December). A joint model of conversational discourse and latent topics on microblogs. Computational Linguistics, MIT Press Journal. *Computational Linguistics*. Advance online publication. doi:10.1162/coli_a_00335

Roesslein, J. (2020). *Tweepy documentation*. Retrieved from https://www.tweepy.org/

Rout, J. K., Choo, K. K. R., Dash, A. K., Bakshi, S., Jena, S. K., & Williams, K. L. (2018). A model for sentiment and emotion analysis of unstructured social media text. Electronic Commerce Research. *Journal Electronic Commerce Research, 18*, 181–199. doi:10.100710660-017-9257-8

Sailunaz, K., & Alhajj, R. (2019). Emotion and sentiment analysis from Twitter text. *Journal of Computational Science, 36*. https://doi.org/ doi:10.1016/j.jocs.2019.05.009

Sarkar, D. (2019). *Text analytics with Python: a practitioner's guide to natural language processing.* Apress. doi:10.1007/978-1-4842-4354-1_6

Seki, Y. (2016, May). Use of twitter for analysis of public sentiment for improvement of local government service. In *2016 IEEE International Conference on Smart Computing (SMARTCOMP)* (pp. 1-3). IEEE.

Sharma, P., & Moh, T. (2016). Prediction of Indian election using sentiment analysis on Hindi Twitter. *2016 IEEE International Conference on Big Data (Big Data)*, 1966-1971. doi: 10.1109/BigData.2016.7840818

Sharma, P., & Moh, T. S. (2016, December). Prediction of Indian election using sentiment analysis on Hindi Twitter. In *2016 IEEE international conference on big data (big data)* (pp. 1966-1971). IEEE.

Trupthi, M., Pabboju, S., & Narasimha, G. (2017). Sentiment Analysis on Twitter Using Streaming API. *2017 IEEE 7th International Advance Computing Conference (IACC)*, 915-919. doi: 10.1109/IACC.2017.0186

Tyagi, P., & Tripathi, R. C. (2019, February). A review towards the sentiment analysis techniques for the analysis of twitter data. *Proceedings of 2nd International Conference on Advanced Computing and Software Engineering (ICACSE).*

Yoo, S., Song, J., & Jeong, O. (2018, March). Social media contents based sentiment analysis and prediction system. Expert Systems with Applications. *Journal Expert Systems with Applications, 105*, 102-111.

Yue, L., Chen, W., Li, X., Zuo, W., & Yin, M. (2018, July). A survey of sentiment analysis in social media. Knowledge and Information Systems. *Journal Knowledge and Information Systems, 60*(2), 617–663. doi:10.100710115-018-1236-4

Chapter 3
Analysis Report for Statistics in the Twitter Network

Parvathi R.
Vellore Institute of Technology, Chennai, India

Yamani Sai Asish
Vellore Institute of Technology, Chennai, India

Pattabiraman V.
(iD) https://orcid.org/0000-0001-8734-2203
Vellore Institute of Technology, Chennai, India

ABSTRACT

Twitter is the most popular social networking service across the world. In Twitter, the messages are known as tweets. Tweets are mainly text-based posts that can be up to 140 characters long which can reach the author's subscribers. These subscribers are also known as followers. Such subscriptions form a direct connection. But these connections are not always symmetric. In this study, the authors have assumed that if two nodes are connected, then the tweet is propagated between them without any other conditions. But using sentiment analysis, the general opinion of people about various things can be figured. The Twitter data set analyzed includes almost 20k nodes and 33k edges, where the visualization is done with software called Gephi. Later a deep dive analysis is done by calculating some of the metrics such as degree centrality and closeness centrality for the obtained Twitter network. Using this analysis, it is easy to find the influencers in the Twitter network and also the various groups involved in the network.

INTRODUCTION

In the past few years people have faced a lot of problems due to the propagation of wrong information in the twitter network. A lot of problems are also faced because certain vital information is not being reached to people in time due to the modularity in the twitter network. Many of these problems can be solved just by analyzing the twitter network and drawing useful conclusions from it. In this analysis, tweet

DOI: 10.4018/978-1-7998-7728-8.ch003

propagation on Twitter social network with 23370 nodes and 33101 edges was analysed. Specific focus on the network influences and how one can use the knowledge about the network for various purposes is been studied through various analysis.

Twitter is the most popular social networking service across the whole world. In Twitter the message passing is known as tweets. Tweets are mainly text-based posts which can be up to 140 characters long which can reach the author's subscribers. These subscribers are also known as followers. Such subscriptions form a direct connection. But these connections are not always symmetric. In this study, we have assumed that if two nodes are connected, then the tweet is propagated between them without any other conditions. But using sentiment analysis the general opinion of people about various things can be figured. The Twitter data set analyzed include almost 20k nodes and 33k edges, where the visualization is done with software called Gephi. Later a dive deep analysis is done by calculating some of the metrics such as degree centrality and closeness centrality for the obtained twitter network. Using this analysis, it is easy to find the influencers in the twitter network and also the various groups involved in the network.

LITERATURE SURVEY

Petrovic (Petrovic et al., 2011) discussed how the tweets are propagated using the Twitter network. They analyzed three categories a) By following users b) By tweeting c) By re-tweeting. The authors argued that the re-tweeting is potentially the best, and proves why it is so by taking examples and by proving using algorithms. And he concludes as follows. The most important task in understanding retweeting is to say if a particular tweet is going to be Re-tweeted or not, which is the main motive of this work. Analysis was performed on humans which has shown a positive result. Machine Learning approach based on passive-aggressive algorithm have substantially outperformed the previous known baseline.

Carlos (Castillo et al., 2011) analyzed the Information credibility on Twitter by analysing the credibility of the twitter information is and how humans react to it.

Information Propagation(Speed and its Patterns) German Tweets has shown that the information travels through a certain pattern in the network. It has also proves that the friend relationships also significantly influence the information propagation speed on the Twitter network. Two approaches was used to evaluate technically as well as based on how a certain topic matches a pattern and how prominent the friends are compared to the rest of the users (Tareaf, et al., 2018).

Twitter presence of (HSS) journal, Titles which are obtained from mainstream citation indices, by analysing how the interaction and communication patterns in them (Raamkumar, et al., 2018). Their research utilizes webometric collection, descriptive analysis, and also the social network analysis. So the results indicate the presence of the HSS journals on Twitter. Sharing of general websites is seen as the key activity that is performed by (HSS) journals on Twitter. Among these the web content from the news portals and magazines are highly different. Sharing of articles and retweeting isn't the most common thing to be observed. Inter-journal communication is also witnessed, But it is less with journals from other indexes.

Shaoshi et al (Ye & Wu, 2010) have evaluated different ways of social influences by measuring their assessments, stabilities and their correlations. This study tells us about all the problems that were faced. The results have given important insights for the future OSN development and research. Bo et al (Wu & Shen, 2015) have used trace-driven experiments, where the data are validated and compared through different prediction model. This proposed model has better performance with respect to that of the regression model. The study showed that the interaction frequency of retweeters and the news source is also correlated with news popularity. The negative sentiment of news also has correlations with retweet popularity but on the other side the positive sentiment has no such correlation. The combination of the overlapping paths in analyzing the twitter data. The Twitter users who have retweeted many tweets has to be identified which is the main goal of this work. Graph was build based on the propagation of retweets, called an Overlap Graph, which shows the information about the people who have shared the same retweets. The proposed work also validated the users appearing on the graph with the help of the frequency attribute (Ota, et al., 2012).

Hana et al (Anber et al., 2016) analysed a a Literature Review on Twitter Data Analysis. The across the board and various sorts of data on Twitter make it one of the most fitting virtual conditions for data observing and following. In the proposed work, the authors audit distinctive data examination strategies; beginning with the investigation of various hashtags, twitter's system topology, event spread over the system, identification of influence, lastly investigation of sentiment. Future innovative work will also be tended to.

PROPOSED WORK

Twitter is the most popular social networking service across the whole world. In Twitter the message passing is known as tweets. Tweets are mainly text-based posts which can be up to 140 characters long which can reach the author's subscribers. These subscribers are also known as followers. Such subscriptions form a direct connection. But these connections are not always symmetric. In this study, we have assumed that if two nodes are connected, then the tweet is propagated between them without any other conditions. But using sentiment analysis the general opinion of people about various things can be figured. The Twitter data set analyzed include almost 20k nodes and 33k edges, where the visualization is done with software called Gephi. Later a dive deep analysis is done by calculating some of the metrics such as degree centrality and closeness centrality for the obtained twitter network. Using this analysis,, it is easy to find the influencers in the twitter network and also the various groups involved in the network. We reason out some of the famous statements such as "You needn't be star to get your tweet to. In today's world it is very important to keep track of the information so that during the become viral today". Some of the applications are:

- In today's world it is very important to keep track of the information so that during the need we could start the propagation from that point for faster and mass spread of the information.
- To track fake messages, to analyse who and how the fake messages are getting viral and how to curb the happenings.
- To find the right person as the brand ambassador for a company.
- To check the authenticity of the tweets by finding its origin.
- To understand human mentality in general, for different age groups, region and race.
- Ability to prove or disprove the statement that most of the viral tweets are from people with the most number of followers like celebrities.
- Finding demographic groups in the twitter network and use this information to segment the market for various products.
- Identifying the groups of disconnected people and help them to connect more to the outside world.

Data Set Description

Dataset: The dataset is named as Twitter Lists categorized as Sparse Networks, the data set included vertex referred as Users and the connection between them is the edge referred as followers. The other important factor is the dataset is an undirected un- weighted data.

Centrality Measures

Centrality measures of the network is identified and from all the influencers of the network can be identified. centrality measures can be plotted to make it easier for people to understand the trends of the twitter network.. First the total degree distribution, in-degree and out-degree distribution of the network is identified . Vincent D Blondel, Jean-Loup Guillaume algorithm is applied to find the modularity of the nodes. The nodes are colored with various colors to visualize the different modularity classes in the network. The diameter, radius, average path length, betweenness centrality, closeness centrality, harmonic closeness centrality, eccentricity distribution using (Ulrik Brandes) algorithm are also computed. To analyse the cluster, the average clustering coefficient and the clustering coefficient distribution of the network using (Matthieu Latapy) algorithm is performed. The eigenvector centrality of the nodes is computed. Finally connected components are made to find the weakly connected nodes in the network using (Robert Tarjan, DFS) algorithm.

Converting the observations into results can be used to solve a lot of real world problems like to find out who can spread emergency messages the fastest. The proposed have analyzed tweet propagation with 23370 nodes and 33101 edges. Many of the centrality metrics were calculated and graphs were are also plotted related to them. The figure 1 shows the nodes and edges for the dataset colored based on the eccentricity measures. Figure 2 shows the modularity classes obtained for the dataset. Figure 3, 4 shows the network colored based on in-degree and network colored based on out-degree. Figure 5,6 shows the number of triangles obtained in the network and the Eigen value centrality measures

Figure 1. The nodes and edges for the dataset colored based on the eccentricity measures

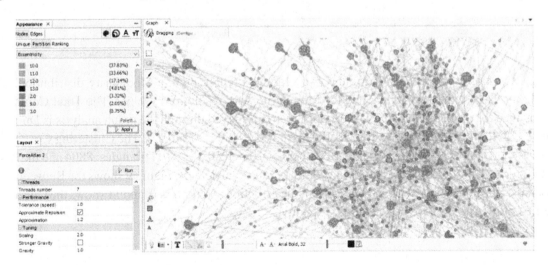

Figure 2. Modularity classes

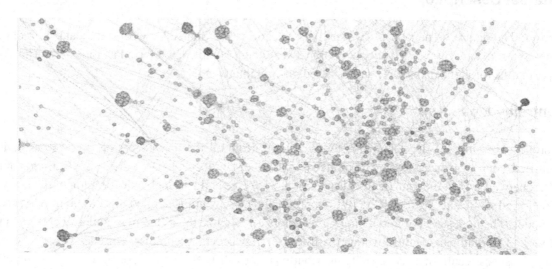

Figure 3. Network colored based on in-degree

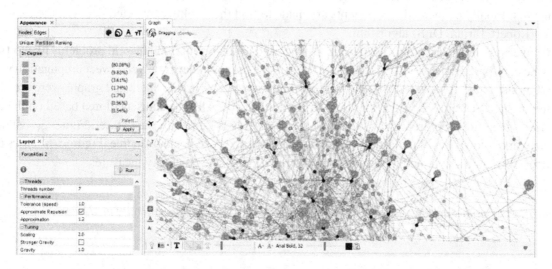

Figure 7 shows the degrees distribution and figure 8 represents the Modularity distribution. The modularity value achieved is 0.892 and the Modularity with resolution is 0.892. The Total Communities obtained for the dataset is 123. The distance metric achieved through the graph analysis is Diameter includes 15, Radius: 1, and the Average Path length is 6.304805597540574. The Clustering Coefficient Metric Report results achieved Average Clustering Coefficient: 0.332, total triangles: 8804 and the Average Clustering Coefficient is the mean value of individual coefficients. Figure 9 shows the Betweenness, Closeness, Harmonic Closeness and Eccentricity Distribution and figure 10, and 11 shows the Clustering Coefficient Metric, Eigenvector Centrality Report.

Figure 4. Network colored based on out-degree

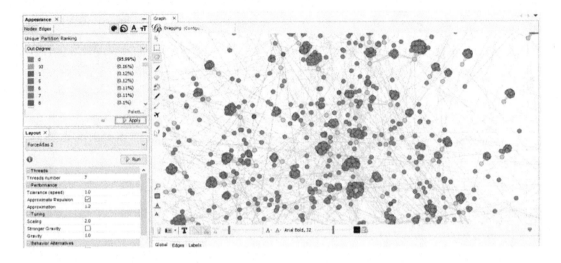

Figure 5. Number of triangles in the network

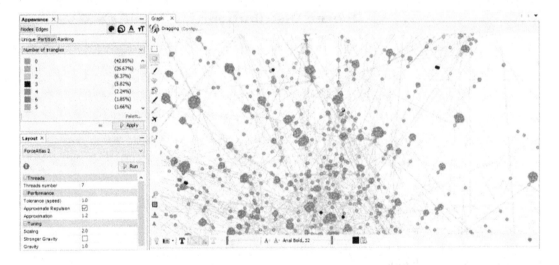

CONCLUSION

The twitter dataset is analyzed using social network metrics like centrality measures like closeness, betweenness, Eigen value centrality measures.etc. Similarly the graph based metrics, distance based metrics were also evaluated to show the performance of the data. But we used gephi which was a better fit for our dataset and needs. Around 20k nodes were analysed in less than more than 20 minutes. The proposed work shows the credibility of the users. The future work includes the evaluation of the false propagation and the speed of the tweets.

Figure 6. Eigenvector centrality of the nodes

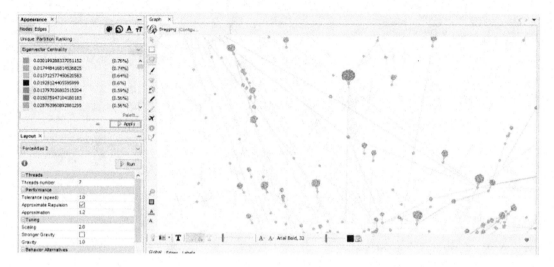

Figure 7. The degrees distribution

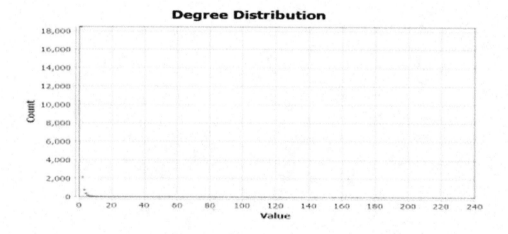

Figure 8. Modularity distribution

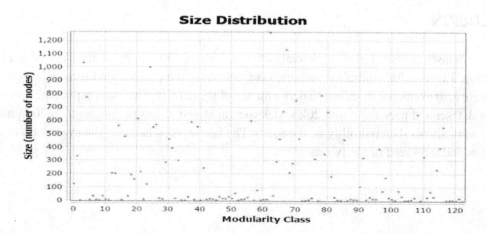

Figure 9. Betweenness, closeness, harmonic closeness and eccentricity distribution

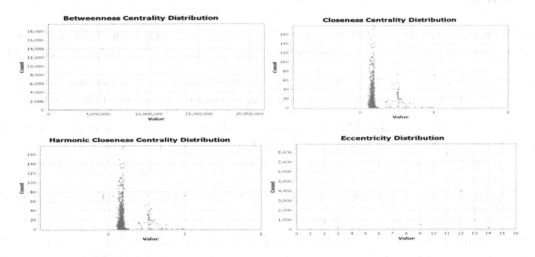

Figure 10. Clustering coefficient metric

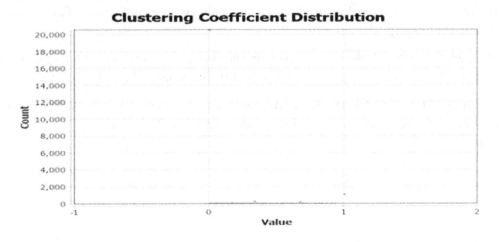

Figure 11. Eigenvector centrality report

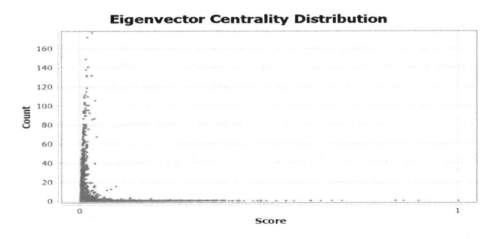

REFERENCES

Anber, H., Salah, A., & Abd El-Aziz, A. A. (2016). A literature review on twitter data analysis. *International Journal of Computer and Electrical Engineering, 8*(3), 241–249. doi:10.17706/IJCEE.2016.8.3.241-249

Castillo, C., Mendoza, M., & Poblete, B. (2011, March). Information credibility on twitter. In *Proceedings of the 20th international conference on World wide web* (pp. 675-684). 10.1145/1963405.1963500

Ota, Y., Maruyama, K., & Terada, M. (2012, December). Discovery of interesting users in twitter by overlapping propagation paths of retweets. In *2012 IEEE/WIC/ACM International Conferences on Web Intelligence and Intelligent Agent Technology* (Vol. 3, pp. 274-279). IEEE. 10.1109/WI-IAT.2012.110

Petrovic, S., Osborne, M., & Lavrenko, V. (2011). Rt to win! predicting message propagation in twitter. *ICWSM, 11*, 586–589.

Sesagiri Raamkumar, A., Erdt, M., Vijayakumar, H., Rasmussen, E., & Theng, Y. L. (2018). *Understanding the Twitter usage of humanities and social sciences academic journals.* Academic Press.

Tareaf, R. B., Berger, P., Hennig, P., Koall, S., Kohstall, J., & Meinel, C. (2018). Information Propagation Speed and Patterns in Social Networks: A Case Study Analysis of German Tweets. *JCP, 13*(7), 761–770. doi:10.17706/jcp.13.7.761-770

Wu, B., & Shen, H. (2015). Analyzing and predicting news popularity on Twitter. *International Journal of Information Management, 35*(6), 702–711. doi:10.1016/j.ijinfomgt.2015.07.003

Ye, S., & Wu, S. F. (2010, October). Measuring message propagation and social influence on Twitter. com. In *International conference on social informatics* (pp. 216-231). Springer. 10.1007/978-3-642-16567-2_16

Chapter 4
Chemical Named Entity Recognition Using Deep Learning Techniques:
A Review

Hema R.
Department of Computer Science, University of Madras, India

Ajantha Devi
https://orcid.org/0000-0002-9455-4826
AP3 Solutions, India

ABSTRACT

Chemical entities can be represented in different forms like chemical names, chemical formulae, and chemical structures. Because of the different classification frameworks for chemical names, the task of distinguishing proof or extraction of chemical elements with less ambiguous is considered a major test. Compound named entity recognition (NER) is the initial phase in any chemical-related data extraction strategy. The majority of the chemical NER is done utilizing dictionary-based, rule-based, and machine learning procedures. Recently, deep learning methods have evolved, and, in this chapter, the authors sketch out the various deep learning techniques applied for chemical NER. First, the authors introduced the fundamental concepts of chemical named entity recognition, the textual contents of chemical documents, and how these chemicals are represented in chemical literature. The chapter concludes with the strengths and weaknesses of the above methods and also the types of the chemical entities extracted.

INTRODUCTION

In this Internet age, enormous measure of digital data is created and partaken as unstructured writings, pictures and recordings. This sort of remarkable development is going on in every single fields of our genuine science through examination articles, specialized reports and digital books. For example, in

DOI: 10.4018/978-1-7998-7728-8.ch004

the event that we think about the field of Chemistry, there are N number of diaries accessible independently for the five essential parts of science, for example, Physical, Organic, Inorganic, Analytical, and Biochemistry. These journals approximately contain over 10 million journal papers. Manually, it is very difficult to organize, manage, identify and to extract the important information like chemical named entities and their relations. In addition, the extracted information is stored in the form of databases such as CHEMDNER corpus (Krallinger et al., 2015), ChemSpider (Krallinger, Leitner, & Rabal, 2013), PubChem (ChemSpider, 2010), ChEBI (Harry, 2010) etc. Notwithstanding, to refresh these information bases, we require broad and persistent manual exertion which is an extravagant and provoking errand and prompts the evolvement of Text Mining (TM) to play out those undertakings.

One significant focal point of Text Mining is on Named Entity Recognition (NER), an absolute first and urgent advance in data extraction. In the specific instance of Chemical Named Entity Recognition (CNER), extra challenges emerge. Most importantly, not all chemical names are having a similar structure. CNER frameworks are especially delicate concerning spelling mistakes and the tokenization technique since chemical substances are generally having hyphenated text portions, variable utilization of enclosures, sections and various punctuation symbols. In addition, compound reports will in general be stacked with many abbreviations and acronyms, which are one of the primary wellsprings of false positives. Another trademark that makes CNER troublesome is the way that the location of limits for chemical substances is particularly lumbering when long compound names are available. A more top to bottom description of challenges in labelling chemicals can be found at (Krallinger et al., 2015).

In chemical databases, it is very difficult to find out the specific information on newly discovered compounds. For example, a new drug development process is based on the knowledge of chemicals like toxic effects, biological properties etc. The chemical entities extracted using Text Mining can be used in many applications such as to find relationships between many entities, mapping the chemical entities to their identical structures, and helps a search engine to retrieve the specific documents which contains one particular entity (Article, 2016). However, the various naming culture of chemical entities makes the task of entity recognition very complex and time consuming. Manual curation of chemical text documents to generate annotations and to use those annotations is also a very laborious process (Kim et al., 2015).

Consequently, a few ChemNER frameworks have been created utilizing various methodologies dependent on standards, dictionary coordinating, Machine Learning (ML) and Deep Learning (DL). Each approach has its own points of interest and disservices relying upon the semantic attributes of the elements being recognized. Applying the best methodologies is preposterous in all cases, since each approach presents diverse specialized necessities (Wang et al., 2009). In any case, when there is a huge volume of information, Deep Learning based arrangements present several advantages over different strategies and give the outcomes best precision. The advancement of DL-based NER arrangements coordinates different complex advances that consolidate distinctive processing pipelines. Hence, along the previous years, an assortment of frameworks was created utilizing the most various structures, procedures and systems.

As we consider the procedures applied in ChemNER, there are four fundamental techniques:

- Rule-based methodologies: Depend with respect to hand-made guidelines thus no requirement for commented on information
- Unsupervised learning approach: Depend on Unsupervised algorithms with no preparation models
- Supervised learning approach: Depend on supervised learning algorithms with cautious component designing;

- Deep-learning based methodologies: Consequently, find the hidden features required for the classification from raw information and fabricate the ChemNER model utilizing layers. We sum up the initial three ChemNER approaches and survey the fourth methodology in detail.

CORPORA AND EVALUATION METRICS

In any domain, the first step required to design a complex relation extraction model is to find mentions of the entities. Specifically, the chemical entities play a vital role in bioinformatics, drug development, medical diagnosis, plant-disease detection etc. High quality annotated datasets are essential for both model learning and evaluation. A corpus may or may not contain annotations of different entity types. That is, some corpus contain annotations for only specific entity sets.

Table 1. List of corpora for ChemNER applications

S.No.	Corpus	Class of Named Entities	Reference
1	IUPAC training corpus	IUPAC names	[15]
2	SCAI	All chemical names	[16]
3	PubMed corpus	Compounds, chemical adjectives, enzymes and reagents	[17]
4	Sciborg corpus	All chemical names	[17]
5	GENIA corpus	Biological entitites and chemical entities	[18]
6	European patent office and ChEBI	All chemical names	[19]
7	CHEMDNER corpus	Chemical compounds and drugs	[20]
8	BioCreative V CDR task corpus	Chemical disease relation	[21]
9	Plant-chemical corpus	Plant-chemical relationships	[22]

The annotated corpora can be divided into two types based on the source of the annotations (Bengio et al., 2013). The first type is Gold Standard Corpora (GSC) in which annotations are performed manually by domain experts by using detailed guidelines. The second type is Silver Standard Corpora (SSC) in which the computerized systems will do the annotations automatically. Table 1 illustrates a list of GSC available for the various types of chemical entities.

Three main information extraction measures are used to evaluate the performance of ChemNER systems namely:

- **Precision**: it refers to the percentage of the ability of a NER system to recognize only the correct chemical entities;

- **Recall**: it refers to the percentage of the ability of a NER system to recognize all the relevant entities; and
- **F-measure:** which combines both the precision and recall and it is a harmonic mean of precision and recall.

APPROACHES IN CHEMICAL NAMED ENTITY RECOGNITION (CNER)

Sixth Message Understanding Conference (MUC6) presented the expression "Named Entity". Named Entity Recognition (NER) is a subtask of data extraction that distinguishes and order named elements in crude content into predefined classifications like people, associations, areas, time articulations, financial qualities and so on Additionally, NER is the center undertaking of Natural Language Processing (NLP) framework (Krallinger, Leitner, Rabal et al, 2013). To build up a ChemNER framework, we need to follow different handling steps and Figure 1 portrays the request for steps to actualize DL-based NER models.

- Corpora: Collection of unstructured texts from various sources related to the chemical domain;
- Preprocessing: To simplify the recognition process, stop word removal, entity boundaries determination by sentence splitting and tokenization are done in this step.
- Feature identification and Classification: Feature extraction is key and time-consuming process. But with deep learning, the features will be automatically identified by the neural network along with classification during learning with huge amount of data.
- Postprocessing: Refinement of annotated entities and removing the multiple occurrences of the same entity are done in this step.
- Output: Raw data or unstructured corpora with annotations in a structured format.

ChemNER has number of challenges. The identification of new chemical entities and the entities mentioned in various representations are considered as the most important challenges. The existing approaches to ChemNER can be grouped into o four: (i) Dictionary-based, (ii) Rule-based, (iii) ML-based and (iv) DL-based NER methods. In this chapter, we will review about the DL-based ChemNER techniques in detail.

Dictionary-Based Methods

Techniques dependent on word references depend on the current rundown of chemical entities found at a particular time. Along these lines, to cover the recently distinguished synthetic elements, it is imperative to refresh the word references constantly. There is additionally an opportunity, with basic English words, of having some un-clear words.

For chemical domain, one dictionary is accessible to distinguish little particles (Li et al., 2016). The string-matching technique is applied by word reference-based frameworks to confirm if a word or a blend of words from the content matches the term in the dictionary. The string matching is of two types:

1. Exact matching: This process looks for an exact match of the term from the text with the dictionary term.

2.   Approximate matching: Like the previous type, this type of string matching does not look for the exact match of the term. Insertion, deletion or substitution can be done in this process and it is used by most NER approaches (Choi et al., n.d.).

Figure 1. Order of steps to implement DL-based ChemNER models

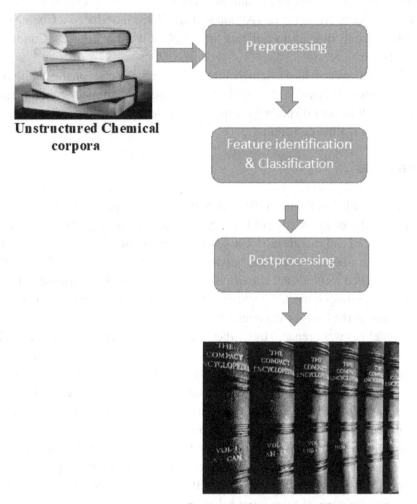

RandDict, an interesting thought for preparing a ChemNER through auto-produced preparing information, was introduced by Su Yan et al., (Mansouri et al., 2008). At the point when this RandDict was contrasted with the prior manual exertion and rule-based frameworks, this idea created better outcomes with less manual endeavors. In joining dictionary based and grammer-based recognizers to distinguish the chemical compounds from text records, Akhondi et al.(Hettne et al., 2009) investigated an ensemble approach. The focal point of this work was principally on characterizing and positioning certain known substance elements. They likewise positioned the different compounds in chemical and non-chemical diaries utilizing a standardized recurrence proportion of terms.

To arrange an enormous number of chemical elements, Daniel and Roger (Klein, 2011) utilized a hybrid technique for fusing the two dictionary based and grammer structure. The recall value was improved by extra truncation discovery and, simultaneously, precision was improved by killing contractions pertinent to non-compound substances. In dictionary based methodologies, progressed procedures incorporate the fuse of numerous information bases, the improvement of example coordinating techniques for the objective class of substances, and the advancement of rules for upgrading results (Yan et al., 2012) Venkata Ravindra Nittala et al. (Akhondi et al., 2013) introduced a ChemNER framework to perceive synthetic elements in licenses utilizing area explicit word references, Conditional Random Fields (CRF) and highlights.

The accuracy of the dictionary-based ChemNER models purely depends on the quality, completeness and the matching algorithm. Generally, the precision achieved by dictionary-based methods are high precision but the recall will be poor if spelling errors are in the text. Due to the maintenance, Dictionary-based systems are costly and time-consuming.

Rule-Based Methods

This technique is also regarded as a handcrafted strategy. In this method, certain rules are constructed by an expert who has a detailed knowledge of the chemistry domain, so that the Chemical Named Entities can be easily recognized and categorized. Based on examples, the rules are formulated and both the grammatical and syntactic rules are taken into account. Sometimes, the set of rules are also combined with dictionaries. Rule-based methods are classified into two types: (i) Pattern-based in which the rules are formulated by using orthographic and morphological features of the words (ii) Context-based in which the rules are built on the basis of the context of words in raw text.

A collection of guidelines was prepared by Corbett (Akhondi et al., 2013) to classify 5 different types of chemical named entities, such as Chemical Compound, Chemical Reaction, Chemical Adjective, Enzyme and Chemical Prefix, and rules were also established to identify particular cases. Later, they sorted key chemical names manually into their subclasses. The chemical entities have been split into six subtypes. EXACT, CLASS and PART (partial compounds) are the three main subtypes, and SPECIES, SURFACE and POLYMER are the three minor subtypes.

Narayanasamy et al., (Lowe & Sayle, 2015) concentrated primarily on the identification of the chemical names of the IUPAC and thus established a set of handmade rules. In this paper, they considered the morphological characteristics based on the structure of IUPAC names, since their purpose was to extract IUPAC chemical names. The manual rules for one domain cannot be extended to another domain, as the features are modified from one domain to another.

ML-Based Methods

In order to learn a model, Machine-learning based methods (Corbett et al., 2007; Narayanaswamy et al., 2003; Sayle et al., 2012) need an annotated corpus and the learned model will be used in the test data sets. This type of methods use statistics to recognize the entity names using features identified from the corpus. The two basic steps in ML-based NER models are: (i) Training in which the designed ML model will be trained using the annotated documents. (ii) Annotation in which records can be annotated to identify entities on the basis of previous experience. The ML algorithms can be classified into three types such as Supervised, Semi-supervised and Unsupervised approaches.

Supervised Learning Algorithms.

In Supervised learning algorithms, feature identification is a very critical step. Feature vectors are represented by Boolean, numeric and nominal values (Bikel et al., 1999; Borthwick, 1999). Machine learning algorithms are trained to learn a model to identify the entities with similar patterns from unseen data. Word-level features (Chieu & Ng, 2002; Nadeau & Sekine, 2007; Sekine & Ranchhod, 2009), list lookup features (Liao & Veeramachaneni, 2009; Mikheev, 1999; Settles, 2004; Zhou & Su, 2002) and document and corpus features (Hoffart et al., 2011; Kazama & Torisawa, 2007; Ravin & Wacholder, 1997; Toral & Munoz, 2006) are the widely used features in most supervised ChemNER systems. Based on the features, many machine learning algorithms like Hidden Markov Models (HMM) (Zhu et al., 2005), Maximum Entropy Models (Ji et al., 2016), Conditional Random Fields (CRF) (Krishnan & Manning, 2006), Decision Trees (Eddy, 1996) and Support Vector Machines (SVM) (Kapur, 1989). A discussion of techniques performed is given in the following subsections.

Semi-Supervised Learning Algorithms

Semi-supervised algorithms use few labelled data to train and try to identify the entities in more unlabelled data. For this type of algorithms, a small degree of manual supervision is needed. This approach needs minimal human supervision to select a small set of feature tagged seed samples to learn simple, long and complex chemical entities. The feature sets of chemical terms based on the orthographic and morphological levels are identified and the seed patterns designed will be used by the algorithm. The components of the seed patterns are masked to generate new patterns. This loop is repeated until no more new patterns are generated (Rebholz-Schuhmann et al., 2008).

Unsupervised Learning Algorithms

Unsupervised learning algorithms are more complicated because, without training the NER method, they attempt to identify the entities and the labels are not understood. The aim of unsupervised learning, therefore, is to construct representations directly from data. Clustering is one example for unsupervised learning which finds the similarities in clusters. In the NER task (Friedrich et al., 2006; Grego et al., 2009), however, unsupervised learning is not common.

In order to create the rules for machine learning approaches, manual effort is not needed. The newly discovered chemical entities can thus be effectively characterized by these approaches. Therefore, nowadays, much of the academic work is conducted using these methods of machine learning. Feature sets and training data are considered essential for these approaches. However, supervised learning algorithms are applied in the majority of NER systems. But in ChemNER implementations, the semi-supervised and unsupervised learning algorithms are not technically implemented.

Deep Learning Techniques on ChemNER

The Machine Learning based ChemNER solutions integrates various complex steps through various processing pipelines. These type of NER models use statistical models to recognize or to identify specific entity names with the help of feature engineering of the previous data. Such features help in identifying new entity names and also new spelling variations of an entity name. But the features should be identified by a domain expert to facilitate the reduction of complexity in data and make patterns for learning by Machine Learning algorithms to work. However, the main drawback of Machine Learning ChemNER solutions depend on annotated documents which are very expensive and hard to obtain. Thus, the absence of annotated resources and the need of feature engineering may limit the applicability of Machine Learning techniques. Recently, DL-based ChemNER models become more popular and dominant.

Figure 2. Processing pipeline of machine learning and deep learning

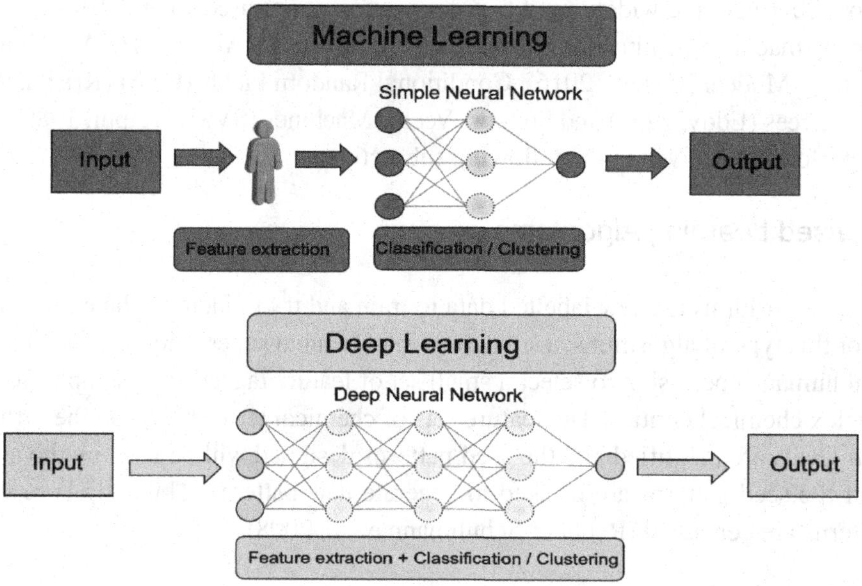

Deep Learning is a subfield of machine learning composed of multiple processing or hidden layers with representation learning of data. Learning can be supervised, semi-supervised or unsupervised (Degtyarenko et al., 2009; Degtyarenko et al., 2008; Klinger et al., 2008).

Deep learning techniques are very good in discovering hidden features automatically from huge volume of data in an incremental manner. This put an end to the need of domain expertise and the necessity for feature extraction.

Problem solving approach is another major difference between Machine Learning and Deep Learning techniques. Machine learning techniques first break the problem statement into different modules, solve the modules and the individual module results will be combined at the final stage. But Deep Learning techniques accomplish a problem end to end. Figure 2 shows the processing pipeline of both the Machine Learning and Deep Learning. Next, we briefly introduce the concept behind Deep Learning and why deep learning for ChemNER. Finally, we then survey DL-based NER approaches.

Why Deep Learning for ChemNER?

There are three main reasons to design ChemNER models using deep learning techniques. First, compared to linear models, Deep Learning techniques automatically identify the complex and hidden features using non linear activation functions. Second, deep learning models are effective in learning representations from raw data and saves effort and time in designing ChemNER features. The feature-based approaches, on the other hand, require domain experts to identify the features. Third, deep neural NER models can be trained in an end-to-end paradigm with the help of gradient descent, which is a first-order iterative optimization algorithm and so it is possible to design very complex ChemNER systems. Nowadays, deep learning architectures are used in many fields such as Natural Language Processing, Medical Image Analysis, Bioinformatics, Drug Design, Board games etc. to produce better results than earlier and in some cases, the performance is surpassing human performance (Eltyeb & Salim, 2014; Hawizy et al., 2011; LeCun et al., 2015).

In order to boost NER efficiency in Chinese Electronic Medical Records, a new bi-directional RNN model combined with deep transfer learning and multitask bi-directional LSTM RNN was proposed by Xishuang Dong et al. The authors concentrated on improving the accuracy of NER tasks with minimal labeled data in the proposed model. Deep transfer learning can use transferred information from other tasks to increase the accuracy of prediction, whereas multi-task deep learning can be seen as data augmentation that could effectively boost the efficiency of the NER. It is noted that in the case of discharge datasets, the proposed model outperforms the baseline model.

The implementation of Named-Entity Recognition (NER) for Indonesian Language is defined by William Gunawan et al. using various deep learning approaches, but mainly based on the architecture of hybrid bidirectional LSTM BLSTM and convolutional neural network (CNN). The newly developed Indonesian NER can able to extract four types of entities such as Person, the information from articles into 4 different classes; they are Organization, Person, Event and Location. The results of the experiment reported that deep learning could achieve good efficiency. BLSTMS-CNNs is considered the best Indonesian-language model for the identification of named entities.

CHEMICAL NER TOOLS

In text mining, there are now several Natural Language Processing (NLP) tools to automate the extraction of relevant data from unstructured text documents. In the field of chemistry, compared to the field of biology, only a few tools have been created. The names of proteins, genes, drugs, diseases and the relationship between drugs and diseases and also between documents will be the information retrieved in the biological domain. In the field of chemistry, the rapid development of NLP tools in biology has motivated many researchers to develop NLP methods. The open-source ChemNER tools are listed in Table 2.

Recent Works In Chemical NER Using Deep Learning Neural Networks

PharmacoNER tagger, a neural NER based on an existing device,NeuroNER, was introduced by Jordi Armengol-Estapé et al., (Dahl et al., 2012). It is an open-source NER program and has achieved state-of-the-art efficiency by introducing three layers of neural architecture: (1) a label prediction layer, (2) a character-enhanced to-ken-embedding layer, and (3) a label sequence optimization layer. The chemical compounds were defined by the tagger in this study, especially in Spanish medical texts. With the SPACCC dataset, the best results are obtained. Finally, 89.06 percent of the F1 score was obtained by this study.

Table 2. Open-source ChemNER tools

S.No.	Chemical NER Tool	Class of Entities	Availability	References
1	OSCAR4	Chemical entity, Chemical reaction, Chemical adjective, Chemical enzyme, Ontology terms and Chemical prefixes	http://apidoc.ch.cam.ac.uk/oscar4-4.0.1	[92]
2	ChemSpot	IUPAC entities, Trivial names, Abbreviations, Drugs and Molecular formulas.	http://www.informatik.hu-berlin.de/wbi/resources	[93]
3	Chemical Tagger	Chemical units, the mixture of chemical compounds, quantity of chemical substances and it's roles as reactants, solvents or products and action phrases in chemical experiments.	https://bitbucket.org/lh359/chemicaltagger	[94]
4	CheNER	Used a set of approaches that combines dictionary, CRFs and regular expression matching in five ways. CheNER is unique because CheNER classifies the annotated chemical terms into the various classes.	http://metres.udl.cat	[95]
5	ChemTok	Rule based tokenizer for Chemical NER	https://doi.org/10.1155/2016/4248026	[96]
6	BERN	genes/proteins, diseases, drugs/chemicals, and species	https://bern.korea.ac.kr.	[97]
7	LSTMVoter	Recognition and classification of chemical named entities	https ://github.com/texttechnologyab/LSTMVoter.	[70]
8	PharmacoTagger	Chemicals and drugs in Spanish medical texts	https://github.com/PlanTL-SANIDAD/PharmacoNER	[81]

ElemNet, a deep neural network model was demonstrated by Dipendra Jha et al., (Berger, n.d.). With only a few thousand training samples, this model bypassed manual function engineering domain awareness and produced much better results. Using artificial intelligence, physical and chemical interactions and similarities between various elements are automatically captured, allowing greater accuracy and speed to predict the properties of materials. ElemNet's speed and accuracy helped to rapidly and robustly screen new material candidates in a vast combinatorial space and to identify hundreds of thousands of undiscovered compounds.

Zainab Awan et al., (Amengol-Estapé et al., 2019) have demonstrated the impact of contextualized embeddings for ChemNER by using Bi-LSTM-CRF networks. In this study, the authors proved that implementing Embedded Language Models (ELMo) embeddings into the static embeddings for a Bi-LSTM-CRF network results in a significant increase in F1 score for all the evaluated corpora. Also, the results produced by training the ELMo on Pubmed is better when compared to the results obtained by pretraining the ELMo on a general domain corpus. This difference in results proved that transfer learning results in higher F1 score if the source dataset is from the target domain. The results are evaluated with the help of four benchmarked ChemNER corpora such as BC5CDR, BC4CHEMDNER, Chemical Entity Mentions in Patents (CEMP) and BioSemantics.

DEEP LEARNING IN OTHER FIELDS OF CHEMISTRY

Till now, we have discussed about the role of various deep learning algorithms for ChemNER. But deep learning has shown it's efficiency in other fields of Chemistry also. In this section, we will discuss how the deep learning had been applied in other areas of Chemistry.

George Edward Dahl (Luo et al., 2018), in his dissertation, applied deep NN models to three different domains such as natural language text processing, speech recognition and computational chemistry. Though each domain has it's unique characteristics, this work used similar methods to get excellent results. The goals of this dissertation is to test the models based on neural networks and Boltzmann machines on three different areas to determine how we can produce successful solutions that generalize across problems and to introduce new techniques to extend the methods as needed. All of the models learn their own features and learn distributed representations. All models are highly expressive and have training algorithms that can be extended in future with high-dimensional datasets.

Cheminformatics plays a vital role in life science. For instance, In disease production and therapy, chemicals interact with genes. Although we have many research papers to explain gene, chemical, and disease relationships, just a few studies derive biomedical literature from disease-gene-chemical relationships. In order to classify the relationships between genes, chemicals, and diseases from Medline abstracts, Jeongkyun Kim et al. proposed a deep learning model based on bidirectional LSTM. They have developed a search engine DigChem, to search disease–gene–chemical relationship for 35,124 genes, 56,382 chemicals, and 5,675 diseases. Finally, by comparing the identified relationships with manual curation and existing databases, this study proves that the retrieved relationships using DigChem are reliable.

Instead of standard machine learning algorithms used in computational chemistry, the principle of applying the hierarchical cascade of non-linear functions differentiated deep learning. This property allows deep learning to learn representations and to extract from raw unstructured data the necessary characteristics that help to predict the particular or required physicochemical property. The wide application of deep learning in many sub-fields of computational chemistry, such as quantum chemistry, computer assisted drug design, material design and computational structural biology, has been found in computational chemistry by Garrett B. Goh et al., (Fooshee et al., 2018). They have analyzed the efficiency of the DNN-based model in recent research papers and conclude that deep learning is superior to conventional machine learning algorithms.

A sample of ML methods supporting computational chemistry was reviewed by Tania F. G. G. Cova and Alberto A. C. C. Pais(Baldi, 2017), but the main focus is on Deep Neural Networks. Such methods have the potential to solve many chemical problems that can not be achieved by traditional methods. Recently, DLN contributions have been growing in computational chemistry. Deep Learning (DL) uses a hierarchical non-linear function to learn representations and automatically detect the required features from raw chemical data which is further used in the prediction of target physicochemical properties. The major challenges are disparity, efficiency and interpretability of the results obtained. In future, the massive growth of chemical information and the sophistication of DL algorithms makes the DLN as a trending algorithm for computational chemistry.

CONCLUSION

As scientific literature expands exponentially in the form of unstructured text, it is essential to mine important words for further study. The manual annotation consumes plenty of time and is inconsistent. In this review study, a few strategies for ChemNER and the correlation of those techniques have been discussed. The study focused on the current frameworks for chemical entity extraction. To begin with, we presented the foundation for ChemNER, for example, the significance of chemical elements, assessment measurements, customary and machine learning approaches to deal with ChemNER and essential ideas in deep learning. Second, we looked into the writing dependent on different deep learning strategies for ChemNER. We found that deep learning is picking up a lot of prevalence because of its incomparability as far as exactness when prepared with enormous measure of data. At long last, we gave a list of open-source ChemNER tools and we present these tools in even structure with joins for simple access. We hope that this literature survey can bring forth an extensive knowledge about the ChemNER and a good platform for the researchers who aim to design Deep learning based ChemNER models.

REFERENCES

Akhondi, S. A., Singh, B., & van der Host, E. (2013). A dictionary-and grammar-based chemical named entity recognizer. BioCreative Challenge Evaluation Workshop, 2, 113.

Amengol-Estapé, J., Soares, F., Marimon, M., & Krallinger, M. (2019). PharmacoNER Tagger: A deep learning-based tool for automatically finding chemicals and drugs in Spanish medical texts. *Genomics & Informatics*, 17(2), e15. doi:10.5808/GI.2019.17.2.e15 PMID:31307130

Article. (2016, January 4). *Nucleic Acids Research*, 44(Database issue), D1202–D1213. PMID:26400175

Baldi, P. (2017). Article. *Data Mining and Knowledge Discovery*, 1–13.

Bengio, Y., Courville, A., & Vincent, P. (2013). Representation Learning: A Review and New Perspectives. *IEEE Transactions on Pattern Analysis and Machine Intelligence*, 35(8), 1798–1828. doi:10.1109/TPAMI.2013.50 PMID:23787338

Berger. (n.d.). *Drug and Chemical Compound Named Entity Recognition using Convolutional Networks*. Academic Press.

Bikel, D. M., Schwartz, R., & Weischedel, R. M. (1999). An algorithm that learns what's in a name. *Machine Learning*, 34(1/3), 211–231. doi:10.1023/A:1007558221122

Borthwick, A. (1999). *A maximum Entropy Approach to Named Entity Recognition* (Ph.D. thesis). New York University.

ChemSpider: An Online Chemical Information Resource. (2010). *Journal of Chemical Education*, 87(11). doi:10.1021/ed100697w

Chieu, H. L., & Ng, H. T. (2002). Named entity recognition: a maximum entropy approach using global information. *Proceedings of the 19th International Conference on Computational Linguistics, 1*, 1–7. 10.3115/1072228.1072253

Choi, Kim, Cho, Lee, & Lee. (n.d.). *A corpus for plant-chemical relationships in the biomedical domain*. Academic Press.

Corbett, P., Batchelor, C., & Teufel, S. (2007). Annotation of Chemical Named Entities. *BioNLP 2007. Biological, translational, and clinical language processing*, 57–64.

Dahl, G. E., Yu, D., Deng, L., & Acero, A. (2012). Context-dependent pre-trained deep neural networks for large-vocabulary speech recognition. *IEEE Transactions on Audio, Speech, and Language Processing, 20*(1), 30–42. doi:10.1109/TASL.2011.2134090

Degtyarenko, Hastings, de Matos, & Ennis. (2009). ChEBI: An open bioinformatics and cheminformatics resource. *Curr Protoc Bioinformatics*. doi:10.1002/0471250953.bi1409s26

Degtyarenko, K., De Matos, P., Ennis, M., Hastings, J., Zbinden, M., McNaught, A., Alcantara, R., Darsow, M., Guedj, M., & Ashburner, M. (2008). ChEBI: A database and ontology for chemical entities of biological interest. *Nucleic Acids Research, 36*(Database), D344–D350. doi:10.1093/nar/gkm791 PMID:17932057

Eddy, S. R. (1996). Hidden Markov models. *Current Opinion in Structural Biology, 6*(3), 361–365. doi:10.1016/S0959-440X(96)80056-X PMID:8804822

Eltyeb, S., & Salim, N. (2014). Chemical named entities recognition: A review on approaches and applications. *Journal of Cheminformatics, 6*(1), 17. doi:10.1186/1758-2946-6-17 PMID:24834132

Fooshee, D., Mood, A., Gutman, E., Tavakoli, M., Urban, G., Liu, F., Huynh, N., Van Vranken, D., & Baldi, P. (2018). Deep learning for chemical reaction prediction. *Molecular Systems Design & Engineering, 3*(3), 442–452. doi:10.1039/C7ME00107J

Friedrich, Revillion, Hofmann, & Fluck. (2006). Biomedical and Chemical Named Entity Recognition with Conditional Random Fields: The Advantage of Dictionary Features. *Proceedings of the Second International Symposium on Semantic Mining in Biomedicine (SMBM 2006)*, 7, 85-89.

Grego, T., Pęzik, P., Couto, F., & Rebholz-Schuhmann, D. (2009). *2009. Identification of chemical entities in patent documents*. Distributed Computing, Artificial Intelligence, Bioinformatics, Soft Computing, and Ambient Assisted Living.

Harry, E. (2010). ChemSpider: An online chemical information resource. *Journal of Chemical Education, 87*(11), 1123–1124. doi:10.1021/ed100697w

Hawizy, L., Jessop, D. M., Adams, N., & Murray-Rust, P. (2011). ChemicalTagger: A tool for semantic text-mining in chemistry. *Journal of Cheminformatics, 3*(1), 17. doi:10.1186/1758-2946-3-17 PMID:21575201

Hettne, K. M., Stierum, R. H., Schuemie, M. J., Hendriksen, P. J., Schijvenaars, B. J., Mulligen, E. M., Kleinjans, J., & Kors, J. A. (2009). A dictionary to identify small molecules and drugs in free text. *Bioinformatics (Oxford, England), 25*(22), 2983–2991. doi:10.1093/bioinformatics/btp535 PMID:19759196

Hoffart, Yosef, Bordino, Fürstenau, Pinkal, Spaniol, Taneva, Thater, & Weikum. (2011). Robust disambiguation of named entities in text. *EMNLP*, 782–792.

Ji, Sun, Cong, & Han. (2016). Joint recognition and linking of fine-grained locations from tweets. *WWW*, 1271–1281.

Kapur, J. N. (1989). *Maximum-entropy models in science and engineering*. John Wiley & Sons.

Kazama & Torisawa. (2007). Exploiting wikipedia as external knowledge for named entity recognition. *EMNLP-CoNLL*.

Kim, Thiessen, Bolton, Chen, Fu, Gindulyte, Han, He, He, Shoemaker, Wang, Yu, Zhang, & Bryant. (2015). *Chem Substance and Compound Databases*. doi:10.1093/nar/gkv951

Klein, C. (2011). *Information Extraction from Text for Improving Research on Small Molecules and Histone Modifications* [Ph.D. thesis]. Bonn, Germany: Universitäts-und Landesbibliothek.

Klinger, R., Kolárik, C., Fluck, J., Hofmann-Apitius, M., & Friedrich, C. M. (2008). Detection of IUPAC and IUPAC-like chemical names. *Bioinformatics (Oxford, England)*, *24*(13), i268–i276. doi:10.1093/bioinformatics/btn181 PMID:18586724

Krallinger, M., Leitner, F., & Rabal, O. (2013). Overview of the chemical compound and drug name recognition (CHEMDNER) task. *BioCreative Challenge Eval. Workshop*, *2*, 2.

Krallinger, M., Leitner, F., Rabal, O., Vazquez, M., Oyarzabal, J., & Valencia, A. (2013). Overview of the chemical compound and drug name recognition (CHEMDNER) task. BioCreative Challenge Evaluation Workshop, 2.

Krallinger, M., Rabal, O., Leitner, F., Vazquez, M., Salgado, D., Lu, Z., Leaman, R., Lu, Y., Ji, D., Lowe, D. M., Sayle, R. A., Batista-Navarro, R. T., Rak, R., Huber, T., Rocktäschel, T., Matos, S., Campos, D., Tang, B., Xu, H., ... Valencia, A. (2015). The CHEMDNER corpus of chemicals and drugs and its annotation principles. *Journal of Cheminformatics*, *7*(S1, Suppl 1), S2. doi:10.1186/1758-2946-7-S1-S2 PMID:25810773

Krishnan & Manning. (2006). An effective two-stage model for exploiting non-local dependencies in named entity recognition. *ACL*, 1121–1128.

LeCun, Y., Bengio, Y., & Hinton, G. (2015). Deep learning. *Nature*, *521*(7553), 436–444. doi:10.1038/nature14539 PMID:26017442

Li, J., Sun, Y., Johnson, R. J., Sciaky, D., Wei, C.-H., Leaman, R., Davis, A. P., Mattingly, C. J., Wiegers, T. C., & Lu, Z. (2016). BioCreative V CDR task corpus: A resource for chemical disease relation extraction. *Database (Oxford)*, *2016*, baw068. Advance online publication. doi:10.1093/database/baw068 PMID:27161011

Liao & Veeramachaneni. (2009). A simple semi-supervised algorithm for named entity recognition. *NAACL-HLT*, 58–65.

Lowe & Sayle. (2015). LeadMine: A grammar and dictionary driven approach to chemical entity recognition. *Proceedings of the fourth BioCreative challenge evaluation workshop*, 2.

Luo, L., Yang, Z., Yang, P., Zhang, Y., Wang, L., Wang, J., & Lin, H. (2018). A neural network approach to chemical and gene/protein entity recognition in patents. *Journal of Cheminformatics*, *10*(1), 65. doi:10.118613321-018-0318-3 PMID:30564940

Mansouri, A., Affendey, L. S., & Mamat, A. (2008). Named entity recognition approaches. *Int J Comp Sci Netw Sec*, *8*, 339–344.

Mikheev. (1999). A knowledge-free method for capitalized word disambiguation. *ACL*, 159–166.

Nadeau, D., & Sekine, S. (2007). A survey of named entity recognition and classification. *Lingvisticae Investigationes*, *30*(1), 3–26. doi:10.1075/li.30.1.03nad

Narayanaswamy, M., Ravikumar, K. E., & Vijay-Shanker, K. (2003). A biological named entity recognizer. *Pacific Symposium on Biocomputing*, 427.

Ravin & Wacholder. (1997). *Extracting names from natural-language text.* IBM Research Report RC 2033.

Rebholz-Schuhmann, Arregui, Gaudan, Kirsch, & Jimeno. (2008). Text processing through Web services: calling Whatizit. *Bioinformatics,* *24*(2), 296-298.

Sayle, R., Xie, P. H., & Muresan, S. (2012). Improved chemical text mining of patents with infinite dictionaries and automatic spelling correction. *Journal of Chemical Information and Modeling*, *52*(1), 51–62. doi:10.1021/ci200463r PMID:22148717

Sekine, S., & Ranchhod, E. (2009). *Named entities: recognition, classification and use* (Vol. 19). John Benjamins Publishing. doi:10.1075/bct.19

Settles. (2004). Biomedical named entity recognition using Conditional Random Fields and rich feature sets. *ACL*, 104–107.

Toral, A., & Munoz, R. (2006). A proposal to automatically build and maintain gazetteers for named entity recognition by using Wikipedia. *Workshop on NEW TEXT Wikis and blogs and other dynamic text sources.*

Wang, Y., Xiao, J., Suzek, T. O., Zhang, J., Wang, J., & Bryant, S. H. (2009). PubChem: A public information system for analyzing bioactivities of small molecules. *Nucleic Acids Research*, *37*(Web Server), W623–W633. doi:10.1093/nar/gkp456 PMID:19498078

Yan, Spangler, & Chen. (2012). Learning to Extract Chemical Names based on Random Text Generation and Incomplete Dictionary. *BIOKDD'12.*

Zhou & Su. (2002). Named entity recognition using an HMM based chunk tagger. *ACL*, 473–480.

Zhu, J., Uren, V., & Motta, E. (2005). *Espotter: Adaptive named entity recognition for web browsing. In WM.* Springer.

Chapter 5
Mathematical Information Retrieval Trends and Techniques

Pankaj Dadure
National Institute of Technology, Silchar, India

Partha Pakray
National Institute of Technology, Silchar, India

Sivaji Bandyopadhyay
National Institute of Technology, Silchar, India

ABSTRACT

Mathematical formulas are widely used to express ideas and fundamental principles of science, technology, engineering, and mathematics. The rapidly growing research in science and engineering leads to a generation of a huge number of scientific documents which contain both textual as well as mathematical terms. In a scientific document, the sense of mathematical formulae is conveyed through the context and the symbolic structure which follows the strong domain specific conventions. In contrast to textual information, developed mathematical information retrieval systems have demonstrated the unique and elite indexing and matching approaches which are beneficial to the retrieval of formulae and scientific term. This chapter discusses the recent advancement in formula-based search engines, various formula representation styles and indexing techniques, benefits of formula-based search engines in various future applications like plagiarism detection, math recommendation system, etc.

INTRODUCTION

Mathematics is a significant factor in the field of science, technology, engineering, and mathematics (STEM) (Greiner-Petter A. A., 2020). Without a single mathematical expression or symbol, a scientific text is often available. In this digital world, with growing numbers of teaching and learning materials

DOI: 10.4018/978-1-7998-7728-8.ch005

being produced, the explosion of knowledge was indeed inevitable. In the last decade, new techniques, concepts, and tools were created to store, maintain and retrieve this vast array of scientific records. In order to ensure, the users can easily access the information according to their information needs, the information needs to be organized and represented in the most efficient way.

Information retrieval (IR) is a subfield of natural language processing (NLP) that aims to retrieve the needed information from the collection of documents. The general IR system takes the user's query as an input, works on the similarity, and based on that returns the rank of relevant documents (Buttcher, 2016). This is a common methodology used by today's retrieval system like Google search, PubMed, or Apple's Spotlight system. Nowadays, most of the available data on the web is sequential text data. Besides, the demand of the users may change: sometimes users may search for image/video data based on the text data, text based on the image data, based on the cause user's looking for effect related documents, some users interested in the linguistically structured documents. In some cases, users are unsure about what exactly they are looking for. To achieve these, several preprocessing operations have been investigated depend on the domain and the user's requirements (Virmani, 2019). Almost all the retrieval systems are specially written programs, as long as researchers can explain their methodology, can be done for particular types of data. Moreover, the domain of information retrieval is explored since the early 1950s, and as a result, many IR models come into the limelight which mainly lies on the boolean model, vector space model, and probabilistic model. The field of textual information retrieval has been extensively investigated for many years, but mathematical information retrieval (MIR) (Hu, 2013) requires distinctive attention since traditional text recuperation systems cannot retrieve mathematical expressions. The mir systems are formula-based search engines that assist to search for knowledge in mathematical documents. The prime aspect of these MIR systems is to retrieve mathematical formulae which are relevant to a queried formula. In this task, the term 'relevant' encompasses two meaning: first considered the structural similarities to query formula, and the second one considered the conceptual meaning of the formula. Each finds not only formulas that are the exact match of the query formula, but also those which share similarities with it. For example, a retrieved result might contain only part of the query equation or might append terms.

Formulas found in web pages are mainly encoded in latex and/or MathML format. The traditional text-based search engines ignore the structure of these encodings by treating formula as normal text. This creates obstacles for a search engine to retrieve the relevant documents due to bounded structural information about the formula in the search index. In terms of query generation, this is a challenging task for an unfamiliar user with latex or MathML. Also, a recent study confirms that presenting raw math encodings in search results can adversely affect the accuracy of relevance assessment for search hits.

Information in mathematics is conveyed through descriptions, scientific terms, mathematical structures, and symbols which can be predefined in a mathematical expression. In this sense, technical terminology has also a significant role to play in mathematics. Moreover, the use of mathematical notation is dialectic. For example, different communities use different conventions for naming variables and defining operators. Individual authors redefine and adapt notation for their immediate needs. This flexibility is beneficial for authors and readers but makes automatic interpretation very difficult. This hypothesis stemmed from the observation that the mathematical discourse is dense with named mathematical objects, structures, properties, and results. An automatic understanding of equations significantly beneficial for analyzing scientific literature. In addition to this, the useful representations of equations can help to draw connections between articles, improve retrieval of scientific texts, and help to create tools for exploring and navigating scientific literature. Furthermore, the successful searching and retrieval of mathematical information provide the future research direction for many natural language processing-artificial intelligence applications like math-based question answering systems, math-based recommender systems, plagiarism detection, etc.

Figure 1. Interaction of mathematical formula and their context

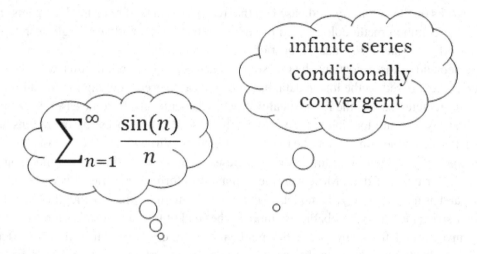

RELATED WORK

This section provides the brief overview about the existing state-of-the-art mathematical information retrieval approaches. Based on the idea of formula representation, existing related work have been classified into four broad categories namely text-based, tree-based, vector-based and neural network-based approach.

1. Text-Based Approach

The prior research study of text-based approaches witness that the retrieval of textual information is different from MIR. To deal with mathematical information, ordinary text-based approaches requires the significant improvement. At NTCIR-10, team MIRMU (Livska M. a., 2013) used conventional full text retrieval approach to retrieve both text and math information. To make the formula compatible for text retrieval system, several preprocessing operations have been adopted. Moreover, team BRKLY (Larson, 2013) has adopt the keyword-based approach to mutate the XML documents into the textual form. For indexing, conventional full text indexing approach has been applied. The type embedding mechanism (Stathopoulos Y. A., 2016) uses the types (sequence of word or words) to communicate the idea of mathematical expression. In which, the type has been created for the collection of documents where mathematical formulae are associated with concepts and object properties. This type of work imparts the use of semantic relationships in the retrieval of mathematical formulae.

2. Tree-Based Approach

In the retrieval of mathematical information, tree-based approaches have divulged the considerable performance and set the benchmark for other approaches. To overcome the restraint of semantic enhancement, the ICST math retrieval system (Gao L. a., 2014) has generates sub-tree from the semi-operator tree of formulas. In which, the layout presentation of tree transformed into a semantic presentation to enrich the retrieval of formula. Tangent-CFT (Mansouri B. a., 2019) uses two distinct hierarchical representations of formulae i.e., Symbol Layout Tree (SLT) and Operator Tree (OPT). The path between the pair of symbols generates the tuples which have then embed using the n-gram embedding model. To achieve the stat-of-the-art results, structural matching has been deployed to retrieves partial similar formulas. The Tangent-CFT-Plus (Mansouri B. a., 2020) is an extended model of Tangent-CFT where each formula represented in two distinct vector form i.e., formula vector and text vector. The vector representation of the formula acquired based on the idea of Tangent-CFT model where vector size of formula is 300 and the vector representation of the textual acquired by considering formula as a word and training the fastText model on the surrounding words of the formula where vector size is 100. As response to final vector, formula and text vector has been concatenated. The result of Wikipedia Formula Browsing Task of NTCIR-12 shown that the Tangent-CFT enhance partial matching compared to exact match. To solve this problem, the extended version of Tangent-CFT (Tangent-CFT with Tree Edit Distance) (Mansouri B. a., 2020) performed re-ranking of the retrieval results based on tree-edit distance. The minimum cost of converting one tree to another is the Tree-Edit Distance. The insertion, deletion and substitution were three editing operations taken into the considered. When measuring the distance cost for tree-editing, each operation has different weight. VMEXT is a free open-sourced platform (Schubotz M. a., 2017) used to visualized expression tree form the parallel MathML. It demonstrates the visualizations in two web-based applications. The first one depicts the curating semantically enriched mathematical content. The second one demonstrates the potential inclusion of visualization techniques into systems for the management of mathematical knowledge and MIR. The approach which converts LATEX input to parallel MathML, computes simple measurements of similarity for mathematical expressions, and uses VMEXT to visualise the output. The variable typing approach (Stathopoulos Y. A., 2018) has assigned the mathematical words to each variable and typing has performed on the sentence level with valid type assignments for variables drawn from the sentences in which they occur, rather than from larger contexts, such as documents.

3. Vector-Based Approach

In MIR, vector-based approach is one of the leading techniques which transformed formula to vector. For instance, the BVTMF approach (Pathak A. a., 2019) generates the binary vector of size 202 where '1' represents the presence and '0' represent the absence of entity in a formula. In this approach, both textual and mathematical information have been incorporated to achieve the better retrieval efficiency. In a vector-based approach, the similarity calculation is one of the time taking task where the system mapped the similarities between the user query and indexed vectors. For instance, cosine similarity calculation between the query and indexed formulas have shown the valuable contribution and leading scope in similarity measurement (Pathak A. a., 2019) (Dadure, An empirical analysis on retrieval of math information from the scientific documents, 2019). Motivated from the concept of formula embedding and term-document matrix, the variable size formula embedding approach (Dadure, 2020) where the formula is transformed into the variable size vector. In a vector, each bit represents their occurrence and corresponds to their position in BPIT (Pathak A. a., 2018). A novel signature-based hashing scheme (Dhar, 2019) has extracted formulas from scientific documents and converted to structure encoded strings. These strings have served as the input for the hash-based indexing scheme, which aimed to converts these strings into a bit vector/signatures. A hash table of these signatures has created which enabled the online searching of formulas.

4. Neural Network-Based Approach

Now a days, a neural network is an emerging field in the domain of IR and natural language processing. While the remarkable performance of the neural network in the retrieval of textual information, many researchers have attempted at formula retrieval and achieves the benchmark results. For instance, Formula2vec based approach (Gao L. a., 2017) explores the proficiency of neural network-based vector representation of mathematical formulas. It uses the Distributed Memory Model of Paragraph Vectors (PV-DM) to learn a different representation of formula. The influence of LSTM in sequence-to-sequence tasks, LSTM based formula entailment approach (Pathak A. a., 2019) has been proposed to formulate the entailment between the user entered math query and the formula contains in a scientific document. MIRMU is one of the research team of Masaryk University and well performed participant of ARQMath CLEF 2020 task. Team MIRMU have designed the two systems named Soft Cosine Measure (SCM) and Formula2Vec for the task of formula retrieval (Novotny, 2020). In which, the SCM system combines TF-IDF with unsupervised word embeddings to produce interpretable representations of math documents and math formulae that enable fast and interpretable information retrieval. The Formula2Vec system that uses Doc2Vec to infer document and formula embeddings for formula search task. In Formula2Vec, documents and formulae are represented by document and formula embeddings produced by training the Doc2Vec DBOW model on text and math data. To learn a distributed representation of equations, the unsupervised approach called equation embeddings (EqEmb) (Krstovski, 2018) where equation is treated as singleton word. In which semantic representations of mathematical equations and their surrounding words is embed and obtained results have compared with the CBOW, PV-DM, GloVe model where EqEmb-U achieves the highest performance. Motivated from the emerging association between mathematical formulas and textual context found in scientific documents, the topic model called (Yasunaga, 2019) has jointly generates mathematical equations and their surrounding text. In this approach, the context has generated from a mixture of latent topics, and the equation has generated by an RNN that depends on the latent topic activation and enables intelligible processing of equations by considering the relationship between the mathematical equations and topics and shown their performance in terms of perplexity metric. The exploratory investigation of the effectiveness and used of word embedding (Greiner-Petter A. a., 2020) where word2vec model has trained on DLMF and arXiv with slightly different approaches. The DLMF trained model discovered the mathematical term similarities and analogies, and generates the query expansions whereas arXiv trained model beneficial to extract the textual descriptive phrases for math terms. The word embedding model mainly focused on term similarity, math analogies, concept modeling, query expansion, and knowledge extraction.

5. Other Approaches

In the retrieval of mathematical information, some of the researchers have uses both text and math-based approaches to achieves the best results. The Tangent math search system (Pattaniyil, 2014) uses two indices to attains their best retrieval results. The first index has based on the concept of TF-IDF textual search and second index based on the concept of query-by-expression. The query-by-expression strategy uses the bag-of-word approach to represent the formula in pairs of symbols which are computed from the symbol layout tree. The SMSG5 research team (Thanda, 2016) from India introduced the math search engine which explores the co-occurrence of formula and keyword. For co-occurrence findings, LDA and doc2vec techniques have been used. Moreover, they have used common patterns between formula and keywords to achieves their best. The approach of combining the textual information and the math expression (Livska M. a., 2015) contained in the documents and the queries have shown the cutting-edge performance of the MIR system. In this, to retrieves the exact match, similar match and sub-formulas, the query expansion technique has been used and finalize the best search results. At NTCIR-12 (Zanibbi, 2016), team MIRNU [34] presented a refinement in the mechanism of unification and query expansion. In this work, two types of unification approaches have been used namely structural unification and operator unification. To obtain more promising results, the system accepts the query in different versions. The inclusion of structural unification leads to impressive recall but has a pessimistic influence on precision. In order to obtain supportive definitions and propositions, the selection method of natural premises (Ferreira, 2020) has generates the informal mathematical proofs to produce a specific argument. This offered that the estimation of the task of selecting the premise of natural language is to be supplied with precise embedding and representation of mathematical formulas.

DIGITAL REPRESENTATION OF FORMULA

The most suitable representation of formula can influence the rate of algorithms, the amount of storage, the accuracy of the system and other factors when developing an any type of information retrieval system. There is no limitation to represent the mathematical content. The numerous formats for mathematical expression encoding are available (Caprotti, 1999). Latex is one of the most common ways to represents the mathematical formulas in scientific documents. Latex represents the mathematical formula in more compact form than other representation formats. However, its processing is not simple because the equations in latex form can contain several commands from various packages. In latex, there are several ways to represent the same symbols using either a unicode or embedded commands. In addition to this, the MathML is another standard to represent the mathematical formulas, which has first offered as the recommended language for web documents in 1998 by the world wide web consortium. One of MathML's advantages over latex is that it is an xml framework that makes algorithmic processing very simple. There are two types MathML representation i.e., Presentation MathML and Content MathML. The first is aimed at the visual representation of the formula and the other at the semantic of the formulas. OpenMath is another formula representation markup language, which can be used to incorporate more semantic information using a complementary MathML presentation. It is mostly used in standard contents dictionaries to describe the math definition. In general, to translate and process mathematical expression in these languages, a complete compiler is needed. The MathML provides a better balance between the representation length and the ease of processing. Table 1 present a comparison on how different language can express the formula $\cos(\pi) = -1$.

Table 1. The different languages for expressing the mathematical content

LATEX	Presentation MathML	Content MathML	OpenMath
\cos(\pi) = -1	<math> <mi> cos </mi> <mo> (</mo> <mi> π </mi> <mo>) </m> <mo> = </mo> <mo> - </mo> <mn> 1 </mn> </math>	<apply><cos/> <apply> <ci> π </ci> </apply> <cn> = </cn> </minus> <cn> = </cn> <cn> 1 </cn> </apply>	<OMA> <OMS cd="relation1" name="eq"/> <OMA> <OMS cd="transc1" name="cos"/> <OMS cd="nums1" name="pi"/> </OMA> <OMI$> -1 </OMI$> </OMA>

CHALLENGES IN MATHEMATICAL INFORMATION RETRIEVAL

The retrieval of mathematical information is qualitatively and quantitively different from textual information retrieval and it requires inclusion of new knowledge processing, indexing, and ranking techniques. Following are some of the key challenges faced by MIR systems (Schubotz M. a., 2015):

- In scientific document/articles, mathematical formulas are mostly represented in MathML and TEX format. However, the traditional text-based search engines have unavailability of precisely designed math editors, which are compulsory for inputting formulas.
- The formulas are immensely structured and are generally seen in layouts presentations, e.g., LATEX or MathML. These features cause difficulties to utilized natural language approaches in the processing and retrieval of mathematical information.
- In return to the query request (for example $\sqrt{a+b}$), end user not only search for documents with an accurate formula match ($\sqrt{a+b}$) but also the documents consist sub-formulae ($\sqrt{a}, \sqrt{b}$), similar formulae (for example $\sqrt{x+y}$) and parent formulae (for example $\dfrac{1}{\sqrt{a+b}}$). Existing systems unable to handle such kind of retrieval.
- The several mathematical formulae have alternative representations. For example, permutation of k items selected from n different items can be expressed in several forms: P_k^n , $P_{n,k}$, and $P(n, k)$. The successful MIR system should have the ability to consider all differently express formulas as identical.
- The several encoding techniques are used (Hu, Wikimirs: a mathematical information retrieval system for wikipedia, 2013) to encode mathematical formulas, like TEX, MathML, OpenMath, SGML, Unicode etc. Almost all these encoding techniques allows the redundant elements and attributes. These redundant entities often aim to create any marvellous formula and no impact on formula semantic. For example, the <mspace> element of MathML is only used for adding a space. Therefore, all such redundant elements and attributes should be excluded from well preprocessed formula.

- In scientific documents, the mathematical formulae are mainly depend on its meaning. For example, f(x) which means that the function of 'x' or the variable 'f' multiples with variable 'x'. These two notions delivered the completely different meaning. Therefore, a retrieval system should definitely require note of the meaning of the formula.
- The mathematical symbols are ambiguous in nature. For example, '.' (dot symbol) in scientific documents delivered the multiple meanings such as multiplication sign, boundary symbol or noise.
- Mathematical formulas are recursive in structure, while the natural language text is generally structurally straightforward.

FORMULA PREPROCESSING

The mathematical expressions are analysed to promote searches not only for exact match formulae, but also for sub-formula (tokenisation) and semantically related formula (unification) (Sojka P. A., 2018). This explores the static existence of full-text search engines and produces a number of representations for input formula, all are indexed uniformly.

- **Segmentation:** The prime task of document segmentation is to segments the documents into the small chunks. Chunks are the user-returned information unit which displayed in the parent document. Formal mathematical formula segmentation is trivial, complex on the websites, and intermediate on books or articles. The NTCIR-11 task, however, provided a collection of segmented documents which could inhibit the future analysis of segmentation techniques.
- **Normalization:** The normalization is the process of reducing the ambiguity of the formulas which have same representational structure with different constants and variables. To handle the variation between the query formula and searched formula, the normalization is performed. The stemming and thesaurus are the normalization operation for text-based information retrieval which reduce the word to their canonical form. Similar to this, formula normalization reduced the formulas which have several representational structures to their canonical form. For example, normalizing the arrangement of symbols imposes a single spatial relationship order. Another example is the listing of variables in operator trees which enables variables to fit without considering their unique symbolic identity.
- Canonicalization: In math digital library, some formulas represent differently but holds the same meaning. For example, $x^{1/2}$ and $\sqrt{x}$, the both formulas have same meaning but different representation. Thus, canonicalization reduces the differently expressed semantically similar formulas into the unified form. This mechanism provides the facility to retrieve the documents which are semantically similar to query formula. Canonicalization also leads to reduced index size, which result to less space and faster retrieval.
- **Ordering:** In digital mathematical library, some formulas have same operands, operators, variables and constants in different order. For example, x+10 and 10+x, both formulas have same operands and operators. To deal with this kind of formulas and for efficient retrieval, the ordering mechanism is used. For above-mentioned example, the variable x denoted as mi and number 10 denoted as mn. In which, the priority is assigned to (mi<mn) which makes the mathematical expression and the query term similar.

- **Tokenization:** Tokenization is a simple method by which sub-formulas are derived from the input formula. The current framework uses the MathML presentation markup where all logical elements are included in XML tags, making it possible to obtain tree traversals in all sub-formulas.

- Unification: The main purpose of unification is to obtained the more generalized form of formulas obtained from tokenization process. This step allows the system to return identical matches to the user request and preserve the structure and α-equality of the formula. In which sub-formulas are collected and eliminate the irrelevant information. The unification operation is performed at two level i.e., variables unification (substitution of variable with unified symbol (id)) and constants unification (substitution of numbers with constant(const)). For instance, after variable unification, such as $x+y^a$ and $a+b^x$ will be $\mathbf{id}_1 + \mathbf{id}_2{}^{id_3}$. The unification operation is performed on indexing and searching side so that it can be easily fit expressions with the same semantic meaning with different variables.

FORMULA BASED SEARCH ENGINE

1. MathDex

MathDex is one of the oldest formulae based full text search engine (Miner, 2007) implemented on apache lucene search engine (Lucene, 2010). It is implemented by National Science Foundation under the National Science Digital Library program lead by Robert. The processing layers of MathDex is implemented on the top of the apache lucene search engine. The prime task of these layers is to analyze the mathematical formula which are express in XML format. It considers the mathematical formula as a text token and follow the searching framework of apache lucene. The key contribution of the MathDex is given below:

a.   Assist to retrieve semantically indigent documents
b.   Assist various math encoding styles for semantically indigent documents
c.   Enables the searching of both mathematical expression and textual data
d.   Seeks to satisfy user search needs instead of addressing the demand solely

2. EgoMath

EgoMath is a full text search engine designed by Jozef Misutka, based on digital mathematical information with little semantic knowledge (Mivsutka, 2008). Furthermore, the extended version of EgoMath has been released named EgoMath2 which enables system to access the mathematical concept from wikipedia digital library. The prime aspect of any formula-based engine is to retrieve the syntactically and semantically similar formulas. To addressed this, Egomath2 (Mivsutka, 2011) and its ancestor worked on the similar goal but various designs are deployed for similarity function, indexing, and searching. In which, the contextual definition of the formula is considered to furnish the similarity search. In addition to this, the EgoMath2 incorporated the augmentation algorithm: takes benefits of full text search engine to accelerate the search into a broad range of words, ordering algorithm: converts each representation to a canonical one. The complete architecture of the EgoMath2 is shown in Figure 2.

Figure 2. EgoMath2 architecture (Mivsutka, 2011)

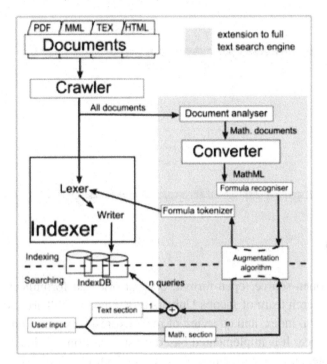

3. LaTeXSearch

LaTeXSearch is an innovative online platform launched by springer which enables the individual to search and discovers latex equation (Pineau, 2016). The user interface of LaTeXSearch is shown in Figure 3 where each individual module works cooperatively to satisfy user's need. LaTeXSearch is presently supported the access of more than 120,000 springer-published papers in the journal of computational neuroscience, journal of experimental, theoretical physics, and journal of materials science. One of the problems faced by readers of mathematical journals is their absence of access to the code that generates the equations. Latexsearch.com solved this problem by a variety of ways to find equations and accessing the latex code with one link. The LaTeXSearch enables the users to type the same equation in a numerous form. To achieved this, springer invested over eight months to normalized the latex equations. In response to user's query, it returned the set of exact match results and semantically similar results (or even exactly the same but written slightly different) under the "similar results" tab. In LaTeXSearch, the users can search the latex equation in three way:

a.   LaTeX Search: By directly typing latex equation as per the need.
b.   Article title search: Searching of research articles which consist latex code.
c.   Digital Object Identifier (DOI) search: If a user knows in which document they wants to see equations.

Figure 3: User Interface of LaTeXSearch (Pineau, 2016)

4. MathWebSearch

MathWebSearch is an open-source, open-format, content-oriented formula based search engine developed by KWARC research team of Jacobs University Bremen (Kohlhase, 2006). This is one of the robust system able to crawl, index, and querying of math expressions based on the operator's structure rather than their appearance. It is implemented based on substitution tree indexing. In addition to this, generalization of variable, and constant unification is also deployed. It offers low-latency responses to the unification of Content MathML formula notation.

5. WikiMirs

WikiMirs system facilitated the search for mathematical formulae based on textual and spatial similarities (Hu, 2013). WikiMirs introduced the hierarchical generalization technique which produces the sub-trees from presentation trees of formulae, and similarity is estimated by performing the text matching and structure matching at different levels of these trees. The extended version of WikiMirs (i.e., WikiMirs 3.0) (Wang, 2015) proposed a novel hybrid indexing and matching model which support the both exact and fuzzy matching. In which users can easily cut formulae and contexts from pdf documents as well as type in queries. This model uses the both the context and structural definition of the formulae. In which, the definition of formula lead to better ranking. The working flow of WikiMirs 3.0 system is shown in Figure 4.

Figure 4. WikiMirs 3.0 architecture (Wang, 2015)

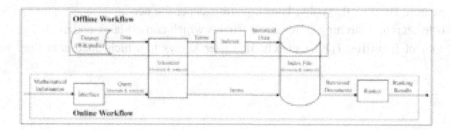

6. Tangent-CFT

The distributive representation of word benefits the many information retrieval and natural language processing activities, vector representation models for mathematical formulations have not yet been adequately examined. Mathematical formulas can express the similar contents in various ways and therefore potentially distributed representations are useful to give the level of abstraction. The Tangent-CFT (Mansouri B. a., 2019) proposed the new embedded format that use with two hierarchical representation, (1) Symbol Layout Trees (SLTs) to preserve the appearance of the formula and (2) Operator Trees (OPTs) to preserve the content of the formula. Based on the approach of graph embedding like DeepWalk, Tangent-CFT produced the tuple which represents the path between pairs of symbols. Afterwards tuples embedded using fastText n-gram embedding model and average of OPT and SLT tuple taken into the consideration. The average tuple vectors lead to state-of-the-art retrieval results compared to individual one. The work flow of the Tangent-CFT system is shown Figure 5.

Figure 5. Tangent-CFT work flow (Mansouri B. a., 2019)

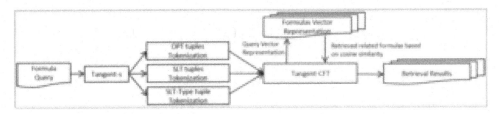

7. MIaS

MIaS (Math Indexer and Searcher) (Sojka P. a., 2011) is one of the most popular open sourced highly-scalable full-text search engine based on apache lucene system and consist the set of tools for the preprocessing of mathematical formulae. The pictorial representation of the MIaS architecture is shown in Figure 6. In 2012, MIaS has been deployed in the Europe Digital Mathematical Library (EUDML) and become the first MIR system deployed in digital mathematical library. MIaS processes the text and mathematical data independently. In which text data is tokenized and stemmed to root word forms. MIaS works on MathML format of formula. For this, the MIaS has uses the Tralics tool which converts the formula in Latex format to formula in MathML format. In addition to this, InftyReader, and Max-Tract tools have been used to convert PDF documents to MathML format. The main constituent of this model is the preprocessing operations on mathematical data which includes Canonicalization, Ordering, Tokenization, and Unification. To built the user interface, MIaS has uses the open-sourced WebMIaS which is shown in Figure 7. Using this, users can enter their text-formula based query. In response to user entered query, the retrieve matches highlighted in the search results.

Figure 6. MIaS architecture (Sojka P. a., 2011)

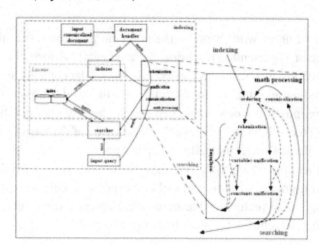

Figure 7. WebMIaS user interface (Sojka P. a., 2011)

8. MathIRs

The retrieval system for scientific documents i.e., MathIRs (Pathak A. a., 2017) performed the retrieval of mathematical and textual information and to performed similarity matching with these contents, three important modules have been deployed: Text-Text Similarity (TS), Math-Math Similarity (MS) and Text-Math Similarity (TMS). The MathIRs system basically depends on the three important modules: Indexing, Math Processing and Similarity. For indexing the textual information, the MathIRs has used the apache lucene open-source information retrieval software library. In addition to this, a substitution tree-based mechanism has been used for indexing mathematical expressions. Afterwards, TS, MS and TMS modules of MathIRs architecture performed text-text, math-math and text-math similarity matching for scientific document retrieval. The first module is a TS module that sets the level of likeness between the text query and the text in the document. In which there are four methods that quantify the resemblance between text and text: lexical, syntactic, wordnet, and distributed semantic. The query is interpreted with synonyms, hypernyms, and hyponyms in the knowledge-based approach. The second module is MS module which finds the similarity between math query and the document containing mathematical expressions. MS module helps to match canonically selected querying expressions with canonical and structurally unified mathematical expressions present in the document. A query expression may not refer to an exact math term in a document but may correspond to one of its structurally unified variants, leading to the retrieval of the subordinate document. The third and final module is the TMS module that reveals correlations between text queries and formulas within the documents. The correspondence between Text and Math can be discovered by assigning correct names to the math expressions at the time of indexing. Text query is compared to indexed mathematical description, and the corresponding document is retried if any acceptable match is found. The work flow of the MathIRs is shown in Figure 8.

Figure 8. MathIRs system architecture (Pathak A. a., 2017)

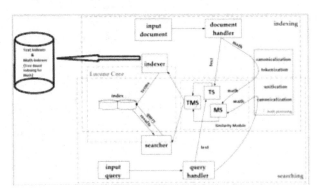

9. Retrieval System Based HFS and BERT

In the retrieval of scientific documents with mathematical formulas as the main content, both mathematical formulas and contextual text need to be taken into account. However, mathematical formulas have a predefined structure, syntax, and semantic. Thus, to integrate these features in a textual information retrieval system is a laborious one. The HFS-BERT based retrieval system (Tian, 2021) has used the concept of Hesitation Fuzzy Sets, and Bidirectional Encoder Representations from Transformer. This system utilized the benefits of HFS in multi-attribute decision making and BERT in context-dependent similarity calculation. The similarity calculation of mathematical formulas is about the measurement of symbols similarity and their corresponding mathematical structures. Sometimes, some mathematical symbols have possessed different attributes, their similarities would also be very different. To achieve this, the capability of HFS has used to processed the multiple attributes. In addition to this, the extracted textual context used by the BERT to calculate textual similarity. Afterward, the recalled documents are sorted according to the context similarity and retrieved the final search results. This system has been tested on the 10,372 Chinese and 11,770 English scientific documents in the NTCIR extended data set. The workflow of the HFS-BERT based retrieval system is shown in Figure 8.

Figure 9. Flow chart of the HFS-BERT based retrieval system (Tian, 2021)

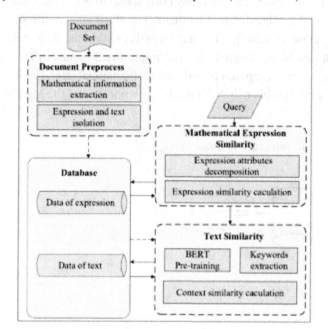

FUTURE APPLICATIONS

Math Recommender System

With YouTube, Amazon, Netflix and many other Web services in recent decades, recommendation systems have been putting more and more of their place in our lives. In order to tackle the growing online knowledge overload issue and strengthen customer experience management, a recommending framework aim to offer users personalized online products and services recommendations. Recommendation systems are algorithms that offer related stuff to users. The numerous information systems (software) were introduced and many real-world recommending system applications were developed with the advancement of recommendation approaches and techniques. Recommendation systems are implemented in the fields of e-commerce, e-learning, e-library, e government and e-business services, and include the recommendations on movies, music, broadcasters, books, papers, blogs, conferences, tourism attractions and learning material. A recommendation system will automatically assist by recommending scientific documents based on the preferences of similar mathematical formulas (Scharpf, 2019). The recommendation system that makes and accelerates formula annotation by showing the most likely nominee candidates. The researcher working in the field of MIR, started to work on recommender system for mathematical information or math-based scientific documents. The research just in early stage and requires inclusion of new ideas and technologies.

Plagiarism Detection

The detection of academic plagiarism is an urgent need of educational, research, publishing and commercial institutes. Instances of copied and mildly redrawn text can be detected by the present plagiarism detection systems (Naik, 2015). However, it is an open issue of study to accurately identify secret plagiarism, such as heavy paraphrasis, translations and mathematical content. In order to establish novel plagiarism detection methods, the research on non-textual content is in limelight which integrates the analyses of the mathematical contents with analyses of academic citations. This framework allows the editor to understand quickly why a document is so suspicious. Visualizing the topical similarity is a crucial element for the future method to accomplish this purpose.

Mathematical Problem Solver

One of the early-stage applications of artificial intelligence is mathematical problem solving, such as the Newell and Simon automatic theorem proofing. The recent research on mathematical problem solving involves structures that address algebraic word issues while offering a problem solving overview and that solve text-math based algebra word problems (Kushman, 2014). To address such issues a system of equations needs to be reasoned across phrased borders in order to model the defined semantic relations in a concise way. Learning end-to-end model to solve word problems only an educational corpus of questions coupled with equations or answers is needed. The researcher working in the field of MIR, started to work on mathematical problem-solving approach. The research just in early stage and requires inclusion of new ideas and technologies.

CONCLUSION AND FUTURE SCOPE

This chapter highlights the key challenges in developing a mathematical information retrieval system that enables access and searches for mathematical formulae in existing information systems. With the rising significance of digital mathematical libraries, the demand for successful MIR systems is growing. This study is designed to confirm the assumption where the development of math-enabled digital libraries essentially blends both users' needs and technological opportunities. The goals of this study were: 1) challenges faced by MIR system, 2) preprocessing operations which enable formulas compatible for retrieval system, 3) working phenomenon of the existing math-based search engine, and 4) future research direction have discussed. In future, there is a need to design novel formula representation and indexing technique which will incorporate the innovative and intelligent formula retrieval properties into the math-based engine.

ACKNOWLEDGMENT

The authors would like to express gratitude to the Department of Computer Science and Engineering and Center for Natural Language Processing, National Institute of Technology Silchar, India for providing infrastructural facilities and support. The authors would also like to thank Mr. Amarnath Pathak for providing the foundation, encouragement, and many fruitful discussions on this work.

REFERENCES

Buttcher, S. a. (2016). *Information retrieval: Implementing and evaluating search engines*. MIT Press.

Caprotti, O. a. (1999). OpenMath and MathML: semantic markup for mathematics. *XRDS: Crossroads. The ACM Magazine for Students, 6*(2), 11–14.

Dadure, P. a. (2019). An empirical analysis on retrieval of math information from the scientific documents. In *International Conference on Communication and Intelligent Systems* (pp. 301-308). Springer.

Dadure, P. a. (2020). An Analysis of Variable-Size Vector Based Approach for Formula Searching. *CLEF 2020 Working Notes Working Notes of CLEF 2020 – Conference and Labs of the Evaluation Forum Thessaloniki, 2696*.

Dhar, S., & Roy, S. (2019). Mathematical document retrieval system based on signature hashing. *Aptikom Journal on Computer Science and Information Technologies, 4*(1), 45–56. doi:10.11591/APTIKOM.J.CSIT.135

Ferreira, D. a. (2020). *Natural language premise selection: Finding supporting statements for mathematical text*. arXiv preprint arXiv:2004.14959.

Gao, L. a. (2014). *ICST Math Retrieval System for NTCIR-11 Math-2 Task*. NTCIR.

Gao, L. a. (2017). *Preliminary Exploration of Formula Embedding for Mathematical Information Retrieval: can mathematical formulae be embedded like a natural language?* arXiv preprint arXiv:1707.05154.

Greiner-Petter, A. a. (2020). Discovering mathematical objects of interest—a study of mathematical notations. *Proceedings of The Web Conference 2020*, 1445-1456. 10.1145/3366423.3380218

Greiner-Petter, A., Youssef, A., Ruas, T., Miller, B. R., Schubotz, M., Aizawa, A., & Gipp, B. (2020). Math-word embedding in math search and semantic extraction. *Scientometrics, 125*(3), 3017–3046. doi:10.100711192-020-03502-9

Hu, X. a. (2013). Wikimirs: a mathematical information retrieval system for wikipedia. *Proceedings of the 13th ACM/IEEE-CS joint conference on Digital libraries*, 11-20. 10.1145/2467696.2467699

Kohlhase, M. a. (2006). A search engine for mathematical formulae. In *International Conference on Artificial Intelligence and Symbolic Computation* (pp. 241-253). Springer. 10.1007/11856290_21

Krstovski, K. a. (2018). *Equation embeddings*. arXiv preprint arXiv:1803.09123.

Kushman, N. a. (2014). Learning to automatically solve algebra word problems. In *Proceedings of the 52nd Annual Meeting of the Association for Computational Linguistics (*Volume 1*: Long Papers)*, (pp. 271-281). 10.3115/v1/P14-1026

Larson, R. R. (2013). *The Abject Failure of Keyword IR for Mathematics Search: Berkeley at NTCIR-10 Math*. NTCIR.

Livska, M. a. (2013). Similarity search for mathematics: Masaryk university team at the ntcir-10 math task. *Proceedings of the 10th NTCIR Conference on Evaluation of Information Access Technologies*, 686-691.

Livska, M. a. (2015). Combining text and formula queries in math information retrieval: Evaluation of query results merging strategies. In *Proceedings of the First International Workshop on Novel Web Search Interfaces and Systems*, (pp. 7-9). 10.1145/2810355.2810359

Lucene, A. (2010). *Apache lucene-overview.* http://lucene. apache. org/iava/docs/

Mansouri, B. a. (2019). Tangent-CFT: An Embedding Model for Mathematical Formulas. In *Proceedings of the 2019 ACM SIGIR international conference on theory of information retrieval*, (pp. 11-18). 10.1145/3341981.3344235

Mansouri, B. a. (2020). DPRL Systems in the CLEF 2020 ARQMath Lab. *Working Notes of CLEF 2020-Conference and Labs of the Evaluation Forum.*

Miner, R. a. (2007). An approach to mathematical search through query formulation and data normalization. In *Towards Mechanized Mathematical Assistants* (pp. 342–355). Springer. doi:10.1007/978-3-540-73086-6_27

Mivsutka, J. a. (2008). *Extending full text search engine for mathematical content.* Towards Digital Mathematics Library.

Mivsutka, J. a. (2011). System description: Egomath2 as a tool for mathematical searching on wikipedia. org. In *International Conference on Intelligent Computer Mathematics* (pp. 307-309). Springer.

Naik, R. R. (2015). A review on plagiarism detection tools. *International Journal of Computers and Applications, 125*(11).

Novotny, V. a. (2020). Three is better than one. *CEUR Workshop Proceedings.*

Pathak, A. a. (2017). Mathirs: Retrieval system for scientific documents. *Computacion y Sistemas, 21*(2), 253-265.

Pathak, A. a. (2018). A formula embedding approach to math information retrieval. *Computacion y Sistemas, 22*(3), 819-833.

Pathak, A. a. (2019). Lstm neural network based math information retrieval. In *Second International Conference on Advanced Computational and Communication Paradigms (ICACCP)* (pp. 1-6). IEEE. 10.1109/ICACCP.2019.8882887

Pathak, A., Pakray, P., & Gelbukh, A. (2019). Binary vector transformation of math formula for mathematical information retrieval. *Journal of Intelligent & Fuzzy Systems, 36*(5), 4685–4695. doi:10.3233/JIFS-179018

Pattaniyil, N. a. (2014). *Combining TF-IDF Text Retrieval with an Inverted Index over Symbol Pairs in Math Expressions: The Tangent Math Search Engine at NTCIR 2014.* NTCIR.

Pineau, D. C. (2016). *Math-aware search engines: Physics applications and overview.* arXiv preprint arXiv:1609.03457.

Scharpf, P. a. (2019). AnnoMathTeX-a formula identifier annotation recommender system for STEM documents. *Proceedings of the 13th ACM Conference on Recommender Systems*, 532-533. 10.1145/3298689.3347042

Schubotz, M. a. (2015). Challenges of mathematical information retrievalin the ntcir-11 math wikipedia task. *Proceedings of the 38th international ACM SIGIR conference on research and development in information retrieval*, 951-954. 10.1145/2766462.2767787

Schubotz, M. a. (2017). VMEXT: a visualization tool for mathematical expression trees. In *International Conference on Intelligent Computer Mathematics* (pp. 340-355). Springer. 10.1007/978-3-319-62075-6_24

Sojka, P. a. (2011). The art of mathematics retrieval. *Proceedings of the 11th ACM symposium on Document engineering*, 57-60. 10.1145/2034691.2034703

Sojka, P. a. (2018). MIaS: math-aware retrieval in digital mathematical libraries. *Proceedings of the 27th ACM International Conference on Information and Knowledge Management*, 1923-1926. 10.1145/3269206.3269233

Stathopoulos, Y. A. (2016). *Mathematical information retrieval based on type embeddings and query expansion*. International Committee on Computational Linguistics.

Stathopoulos, Y. A. (2018). *Variable typing: Assigning meaning to variables in mathematical text*. Academic Press.

Thanda, A. a. (2016). *A Document Retrieval System for Math Queries*. NTCIR.

Tian, X., & Wang, J. (2021). Retrieval of Scientific Documents Based on HFS and BERT. *IEEE Access: Practical Innovations, Open Solutions*, 9, 8708–8717. doi:10.1109/ACCESS.2021.3049391

Virmani, D. a. (2019). A text preprocessing approach for efficacious information retrieval. In *Smart Innovations in Communication and Computational Sciences* (pp. 13–22). Springer. doi:10.1007/978-981-10-8968-8_2

Wang, Y. a. (2015). WikiMirs 3.0: a hybrid MIR system based on the context, structure and importance of formulae in a document. *Proceedings of the 15th ACM/IEEE-CS joint conference on digital libraries*, 173-182. 10.1145/2756406.2756918

Yasunaga, M., & Lafferty, J. D. (2019). Topiceq: A joint topic and mathematical equation model for scientific texts. *Proceedings of the AAAI Conference on Artificial Intelligence*, 23, 7394–7401. doi:10.1609/aaai.v33i01.33017394

Zanibbi, R. a. (2016). *NTCIR-12 MathIR Task Overview*. NTCIR.

Chapter 6
Language Processing and Python

Belsini Glad Shiya V.
Agurchand Manmull Jain College, India

Sharmila K.
VISTAS, India

ABSTRACT

Natural language processing is the communication between the humans and the computers. It is the field of computer science which incorporates artificial intelligence and linguistics where machine learning algorithms are used to analyze and process the enormous variety of data. This chapter delivers the fundamental concepts of language processing in Python such as text and word operations. It also gives the details about the preference of Python language for language processing and its advantages. It specifies the basic concept of variables, list, operators, looping statements in Python and explains how it can be implemented in language processing. It also specifies how a structured program can be written using Python, categorizing and tagging of words, how an information can be extracted from a text, syntactic and semantic analysis, and NLP applications. It also concentrates some of the research applications where NLP is applied and the challenges of NLP processing in the real-time area of applications.

INTRODUCTION

Nowadays data gathering and analysis of data are essential in every field of business for understanding the needs and passions of the user so that the organizations and companies can satisfy their customer's essentials and expectations. For data analytics different fields of computer Science, technologies, statistics, algorithms, analytical tools are used according to the types of data to be processed and depending on the field that data belongs. Natural Language Processing is one of the data analytical fields of computer science which comprises linguistics and artificial intelligence which mainly concentrates the communications between computers and humans (Vismaya & Reynald, 2017). It processes and analyze huge natural language data which inference the computers to understand the documents and gives in forma-

DOI: 10.4018/978-1-7998-7728-8.ch006

tions about that documents. NLP supports computers to interact with humans in their own language and process other language related methods to help computers to read text data, hear voice data and interpret it. NLP emprise utilization of algorithms to recognize and draw out the rules of natural language which is in the form of unstructured data format in turn processed and changed into structured data in which the computer can easily understand.

NLP process functions based on rules which can take more time and effort of people. Some other performs with plenty of data using Statistical methods and use machine learning algorithms to obtain the inferences according to the data. The set of data is trained by the machine learning algorithms. With the help of the trained data model the data can be tested to predict the outcome or the result(Thanaki 2017)

NLP plays an important role in research. The research includes speech recognition, text classification, machine translation, question answering. The researches work on Natural Language Processing (NLP) collect the data related to the behavior of human being to process the language by understanding and hence to use the suitable tools and techniques to put together the computers to recognize and process the natural language(Vismaya, Reynald,2017). They converts the linguistic knowledge of data into a rule based implementation by means of Machine learning and Deep learning algorithms for simple manipulation and distribution of data in language processing.

In certain cases the machine learning program in python will be implemented by three step processing to look with the key words relating the event. The first step the NLP cleans the data as the initial stage. In the second step another form of cleaning such as vectorization or tokenization will be performed where the text is converted into tokens and in the third step the data is split to train and test for further processing.(Szlosek, Ferrett, 2016)

This chapter delivers the fundamental concepts of Language processing in Python such as text and word operations. It also gives the details about the preference of Python language for Language Processing and its advantages. It specifies the basic concept of variables, list, operators, looping statements in Python and explains how it can be implemented in language processing. It outlines the knowledge attainment of basic applications of NLP in Python, preparing the data set for NLP applications, Context free grammar, Stepping into NLTK, Raw text processing . It also specify how a structured program can be written using python, Categorizing and tagging of words, how an information can be extracted from a text, Syntactic and Semantic analysis and NLP applications. It also concentrates some of the research applications where NLP is applied and the challenges of NLP processing in the real time area of applications.

NATURAL LANGUAGE PROCESSING WITH PYTHON

Python is an interactive, interpreted, object oriented programming language which is easy to learn and develop applications and algorithms to analyze and process huge natural language data. (Menzenski, 2015). It was developed by Guido Van Rossum in the year 1991. Python allows easy encapsulation of methods and data and hence the code can be repeatedly used. The variables can be used as dynamic in our program to improve fast development of program codes. It also contains standard library which contains a collection of build-in modules for performing specific functions which includes a core part of the language. It also contains components for Graphical Programming, Web Connectivity and processing numerical data. The Syntax and Semantics are well defined in Python which gives special meaning to the language. Python is a open source software and hence it is easily downloaded according to the operating systems used by the user. It furnish the programmers with various NLP tools and libraries to develop applications and tasks related to NLP such as document classification, part of speech(POS) tagging, word vectors, sentiment analysis etc. It furnishes the programmers with various NLP tools and libraries to develop tasks relating to NLP such as document classification, part of speech (POS), tagging word vectors, sentiment analysis etc .

Python –Features

- ◦ Python can run in different platforms such as windows, Mac, Linux etc
- ◦ Python programs can be expressed in simple syntax like English language.
- ◦ Python has the facility of syntax which helps the programmers to write sprinkling of codes.
- ◦ Python can be implemented as a procedural language or object oriented or functional language.
- ◦ The code of python will be executed by means of interpreter hence it has fast prototyping.

Python –Getting Started

Python interpreter can be accessed by a graphical interface called Interactive Development Environment (IDLE).(Loper et al., 2009). In window we use All programs--------> Python. In Mac operating system Mac python is used. In UNIX we can run from the shell by typing idle. The >>> (prompt) shows that Python interpreter is ready for getting the input. After the interpreter is displaying the answer the prompt reappears. (Loper et al., 2009)

NLTK (NATURAL LANGUAGE TOOL KIT)

Natural Language tool kit (NLTK) is the fundamental and supporting platform for implementing python coding with Language Processing. It consists of number of libraries for text processing such as classification, stemming, tokenization, tagging, passing, semantic reasoning etc which is very useful for linguists, engineers, students, researchers and educators to take part or proceed their task or research with natural language using NLTK. It is a free open source tool available and it contains large number of standard libraries to handle natural language.

Installing NLTK

NLTK requires latest versions of Python. Here the NLTK down Loaded methods will be shown.

Step 1: NLTK can be downloaded from the internet using the linkhttps://www.python.org/downloads/, and the latest version of Python is selected for windows.(Loper et al., 2009)

Step 2: Click Download Python 3.9.1 button and select the downloaded file. The file will be opened. In that select Customize Installation.

Step 3: Click next button and then select Optional features and advanced options and then install.

Step 4: The step was successfully installed and click the close button.

Step 5: Copy the path of Script folder and navigate the location of the pip folder to the command prompt to install NLTK.

```
Command Prompt
icrosoft Windows [Version 10.0.18363.1316]
c) 2019 Microsoft Corporation. All rights reserved.

:\Users\Home PC>cd C:\Python\Scripts

:\Python\Scripts>pip3 install nltk
```

Step 6: The message successfully installed will be shown . We can verify whether the installation is accurate supplying the below command

import nltk

If no error occurs indicates Installation is complete.

Python 3.9 (64-bit)

```
Python 3.9.1 (tags/v3.9.1:1e5d33e, Dec  7 2020, 17:08:21) [MSC v.1927 64 bit (AMD64)] on win32
Type "help", "copyright", "credits" or "license" for more information.
>>> import nltk
>>>
```

No error message. The prompt appears, hence nltk is installed.

Python Packages

The python packages used for nltk should also be downloaded for execution. The first step is to run the python interpreter in operating system. Enter the commands

import nltk
nltk.download ()

The packages will start downloading as shown below. The change of green color indicates that all the packages have installed (Figures 1 and 2).

Figure 1. Downloading the nltk packages

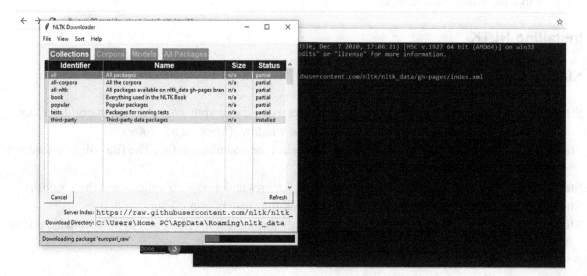

Figure 2. Installing the nltk packages

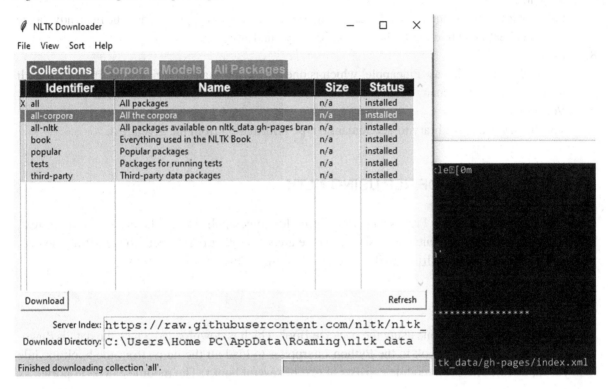

The change of green color indicates that all the packages have installed.

NLP Libraries

Here are some of the NLP libraries which is used for the processing of Natural Language.

1. NLTK:
   This is the most common and important libraries of NLP.
2. spaCy:
   This library is highly accurate and commonly used in Deep learning.
3. tanford CoreNLP Python:
   This library is best for client –server architecture. It provides modularity to use in python.
4. TextBlob:
   This is an NLP library used for textual data processing providing all types of operation in the form of API which is commonly used in Python 2 and 3.
5. Gensim:
   A high efficient and scalable robust open source in NLP library supporting python is Genism .
6. Pattern:
   The light-weighted NLP module used in Web-mining, crawling or such type of spidering task is considered by the library Pattern.

7. Polyglot:
   Polyglot is the best suitable NLP library for massive multilingual applications. The main advantage of this is Feature extraction in the way on Identity and Entity.
8. PyNLPl:
   PyNLPI is also called as 'Pineapple' which is one of the important libraries supporting Python. It provides a parser for many data format like FoLiA/Giza/Moses/ARPA/Timbl/CQL.
9. Vocabulary:
   Vocabulary is a best library to get Semantic type information from the given text.

BASIC OPERATIONS OF NLP USING NLTK

Using nltk Natural Language Processing can be used for some applications like classification of text, language translation, Sentimental analysis etc. There are some other basic operations relating the text, words, sentences etc(Shukla, Iriondo2021). Here we discuss some basic operations.

Text Processing

The text processing can be done using the package Book which is downloaded .Once the data is downloaded import the package book in the Python interpreter to load all the items from the book module (Davydova, 2018). The book module consists of text of several books. The module can be imported as

>>> from nltk.book import * in the prompt of python.

```
>>> from nltk.book import *
*** Introductory Examples for the NLTK Book ***
Loading text1, ..., text9 and sent1, ..., sent9
Type the name of the text or sentence to view it.
Type: 'texts()' or 'sents()' to list the materials.
text1: Moby Dick by Herman Melville 1851
text2: Sense and Sensibility by Jane Austen 1811
text3: The Book of Genesis
text4: Inaugural Address Corpus
text5: Chat Corpus
text6: Monty Python and the Holy Grail
text7: Wall Street Journal
text8: Personals Corpus
text9: The Man Who Was Thursday by G . K . Chesterton 1908
```

   ◦ Showing the text:
If we need to see the text which is displayed in the book module we can give the command text1, text2, text3 ....

```
>>> text1
<Text: Moby Dick by Herman Melville 1851>
>>> text5
<Text: Chat Corpus>
>>> text3
<Text: The Book of Genesis>
```

   ◦ Searching the text:

The text the user need to be searched by the use of concordance command . The text3 contains the book of Genesis . If the word "Adam" is to be searched then the command can be given as text3.concordance("Adam")

Figure 3. Searching the text from book module

```
>>> text3.concordance("Adam")
Displaying 18 of 18 matches:
l of the air ; and brought them unto Adam to see what he would call th and wha
what he would call th and whatsoever Adam called every living creature , that
re , that was the name thereof . And Adam gave names to all cattle , and to th
o every beast of the field ; but for Adam there was not found an help meet for
God caused a deep sleep to fall upon Adam , and he sle and he took one of his
, and brought her unto the man . And Adam said , This is now bone of my bones
 the garden in the cool of the d and Adam and his wife hid themselves from the
arden . And the LORD God called unto Adam , and said unto him , Where art thou
d he shall rule over thee . And unto Adam he said , Because thou hast hearkene
nd unto dust shalt thou return . And Adam called his wife ' s name Eve ; becau
 was the mother of all living . Unto Adam also and to his wife did the LORD Go
ep the way of the tree of life . And Adam knew Eve his wife ; and she conceive
y Lamech seventy and sevenfold . And Adam knew his wife again ; and she bare a
is is the book of the generations of Adam . In the day that God created man ,
blessed them , and called their name Adam , in the day when they were created
the day when they were created . And Adam lived an hundred and thirty years ,
d called his name Se And the days of Adam after he had begotten Seth were eigh
nd daughters : And all the days that Adam lived were nine hundred and thirty y
>>>
```

- Counting Vocabulary:

This shows the length of the text . This indicates the number of words, spaces, special characters the text contains. This can be implemented by using the term len as

>>> len(text2)

It shows the numbers of text in text2

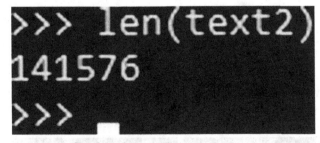

```
>>> len(text2)
141576
>>>
```

○ Sorting the text:
The vocabulary present in the text can be sorted using the command
>>> sorted(set(text2))

Figure 4. Showing the text from book module in a sorted order

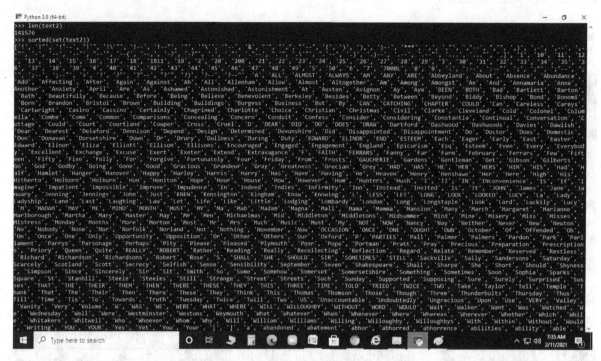

This shows all the words in the text file in a sorted order.

Note:

If the command >>> len(set(text2)) is given it gives the result of number of words present in the text file. So the count of words can be identified.

```
>>> len(set(text2))
6833
>>>
```

In this text 2 file although we have 141576 counting of characters the word count will be 6833.

• Concatenation of Strings:

In NLP using the NLTK we can concatenate two sentences or phrases in Python. In this book module the sentence from two books can be added using the commands as

```
>>> sent1
['Call', 'me', 'Ishmael', '.']
>>> sent3
['In', 'the', 'beginning', 'God', 'created', 'the', 'heaven', 'and', 'the', 'earth', '.']
>>> sent3+sent1
['In', 'the', 'beginning', 'God', 'created', 'the', 'heaven', 'and', 'the', 'earth', '.', 'Call', 'me', 'Ishmael', '.']
>>>
```

In this the sentence 3 and 1 are added.

● Appending the String:

Using append() command a new string can be appended at the end of the original sentence or string.

```
>> sent2
'The', 'family', 'of', 'Dashwood', 'had', 'long', 'been', 'settled', 'in', 'Sussex', '.']
>> sent2.append("great things")
>> sent2
'The', 'family', 'of', 'Dashwood', 'had', 'long', 'been', 'settled', 'in', 'Sussex', '.', 'great things']
>>
```

Here the new word "great things" had appended at the end of the sent 2.

● Indexing the Strings:

The Strings present in the book package has indexed and using the index the corresponding text can be taken. It can be shown as

```
>>> text3[150]
'the'
>>> text4[23]
'filled'
>>> text1[1234]
'HENRY'
>>>
```

It shows that the 150th string in text3 is "the" and likewise the text corresponding to the index are shown . Normally the index can be created like an array of structures or a list of strings starting from zero to the previous number of the last string. It can be created as

```
>>> sent=["God","is","Good","all","the","times"]
>>> sent[0]
```

A sentence is created. To identify the index value, check the code as given below

```
>> sent[0]
'God'
>> sent[1]
'is'
>> sent[3]
'all'
>> sent[5]
'times'
>>
```

Tokenization

The process of dividing the big quantity of data into small piece of text as tokens is called tokenization. The tokens are used to find patterns and it is the basic step for Stemming and lemmatization (Singh 2019).

Word Tokenization

NLTK has a module tokenize which is used for making the large data to tokens. It has two sub modules namely word tokenize and sentence tokenize. A Word can be tokenized from the sentence using the method word_tokenize().

Figure 5. Word Tokenization

```
Python 3.9 (64-bit)
Python 3.9.1 (tags/v3.9.1:1e5d33e, Dec  7 2020, 17:08:21) [MSC v.1927 64 bit (AMD64)] on win32
Type "help", "copyright", "credits" or "license" for more information.
>>> from nltk.tokenize import word_tokenize
>>> text="Hello, how are you .Be happy always."
>>> print(word_tokenize(text))
['Hello', ',', 'how', 'are', 'you', '.Be', 'happy', 'always', '.']
>>>
```

Code Explanation:
1. word_tokenize is the module from the NLTK library.
2. "text" is a variable initialized with sentences.
3. The variable "text" is passed in word_tokenize module and the result is printed. This module breaks the sentence in to each word with punctuation which is given as the output.

Sentence Tokenization

NLTK has another facility of tokenizing the sentence also. This action can be done by importing the method sent_tokenize. The main use of this kind of tokenization is to find the average value of the sentence.

Figure 6. Sentence tokenization

```
Python 3.9 (64-bit)
Python 3.9.1 (tags/v3.9.1:1e5d33e, Dec  7 2020, 17:08:21) [MSC v.1927 64 bit (AMD64)] on win32
Type "help", "copyright", "credits" or "license" for more information.
>>> from nltk.tokenize import sent_tokenize
>>> text="Be happy always . God with us!"
>>> print(sent_tokenize(text))
['Be happy always .', 'God with us!']
>>>
```

Code Explanation:
1. sent_tokenize is the module from NLTK library.
2. "text" is the variable initialized with sentences .
3. The variable "text" is passed in sent_tokenize module and the result is printed. This module breaks the single sentence as two sentences which is the desired output.

Text Normalization

The process of modifying or transforming a text into its standard form by means of grammar or spelling is called Normalization.

For example, the word "but ter" and "budder" can be transformed to "butter", its standard form with correct spelling and, meaning.

Some of the normalization methods can be discussed here.

- Changing the upper case into Lower case:

   The uppercase letters will be converted into lower case by using the lower() function.

```
>>> input_str="India  is the Country having its own Traditions,and Trades"
>>> input_str=input_str.lower()
>>> print(input_str)
india  is the country having its own traditions,and trades
>>>
```

Here the upper case letters are converted into lower case.

- Removing Numbers from strings:

The method of normalize a string without numbers if its original sting is a mixed of numbers and strings by importing the re package in NLP which indicates the Regular Expression.

```
>>> import re
>>> input_str="A class contains 50 students in which 30 are boys and 20 are girls"
>>> output = re.sub(r'\d+', '',input_str)
>>> print(output)
A class contains  students in which  are boys and  are girls
>>>
```

The output is shown without the numbers. Thus unnecessary numbers can be removed while processing and analyzing the data.

- Removal of White spaces:
  The white spaces present in the string can be removed using the strip() command.

```
>>> input_str = " \t a string example\t "
>>> input_str = input_str.strip()
>>> input_str
'a string example'
>>>
```

- Removing Stop words:

Stop words are words we often use in the sentences such as a, the, is, on etc. These words have no meaning in the sentences and hence these words can be removed.

```
>>> import nltk
>>> from nltk.corpus import stopwords
>>> input_str="Python is a programming language which is used for Natural Language Processing."
>>> stop_words=set(stopwords.words('english'))
>>> from nltk.tokenize import word_tokenize
>>> tokens=word_tokenize(input_str)
>>> output=[i for i in tokens if not i in stop_words]
>>> print(output)
['Python', 'programming', 'language', 'used', 'Natural', 'Language', 'Processing', '.']
>>>
```

Stemming

Like normalization Stemming is a process of converting the set of words or sentences to a shorten sequence in its structure. There are words having the same meaning but have some variation according to the context or sentence. In other way, there is a root word, having variations of the same words. For example, the root word is "learn" and it's variations are "learning, learnt etc and like this". With the help of Stemming, the root word of any variations can be found (Jabeen, 2018).

. Stemming is needed because a human can easily understand the meaning of the sentences if the words are different with some variations. But machines will think that that the sentences are different.

Thus it is difficult to convert the same data row. In such cases the machine will fails to predict due to some variations in the words. In such situations stemming categorize the same type of data by getting its root word and prepare the data set for machine learning processing.

Example: 1

```
>>> from nltk.stem import PorterStemmer
>>> e_words= ["sleep", "sleeping", "slept", "sleeps"]
>>> ps =PorterStemmer()
>>> for s in e_words:
...     rootWord=ps.stem(s)
...     print(rootWord)
...
sleep
sleep
slept
sleep
>>>
```

The stemming can be done by an algorithm called "PorterStemmer". This accepts all the words and converts the words in to its root word and allows the data for machine learning processing. Hence Stemming is considered as a preprocessing the data so that the redundancy is removed and variations with relating to the words also changed resulting the data is filtered and ready for processing.

Stemming of a sentence:

```
>>> from nltk.stem import PorterStemmer
>>> from nltk.tokenize import sent_tokenize, word_tokenize
>>> sentence="Hello everybody,NLTK is a tool used for natural language processing."
>>> words = word_tokenize(sentence)
>>> ps = PorterStemmer()
>>> for w in words:
...     rootWord=ps.stem(w)
...     print(rootWord)
...
hello
everybodi
,
nltk
is
a
tool
use
for
natur
languag
process
.
```

Code Explanation
  ◦ Import the Package PorterStemer from module stem
  ◦ Import the Packages for tokenization of sentence and also for word
  ◦ An input sentence is given which is to be tokenized in the next step.
  ◦ Implementation of Word tokenization.
  ◦ In this step create an object for PorterStemmer .

   ◦   Loop will be running and the process of stemming each word is done using the object which is created in the code line number 5.

Lemmatization

Lemmatization is the algorithmic process of identifying the lemma of a word depending on their meaning. Lemma is the word indicating the subject or argument of a literary composition or annotation or a word or phrase defined in a dictionary or entered in a word list. It is often derives the morphological analysis of words, which aims to remove inflectional endings. (Jabeen, 2018).The NLTK Lemmatization of data is the method based on WorldNet's built-in morph function. Text preprocessing before machine learning includes the process of stemming and also lemmatization. Many considered that these two are same and some find the two terms with confusion. But these two terms are not same. There are some differences between the two terms.

- Stemming vs. Lemmatization

Stemming algorithm cuts the suffix or in a broader way cuts the beginning or end of the word to give the root word. But lemmatization is a process which takes two things into consideration. The first thing is the morphological analysis of the words. Morphological analysis is the study of words and its parts such as prefixes, suffixes, base words as well as smallest units of meaning. Morphemes are useful for phonics in English for reading, spelling and also in vocabulary and comprehension. The second feature is returning the lemma which is the base for text. It is also required to create dictionaries and outlook for the appropriate form of the word.

Stemming is the general operation of tokenize the word while lemmatization is an intelligent operation in which a correct format will be looked in the dictionary. Hence Lemmatization performs best in machine learning process of data.

Program illustrating Stemming

```
>>> import nltk
>>> from nltk.stem.porter import PorterStemmer
>>> porter_stemmer = PorterStemmer()
>>> text = "tries try studies studying"
>>> tokenization = nltk.word_tokenize(text)
>>> for w in tokenization:
...     print("Stemming for {} is {}".format(w,porter_stemmer.stem(w)))
...
...
Stemming for tries is tri
Stemming for try is tri
Stemming for studies is studi
Stemming for studying is studi
>>>
```

Program illustrating Lemmatization:

```
>>> import nltk
>>> from nltk.stem import WordNetLemmatizer
>>> wordnet_lemmatizer = WordNetLemmatizer()
>>> text = "tries try studies studying"
>>> tokenization = nltk.word_tokenize(text)
>>> for w in tokenization:
...     print("Lemma for {} is {}".format(w, wordnet_lemmatizer.lemmatize(w)))
...
Lemma for tries is try
Lemma for try is try
Lemma for studies is study
Lemma for studying is studying
```

From the above examples it is clearly shown that the stemming for tries is tri and in lemmatization it is indicated as try which is the original spelling of the word .Hence lemmatization is preferred to make use in machine learning so that the correct predictions can be occurred.

Advantages of Lemmatization:

- Lemmatization algorithms reduce the ambiguity of text.
- It converts all the words with same meaning but give different representations to their base form.
- The density of the given word can be minimized which helps to prepare the accurate features for machine learning purposes.
- The data will be cleaned and very well intelligent to attain accurate machine learning model.
- It also reduces the computational cost and saves memory.

Bag of Words

Bag of words is a technique used in <u>Natural Language Processing</u> for modeling the text. This method is a easy and flexible to extract the features from the text which is given as the input for processing in machine learning algorithms (<u>Mujtaba</u>, 2020).It is the text representation which identifies the word existence in the given document.

In machine learning algorithms for natural language processing the difficulty is that the document or the text will be unstructured. But for analyzing the text or any prediction the text needed should be in a structured and clearly defined length to be given as inputs. This Bag –of-words technique will change the variable length texts into fixed length vector which can be easily processed by the machine learning algorithms.

The steps of processing occurred in Bag of Words technique are

- Text Input
- Tokenization
- Creating Vocabulary
- Vector Generation

Figure 7. Steps involved in bag of words

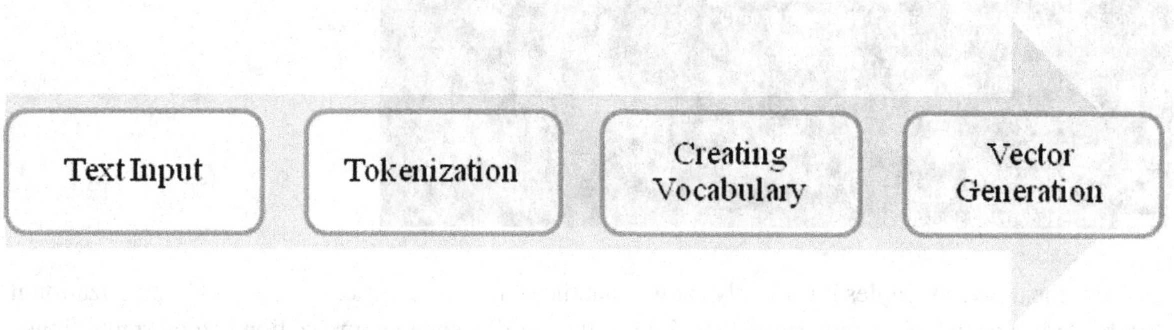

Text Processing Using Bag of Words

Step 1.

The text or document which we need to process for analysis will be given as input for modeling.

Step 2

The text should be converted into lowercase letters since there will be a mismatch when the same text appear in case of upper and lower cases.(e.g noun, Noun). The lower case text will be then converted into tokens in this step by using the word_tokenizer so that the large sentence or document will be made into separate words.

Figure 8. Tokenization

```
import pandas as pd
from sklearn.feature_extraction.text import CountVectorizer
text_1="Proper Noun is the name of the particular person or a place"
text_2="common noun is a name given in Common to every person or thing of the same class or kind."
text_1=text_1.lower()
text_2=text_2.lower()
token1=text_1.split()
token2=text_2.split()
print(text_1)
print(text_2)
print(token1)
print(token2)
```

```
proper noun is the name of the particular person or a place
common noun is a name given in common to every person or thing of the same class or kind.
['proper', 'noun', 'is', 'the', 'name', 'of', 'the', 'particular', 'person', 'or', 'a', 'place']
['common', 'noun', 'is', 'a', 'name', 'given', 'in', 'common', 'to', 'every', 'person', 'or', 'thing', 'of', 'the', 'same', 'cl
ass', 'or', 'kind.']
```

Step 3

After tokenization the vocabulary of the text is created by removing the stop words such as a, the, is etc. Removing the stop words makes the text clean without text repetitions and easy to process in to the next step.

Figure 9. Creating vocabulary

```
import nltk
from nltk.corpus import stopwords
text_1="Proper Noun is the name of the particular person or a place"
text_2="common noun is a name given in Common to every person or thing of the same class or kind."
stop_words=set(stopwords.words('english'))
from nltk.tokenize import word_tokenize
tokens1=word_tokenize(text_1)
tokens2=word_tokenize(text_2)
output1=[i for i in tokens1 if not i in stop_words]
output2=[i for i in tokens2 if not i in stop_words]
print(output1)
print(output2)

['Proper', 'Noun', 'name', 'particular', 'person', 'place']
['common', 'noun', 'name', 'given', 'Common', 'every', 'person', 'thing', 'class', 'kind', '.']
```

Step 4

This is the step in which the text is converted into numerical values called vectors by importing the method count_vectorizer. This indicates if the word is present in the list it indicates the value as 1 and if it is not present in the list it shows zero.

Figure 10. Vector generation

```
import pandas as pd
from sklearn.feature_extraction.text import CountVectorizer
sentence_1="proper noun is the name of the particular person or a place"
sentence_2="common noun is a name given in common to every person or thing of the same class or kind."
CountVec = CountVectorizer(ngram_range=(1,1),
                           stop_words='english')
Count_data = CountVec.fit_transform([sentence_1,sentence_2])
cv_dataframe=pd.DataFrame(Count_data.toarray(),columns=CountVec.get_feature_names())
print(cv_dataframe)
```

	class	common	given	kind	noun	particular	person	place	proper	thing
0	0	0	0	0	0	1	1	1	1	1	0
1	1	1	2	1	1	1	0	1	0	0	1

Hence the text can be processed or modeled for the implementations of machine learning algorithms.

Advantages of Bag of Words:
- ○ Easy to understand
- ○ Easy to implement
- ○ Easy to convert the text data to numeric data
- ○ Simplicity in code.

Disadvantages of Bag of Words:
- ○ Due to large vocabulary size it leads to high dimensional vector.
- ○ Bag of words assumes that all the words are independent to one another hence do not support co-occurrence statistics between words.

POS TAGGING AND CHUNKING

The process of assigning the parts of speech to the words in a sentences indicating whether the word is a noun, adjective, verb and so on. It is also responsible to read the text with grammatical categories such as tense, singular or plural, gender etc. It is commonly used in machine learning and deep learning for text analysis tools and algorithms.

Here is the table which gives some of the abbreviations and its meanings used in POS tagging.

Table 1. Abbreviations and its meanings used in POS tagging.

Abbreviation	Meaning
NN	Singular Noun (man, book)
NNS	Plural Noun (men, books)
NNP	Singular Proper Noun(Rani)
NNPS	Plural Proper Noun(Indians)
PRP	Personal pronoun (hers, herself, him, himself)
PRP$	Possessive pronoun (her, his, mine, my, our)
RB	Adverb (beautifully, greedily)
RBR	Comparative Adverb (smaller)
RBS	Superlative Adverb(largest)
VB	Verb(sing)
VBG	Gerund Verb(reading)
VBD	Verb Past Tense(Pleased)
VBN	Verb Past participle(unified)
VBP	Verb Present tense but not third person singular(run)
VBZ	Verb Present tense with third person singular(plays)
WDT	Wh-determinar(What)
WP	Wh-pronoun(Who)
WRB	Wh-adverb(How)
IN	Preposition
JJ	Adjective(tall)
JJR	Adjective, Comparative(taller)
JJS	Adjective, Superlative(tallest)

POS Tagging

The process of Parts of speech tagging is done by two steps in NLTK.

Step 1 - Tokenize the sentence into words using the word_tokenize method.
Step 2 -pos_tag is applied to step1 to make the sentence with its partsof speech .

```
>>> from nltk import pos_tag
>>> text="Sita is dancing beautifully with greatest expressions".split()
>>> print("After Split:",text)
After Split: ['Sita', 'is', 'dancing', 'beautifully', 'with', 'greatest', 'expressions']
>>> tokens_tag = pos_tag(text)
>>> print("After Token:",tokens_tag)
After Token: [('Sita', 'NNP'), ('is', 'VBZ'), ('dancing', 'VBG'), ('beautifully', 'RB'), ('with', 'IN'), ('greatest', 'JJS'), ('expressions', 'NNS')]
>>>
```

In this program a sentence is made into tokens using the split () command and then its POS is assigned to each word by the use of pos_tag() command.

Chunking

The process of adding more structures to a sentence following the parts of speech is called chunking or shallow parsing. The final grouping of words is called chunks. It is also called as light parsing. The main advantage of chunking is to make a group of POS such as taking of noun phrases, verbs etc. They can be combined according to the requirements and needs of the users.

Syntax:
Chunk:{NN.?>*<VBG.?>*<RB.?>}

The symbol used for identifying the chunk represents some meaning. The name and the description of the symbol is given in the table.

Table 2. Name and the description of the symbols.

Name of the symbol	Description
.(dot)	Any character except new line
*(asterisk)	Match 0 or more repetitions
?(Question mark)	Match 0 or 1 repetitions

A sentence can be chunked as

```
>>> CHUNKRULE: '{NN.?>*<VBG.?>*<RB.?>}'
>>> from nltk import pos_tag
>>> from nltk import RegexpParser
>>> text="Sita is dancing beautifully with greatest expressions.Vanitha is singing a song pleasantly with her amazing voice".split()
>>> print("After Split:",text)
After split: ['Sita', 'is', 'dancing', 'beautifully', 'with', 'greatest', 'expressions.Vanitha', 'is', 'singing', 'a', 'song', 'pleasantly', 'with', 'her', 'amazing', 'voice']
>>> tokens_tag = pos_tag(text)
>>> print("After Token:",tokens_tag)
After Token: [('Sita', 'NNP'), ('is', 'VBZ'), ('dancing', 'VBG'), ('beautifully', 'RB'), ('with', 'IN'), ('greatest', 'JJS'), ('expressions.Vanitha', 'NN'), ('is', 'VBZ'), ('singing', 'VBG'), ('a', 'DT'), ('song', 'NN'), ('pleasantly', 'RB'), ('with', 'IN'), ('her', 'PRP$'), ('amazing', 'JJ'), ('voice', 'NN')]
>>> pattern= """mychunk:{<NN.?>*<VBG.?>*<VBZ.?>*<NNP.?>*<RB>?}"""
>>> chunk = RegexpParser(pattern)
>>> print("After Regex:",chunk)
After Regex: chunk.RegexpParser with 1 stages:
RegexpChunkParser with 1 rules:
       <ChunkRule: '<NN.?>*<VBG.?>*<VBZ.?>*<NNP.?>*<RB>?'>
>>> output = chunk.parse(tokens_tag)
>>> print("After Chunking",output)
After Chunking (S
(mychunk Sita/NNP is/VBZ)
(mychunk dancing/VBG beautifully/RB)
with/IN
greatest/JJS
(mychunk expressions.Vanitha/NN is/VBZ)
(mychunk singing/VBG)
a/DT
(mychunk song/NN pleasantly/RB)
with/IN
her/PRP$
amazing/JJ
(mychunk voice/NN))
>>>
```

TEXT CLASSIFICATION

The process of classifying the text into group of words is called text classification. In NLP the text classification is done by analyzing the text and assigning the set of predefined tags or categories based on the text (boukkouri, 2018)

Text Classification Approaches

The text classification approaches are

- Rule-based System,
- Machine System
- Hybrid System.

Rule –Based System

In rule based systems some linguistic rules have been used for classifying the text. These rules define the list of words that are characterized by words. For example the words such as apple, banana should be categorized as fruits and Lotus, sunflowers should be under flowers.

Rule based classifiers makes the decision using the if-else rules. Hence these rules can be easily accessible; these classifiers are used for generating descriptive models. The condition used with if is known as antecedent and the rule predicted is called as consequent. The generated rule is not mutually exclusive and not exhaustive.

The rules having the highest priority will be taken for the final class otherwise votes can be assigned for the class so that the rules will not change.

Machine Based Classifier

The classification of text can be done based on the past observation from the data sets using machine learning algorithms is called Machine based classifier. It collects the classification method of the previous data which is called the trained data and with the help of the trained data the new text is given as input or the test data for classification. Machine based classification algorithms such as Logistic regression, Naïve bayes, Support vector machine are used for classification.

The first step in training the dataset for classification is by converting each text into numeric representations as vectors. Once the data is trained suitable machine learning algorithms are used for predictions and text analysis.

Hybrid Approach

The approach which combines the rule based and machine based classifier is called Hybrid approach of text classification. It uses the rule based approach to create the training set of text and use machine learning algorithms to create the model.

Language Translation

The process of converting one natural language to another language automatically without altering the meaning of the input text and producing the output is called Language Translation or Machine Translation.

The steps involved in Language translation are
- The source text will be given as the input for translation.
- The text will be De-formatted such as converting the text into lower case and other formats according to the need.
- The text is analyzed with morphologically, syntactically and semantically so that the meaning of the text will not be changed.
- The text is again reformatted and the target text will be given as the output.

Types of Machine Translation

There are two types of Machine translation.

Bilingual Machine Translation

The translation between two particular languages is called Bilingual Machine Translation.

Multilingual Machine Translation

The translation takes place between any pair of languages which may be unidirectional or bidirectional is said as Multilingual Machine translation.

Machine Translation Approaches

There are some ways in which the language is translated is said to the machine translation approaches.

- Direct MT Approach
  It is the oldest approach in which the source language is directly translated into target language. This type of systems may be bi-lingual and uni-directional.
- Interlingua Approach
  In this approach the source language is translated into an intermediate language called Interlingua and then it is converted into the target language.
- Transfer Approach
  This approach will be done by three steps in which the source language is converted into abstract Source language oriented representations. These Source language representations will be converted into its target language oriented representations. This target orientation is then converted into final target language.

- Empirical MT Approach

  The emerging approach for Language translation is Empirical MT approach. It uses large raw data consisting text and translations. The machine translation techniques such as Analogy based, example based, memory based are used to translate the text.

Semantic Analysis

The process of understanding the natural language in which the way of communication by the humans based on the meaning and context is called Semantic analysis. It relates the syntactic structure, levels of phrases, clauses, sentences to their independent meanings. Semantic analysis gives the relationship among each word. (boukkouri, 2018)

The Semantic analysis analyses by reading all the words in the paragraph or content to identify the real meaning of the text. It finds the elements of the text and assigns them to its logical and grammatical field to identify the commonly used elements in the text to understand the topic. It also relates different concepts in the text such that if it understands that the text is about "business" even it does not contain the actual words but related words such as sales, purchase, product etc.

Semantic analysis and Natural Language Processing helps machines understanding the text automatically this may be an important aspect in business and support corporate intelligence and knowledge management.

Working of Semantic Analysis:

Semantic analysis helps to understand the relationship between the words, verbs, phrases etc. During semantic analysis the following concepts should be considered as relations of words.

- **Hyponyms:** It is the generic lexical item (hypernym) of the text. E.g. Apple is a hyponym of fruit (hypernym).
- **Meronomy:** The text and words are logically arranged to denote a constituent part of or member of something e.g., piece of an apple
- **Polysemy:** It indicates the relationship between the meanings of words or phrases, although it is slightly different, which shares a common core meaning e.g. I sing a song, and I read a song)
- **Synonyms:** It means the meaning of the words e.g., handsome, beautiful, fair
- **Antonyms:** It indicates the opposite words of a text e.g., come, go
- **Homonyms**: Two words having the same sound and spelling but with different meaning. e.g., bat(animal), bat (thing)

Semantic Analysis Techniques

There are two semantic analysis techniques depending on the type of text or information.

Text Classification Model: This is used to assign the predefined categories of the text.

Text Extractor Model: This takes or extract out specific information from the text.

Semantic Classification Models

There are some of the Semantic classification models for text analysis which support the machines to process the text.

- Topic classification:

  In this model the text is sorted into predefined categories according to its content.

  In companies the customer service persons need to classify the tickets which are supporting to them. This semantic analysis indicates the classification of tickets for payment or shipping.

- Sentiment analysis:
  This analysis detects positive, negative, or neutral emotions in a text to denote urgency. It gives the positive and negative feedbacks of the customers about a product or about the Medias in real time.
- Intent classification:
  The classification of text based on what customers want to do next. The companies can use the tag sales emails as *"Interested"* and *"Not Interested"* to the customers to identify who may want to try their product.

Semantic Extraction Models

- Keyword extraction:
  The process of finding the relevant words and expressions in a text is called as keyword extraction. This is used get more granular insights about the product or text. For example the keywords can be analyzed from a group of tweets which is categorized as positive and detects the words or topics according to that which is often used.

- Entity extraction:
  This process identifies the entities such as name of the people, company, place etc. A customer service team can extract the name of the customers, products, emails and other data about their customers for doing healthy support service.
  Semantic analysis in combination of Machine Learning delivers the customer data by enabling the machines to extract meaning from unstructured text at scale and in real time. The semantic machine learning tools had powerful effect and delivers valuable inputs gives better decision making improvements for language processing.

Advantages of NLP
- Using Natural Language Processing, computers can analyze human language with suitable meanings instead of getting the input and generating the output using Programs. In this manner Natural Language processing extends proper use and makes interactions with humans resulting natural conversations.

○ The Chat bots applications of Natural Language processing made advantages for customers and employees. The employees can increase the productivity and get focused in their work by getting immediate responses from the NLP chat pot that understand and gives responses like a co employee. The implementation of chat bots also leads the satisfaction of customers providing the responses of the product by visiting the websites improving better communication between customer and prospects.

Applications of NLP

- **Search Autocorrect and Auto complete:**

It is a important application on NLP that everyone use daily .Search autocorrect and auto complete helps everyone to find accurate result in an efficient manner.

These features are used in the websites, face book and Quora. Language models are the driving engine which is behind the auto complete and auto search.

- **Language Translator:**

The process of translating the text from one language to another without the change of meaning is the Language translator. In the field of neural networks, machine translation technique plays an eminent role in converting the text from one language to another. Tools like Google translate work under this principle and help the number o people and business by breaking the barrier in language and made successful.

- **Social Media Monitoring:**

Nowadays more people use social media for posting their articles and their thoughts about a technology or a product or about their interest. They could get some useful information from others who view their work by giving likes and dislikes. Natural Language processing techniques used by the companies identifies the likes and dislikes of the people about their products by analyzing the unstructured data to give valuable insights which makes their growth and gives satisfaction for the customers.

- **Chatbots**

Customers are more essential for a company to survive. A company can be better if it dies the customer service well and good by keeping the customers satisfied. But dealing with the customers manually is a difficult process. To overcome this, chatbots which is the application of Natural Language Processing serves the companies in attaining their goals and profits by smooth handling of the customers.

- **Survey Analysis:**

To identify the growth of the company surveys plays a vital role. The survey related to the feedback of the customers made the companies to understand the lacking areas and made them to improve. There may be a number of customers giving their feedback about the company. Hence a person cannot read all the feedbacks and give the conclusion. The Natural Language Processing helps the companies to analyze the surveys and identifying the sentiments of the users about their products or some events by generating the insights. This gives the useful and true information so that the companies can improve and find the lacking areas.

- **Targeted Advertising**

Targeted Advertising is an online advertising where ads are shown according to the activity or likes of the user. This work is done by Keyword matching in Natural Language Processing. The ads are matched with the keywords searched by the users and it is shown to them. It is easy for the companies to advertise their products to the suitable persons who are in need of that particular product.

- **Hiring and Recruitment**

The human Resource department in a company has the most important part to recruit the qualified, talented, skilled employees for the job. It is very difficult to finding the people with correct eligibilities and filtering and short listing the candidates. Natural Language Processing helps the recruiters to identify the right candidate. The techniques used are information extraction and entity recognition which are used to extract the qualifications, education. These features classified the resume of the candidate and find whether the person is suitable for that particular job.

- **Voice Assistants**

Voice assistant is software that works under the concepts of speech recognition, understanding natural language to understand the verbal commands of the user to do the actions according to their needs. Google Assistant, Apple Siri, Amazon Alexa, and ring a bell is some of the voice assistant used today.

- **Grammar Checkers**

Grammar Checkers are the most efficiently used applications of natural language processing. The tool such as Grammar which is a grammar checking tool has number of features to help a person in writing better content. They can change any simple content of text into systematic literature. These tools also correct grammar, spellings, suggest better synonyms, helping in delivering the content with better clarity and beautiful phrase. They also improve the readability of content and convey your message in the best possible manner. It really helps the authors and writers to implement their views and writings in a better linguistic way.

- **Email Filtering**

The email filtering helps the users to get their important mails correctly in their inbox by filtering the unwanted mails. Text classification technique in Natural Language Processing is the back bone of this process which classifies the text into pre defined categories. Whenever a mail arrives it is classified as primary, social and promotions and also the spam emails which is classified into a separate section.

CONCLUSION

The Natural Language Processing is the field of computer science mainly focusing the interaction among the humans and the computers. It is designed to perform many tasks which help the computer analyzing the text and performs automatic summarization, text analysis, normalization, stemming, tokenization, machine translation, speech recognition etc. These techniques used in this Language processing helps the people to do various task in the field of computers, Artificial Networks, Neural networks by making the machines to understand and work according to the need of the people and also to improve the economy and job opportunities of the society.

Natural Language Processing is the highlighted concept on Machine Learning and Deep learning. Using machine learning algorithms the large amount of text and documents can be analyzed, classified, categorized and predictions can be done according to the data collected .Hence it holds a remarkable position in the field of data science which gives opportunities for the researchers to implement their research programs and data scientists to identify the future explosion in machines to learn and work like humans.

REFERENCES

Boukkouri. (2018). *Text classification the first step Toward NLP Mastery*. medium.com

Davydova, O. (2018). *Text Preprocessing in Python: Steps, Tools, and Examples*. Data Monsters.

Hardeniya, N., Perkins, J., Chopra, D., Joshi, N., & Mathur, I. (2016). *Natural Language Processing: Python and NLTK*. books.google.com

Jabeen, H. (2018). *Stemming and Lemmatization in Python*. https://www.datacamp.com

Loper, E., Klein, E., & Bird, S. (2009). *Natural language processing with Python: analyzing text with the natural language toolkit*. books.google.com

Menzenski. (2015). *Introduction to text analysis With Python and the Natural Language Toolkit*. Academic Press.

Mujtaba. (2020). *An Introduction to Bag of Words (BoW) | What is Bag of Words?* https://www.mygreatlearning.com

Shukla, P., & Iriondo, R. (2021). *Natural Language Processing (NLP) with Python Tutorial on the basics of natural language processing (NLP) with sample coding implementations in Python*. Academic Press.

Singh, S. (2019). *How to Get Started with NLP – 6 Unique Methods to Perform Tokenization*. https://www.analyticsvidhya.com

Szlosek, D., & Ferrett, J. (2016). *Using Machine Learning and Natural Language Processing Algorithms to Automate the Evaluation of Clinical Decision Support in Electronic Medical Record Systems.* www.semanticscholar.org

Thanaki, J. (2017). *Python natural language processing.* books.google.com

Vismaya & Reynald. (2017). Natural language processing using python. *International Journal of Scientific & Engineering Research, 8*(5).

Chapter 7
Creditworthiness Assessment Using Natural Language Processing

Somya Goyal
Delhi Technological University, India

Arti Saxena
(iD) https://orcid.org/0000-0002-4162-793X
Manav Rachna International Institute of Research and Studies, India

ABSTRACT

NLP is a wide and quickly developing segment of today's new digital technology, which falls under the domain of artificial intelligence. Alternative approaches for qualifying and quantifying an individual's creditworthiness have emerged in recent years as a result of recent advancements in AI. Banks and creditors may use AI to rate potential borrowers' creditworthiness based on alternative data, such as social media messages and internet usage, such as which websites people visit and what they buy from e-commerce stores. These digital footprints may show whether or not an individual is able to repay their debts. In this chapter, how the approaches of NLP could offer financial solutions to unbanked communities is explored. This chapter includes the use of various machine learning algorithms and deep learning to find the most accurate credit score of a user. Since NLP is less intrusive than providing direct access to a person's entire contact list or a social media site, it is a more accessible way to measure risk while still having the potential to target a larger audience.

NATURAL LANGUAGE PROCESSING

Computational approaches are used to read, interpret, and generate human language knowledge in natural language processing. The aim of early computational approaches to language science was to automate linguistic structure analysis and advance fundamental technologies such as speech recognition, machine translation, and speech synthesis. One of the most important operations in the advancing machine learn-

DOI: 10.4018/978-1-7998-7728-8.ch007

ing field is natural language processing (NLP). Natural Language Processing (NLP) is concerned with the use of computers to process and comprehend human text/speech, also known as Natural Languages (Julia Hirschberg, 2020).

Today's researchers are refining and applying these techniques in real-world applications, such as developing spoken dialogue systems and speech-to-speech translation engines, mining social media for health and finance information, and predicting sentiment and emotion against products and services.

CREDITWORTHINESS ASSESSMENT

Several organizations provides AI-based credit scoring applications to banks and business creditors who want to better consider the risk involved with their future borrowers. Traditional credit scoring strategies take into account prospective borrower's credit history, although this can prevent certain individuals from obtaining credit despite their ability to repay their loans as they are due.

Banks and creditors uses AI technologies to create a credit score of an individual based on alternate data, such as social media messages and Internet usage, such as which websites people visit and what they buy from e-Commerce stores. These digital footprints help to gather information regarding the probabilities and risks associated with a borrower. Data is generated through these digital footprints that may show whether or not an individual is able to repay their debts.

What Is Creditworthiness?

Creditworthiness is how a lender determines that whether you will be able to repay your debts, or how much worthy you are to receive new credit. Your creditworthiness provides you credibility to receive credit from any provider.

The creditworthiness or credit score is calculated using a number of variables, one of which is the user's repayment history. When determining the likelihood of default, certain credit firms take into account the available assets as well as the number of liabilities you have.

Key Takeaways:
- A lender's creditworthiness determines whether or not you can default on your mortgage obligations.
- Several considerations, including your debt history and credit score, go into determining your creditworthiness.
- Having on-time payments is an easy way to improve or preserve your creditworthiness.

Why is an AI-based Creditworthiness Assessment Needed?

About 90% of today's global data is generated in just the past two years alone (Niccolo Mejia, 2019). According to the most current estimates, 80% of all known data is unstructured. This massive amount of data provides useful knowledge that can be used to improve a variety of financial practices, including fraud prevention, demand forecasting, customer relationship management, and credit scoring.

Currently, financial agencies and institutions rely heavily on financial records, or creditworthiness, such as FICO scores, when assessing credit risk. About 90% of top lenders in the United States. The FICO score creators have kept the formula for calculating the scores a secret. They did, however, disseminate the weights of the metrics they consider, which are as follows: 35% payment history, 30% sum due, 15% duration of history, 10% new credit, and 10% forms of credit used. As a result of their limited ability to provide this sort of knowledge, "two billion adults - more than half of the world's working adults - are still excluded from formal financial services" according to the UNCDF Annual report.

In developing markets like India, such scoring models are much less valid because the bulk of the population is unbanked. According to the BSP, the Philippine Central Bank, 77% of the population in the Philippines were considered unbanked, meaning they do not have a bank account.

Here are a few reasons why the old credit score model has to be replaced:
1. Traditional credit bureau data may be forged or compromised. The main deterrents to conventional credit score models, for example, are identity theft and synthetic ID fraud.
2. They leave no stone unturned when it comes to borrowing money from financial loaning firms that don't have adequate security mechanisms in place.
3. Many frauds go so far as to verify data via background check systems such as premium online credit check services. Fraudsters often use a stolen credit card to create their application file, which they then access via online resources. They deliberately employ methods to raise their credit scores to apply for loans in order to ensure that their repayment rate is greater than that of most loan borrowers.

Creditworthiness Evaluated via Machine Learning Approaches

In the last few years, developments in Machine Learning and Artificial Intelligence, have allowed the advent of new strategies for qualifying and quantifying an individual's creditworthiness, using non-financial knowledge groundbreaking approaches such as phone log analysis or social network analysis (Charles Crouspeyre, 2019). Several startups have arisen as a result of these efforts, with promising outcomes in helping to address the issue of financial inclusion for developing markets, such as LenddoEFL in Singapore and Sesame Credit in China.

Nonetheless, these methods prove to be intrusive, with no regard for the privacy of users, such as asking users to share personal contacts with the device, and so on. As a result, a modern paradigm focused on Natural Language Processing (NLP) and Natural Language Understanding (NLU) software could be able to include a new benchmark for quantifying danger in terms of forecasting borrower repayment behavior by still accessing knowledge specifically applicable to the consumer. This method would also allow for a paradigm shift, from assessing an individual's creditworthiness to assessing his trustworthiness.

In the healthcare sector, creating NLP mechanisms that respect privacy has been discussed. The Lister Hill National Center for Biomedical Communications of the US National Library of Medicine employs natural language processing to "de-identify" health facts in narrative medical records, maintaining the patient identity and retaining clinical experience. NLP was used in this situation to ensure that any material relating to particular private information could be classified and then "de-identified."

What is Digital Footprint Data?

A digital footprint (Oded Netzer, 2018) is a set of data that may be used to identify a single person, such as social media accounts, web cookies, or even specific trends of online behavior. Factors like transaction history, browser used, and IP address are also valuable components of an individual's digital footprint data when it comes to fraud prevention.

Limitations of Digital Footprint Data

Even though financial services have been more widely available in recent years, some people still do not have access to them and are still unbanked. For example, there is a severe scarcity of digital footprint data for loan companies to access in developed countries where a large portion of the population is still unbanked. Except in developed countries, some citizens can't afford to pay banking fees, don't trust financial institutions, lack sufficient paperwork, and depends on a friend's or family member's account to conduct business.

How is Digital Footprint Data Shaping the Future of Credit Scoring?

1. Alternative Data for Credit Scoring

Digital footprint analysis (Finezza, 2020) is a process that uses information from individuals' Internet usage patterns to understand who they are. As the adoption of digital mediums is increasing day in day out, this can be a valuable source of useful data, even in countries where the percentage of unbanked citizens is high.

KYC (know your customer) is an excellent example of how a digital footprint can be accessed. The device used to fill out a KYC form can be useful for lenders. The equipment used to connect to the lending website presents info about whether an applicant is using a private mode or emulator. Through KYC form, lenders can also assess email profiles and check if it is from a suspicious domain or if it requires any additional verification during the sign-up process. Phone analysis allows lenders to check if applicants are signing up with a real phone number, regardless of whether it is from a fixed line or mobile, and also if they are using that number for messaging services. KYC also facilitates IP analysis that verifies the origin of the connection.

Although using alternative data making up for digital footprint may seem extra, it can help ward fraudsters away. Newer credit score evaluation algorithms can easily multivariate, mine, structure, weigh and use rich data for futuristic credit scoring. Modern lending companies analyze various data sets to assess the creditworthiness of consumers applying for loans. Other alternative data sources include online presence, smartphone metadata, psychometric data, social media data, remittance history, utility bill payments, e-commerce merchant rating, etc.

2. Predict Credit Behaviour

Borrowers in emerging financial markets often have a negligible credit history. Digital footprint data can help lending institutions sanction loans to such individuals. Moreover, the use of advanced data helps Fintechs leverage a mix of historical data with new consumer data to predict credit behavior aptly. With the use of data analytics, these diverse data sets can be used to derive relevant consumer insights.

The use of Artificial Intelligence technologies has helped Fintechs shape a new wave of credit accessibility for consumers and small businesses alike. AI can help financial institutions 'learn' more about their consumers to make intelligent credit decisions. Combined with ML, AI can help screen prospective borrowers by predicting their spending and saving behavior accurately. Lenders benefit from lower NPAs, easy turnaround times for processing loans, and better ROIs.

3. Better Customer Experience

Lenders struggle to find a competitive edge in the markets with an increase in the number of players. Trying to deliver the best in class customer experience, Fintechs can leverage digital footprint data for personalization and high-quality customer experience. Efficient data mining and analytics help loan origination systems in assessing the risk level that a prospect faces and can suggest ways to personalize a loan product to suit their needs in the best possible manner. Financial lending institutions can also devise collection strategies according to the customer's credit risk level.

A COMPARATIVE STUDY OF COMPANIES SELLING AI BASED CREDIT SCORING SOFTWARES

There are many companies who are marketing AI credit scoring software or use it internally, and they have the necessary recourses for developing and operating machine learning software. There are also a few vendors offering AI applications for a variety of financial uses, but these firms often lack the sort of AI talent we search for when vetting a firm's AI statements.

Of the companies in this report (Niccolo Mejia, 2019), The companies with most data processing talent are ZestFinance and Kreditech. These data scientists have masters and doctoral degrees in computer science, statistics, and artificial intelligence, as well as one in artificial intelligence.

Here is a comparative study of 4 such companies -

1. LenddoEFL

LenddoEFL provides a tool named LenddoScore. Using predictive analytics and natural language processing, the firm believes that its tools could assist banks in determining the creditworthiness of prospective borrowers. Since their software considers data from internet operations rather than credit records, Lenddo advertises that their software will be used to target prospects who are unable to obtain credit.

According to the company, users can download LenddoEFL's software to their smartphones. Natural language processing is used by the app to look for signs of commitment or risk-taking in users' social media messages and what they type into their browser. This data is then fed into a predictive analytics algorithm that generates a credit score. Banks and credit unions will then use the LenddoScores of their customers to help consider the risk of them defaulting on their loans.

It has been deduced that the software's machine learning algorithm was trained on thousands of consumer data points, such as social media messages and internet surfing habits. From the viewpoint of banks and borrowers, this data may have been labeled as representative of liability or risk. After that, the data will be fed into the software's machine learning algorithm. This has shown the algorithm could data points are associated with creditworthiness. After that, the program was able to determine which customers are more likely to repay their loans. Golden Gate Ventures has funded LenddoEFL, which has raised $14 million.

2.   ZestFinance

Using predictive analytics and natural language processing, ZestFinance says that its app, ZAML, will help financial institutions assess the creditworthiness of prospective borrowers and reduce loan default.

It could be deduced that the software's deep learning model was educated on tens of thousands of social media messages, geo locations, surfing habits, and other data points. From the standpoint of a bank or borrower, this information may have been labelled as risky. After that, the data will be fed into the software's machine learning algorithm. This will teach the algorithm the data points corresponding to the groups of creditors that are more and least likely to default.

The app will then be able to determine whether or not loan borrowers are expected to repay their loans. Prestige Financial Services says that ZestFinance helps them limit loan losses and defaults without losing credit approval rates. ZestFinance's platform was used to supplement Prestige's standard underwriting approaches. Prestige saw a 33% decrease in loan defaults and a 14% rise in creditor satisfaction ratings, according to the case report. Ford Credit is also mentioned as a previous customer of ZestFinance.

3.   Kreditech

Internally, Kreditech employs the namesake application, which utilizes statistical analytics and likely natural language processing to help the business assess the creditworthiness of prospective customers without detailed banking histories.

We can deduce that the software's deep learning algorithm was trained on hundreds of thousands of consumer data points obtained from social networking and web surfing records. Conversations around cash transactions, as well as data points from e-Commerce and payment processing platforms like Amazon and Paypal, would be included. Positive and negative indices of liability and creditworthiness may have been assigned to these results. The software's machine learning algorithm will then be applied to the labeled results. This will teach the algorithm how to recognize data related to creditworthiness.

A consumer could then feed the software social media messages from a possible creditor, and the algorithm would look for signs of liability for creditworthiness. For example, the software might browse through a prospective borrower's social media conversations and discover that they told a coworker that they would be paid back by a certain date. This operation will then be labeled as a positive measure of obligation by the algorithm.

4.   SAS

SAS provides Credit Scoring for SAS Enterprise Miner, a piece of software that the company says can help banks and financial institutions forecast credit risk using predictive analytics.

We may deduce that the software's deep learning algorithm was trained on thousands of borrower profiles and credit histories. After that, the data will be fed into the software's machine learning algorithm. This would have taught the algorithm which data points are associated with a creditor who is a greater risk to business than others. The software would be able to estimate how much danger a possible borrower poses.

Piraeus Bank Group says that SAS Institute assisted them in speeding up data analysis and report generation. The SAS Institute's software was incorporated into Piraeus Bank Group's core banking framework so that it could access its results. The Piraeus Bank Group was able to increase the data analysis pace by 30%.

Analysis - LenddoEFL has a good chance of successfully implementing a machine learning approach. When it comes to AI talent, their business isn't as powerful as ZestFinance and Kreditech, but they're more likely to be honest about their AI technology. Furthermore, LenddoEFL's final figures are more satisfactory and attractive.

Of the companies in this paper, SAS is by far the most developed, and they definitely have the financial resources to hire the necessary data scientists. Many businesses employ data scientists solely to say that they are using AI. They then refuse to give any useful work to their data scientists because they are unable to communicate with them in a language that they understand. In other words, their subject-matter experts and data scientists are unable to collaborate effectively, which is critical while developing machine learning applications. Also, workers who aren't data or computer scientists at organizations like Google, Facebook, and Amazon find growth in their AI efforts, in part because they know how to speak the language in a way that helps them to inform the AI goods that data scientists produce.

CREDITWORTHINESS ASSESSMENT USING MACHINE LEARNING AND DEEP LEARNING ALGORITHMS

Data Generation

We generate massive quantities of data every second in today's world (Bernard Marr, 2018). We create data corpses when texting, talking, writing, or even speaking. The majority of the information is in a written and unstructured format. As a result, we must process this data in order for it to be understandable by a robot. The NLP technique aids in the retrieval of data and the extraction of valuable information from it.

Take a peek at how much data is processed every second.

- Google currently processes over 40,000 requests a second (3.5 billion searches a day) on average!
- Though Google accounts for 77 percent of searches, it's important to note that other search engines still contribute to our everyday data production. Every day, 5 billion searches are conducted around the world.

These are the numbers created every minute of the day on social media sites, according to Domo's Data Never Sleeps 5.0 study (Domo, 2017):

- 527,760 images have been shared on Snapchat by people.
- About 120 practitioners have joined LinkedIn.
- YouTube videos were viewed by 4,146,600 people.
- Twitter receives 456,000 tweets a day.
- There are 46,740 pictures posted on Instagram by users.

There are 2 billion active users on the platform. Facebook remains the most popular social media website. Let that sink in for a moment: Facebook is used by more than a fifth of the world's 7 billion people! Here are some more fascinating Facebook facts:

- Every day, 1.5 billion people use Facebook.
- Facebook has over 307 million users in Europe.
- Every second, five new Facebook profiles are created!
- Every day, over 300 million pictures are posted.
- 510,000 messages are written every minute, and 293,000 statuses are changed every minute.

About the fact that Facebook remains the most popular social media platform, Instagram (which is now owned by Facebook) has seen rapid growth. Here's how this photo-sharing site contributes to our data avalanche:

- There are 600 million Instagram users, with 400 million of them operating on a daily basis.
- On Instagram, 95 million images and videos are posted every day.
- Every day, 100 million people use Instagram's "stories" feature.

When we use our preferred networking tools now, such as texting and emailing, we leave a data trail (Chetna Tripathi, 2020). Here are some astonishing statistics about the amount of contact we send out per minute:

- We send out 16 million text messages per month.
- There are 990,000 swipes on Tinder.
- There are 156 million emails received each day; by 2019, it is estimated that there will be 2.9 billion email users worldwide.
- Facebook Messenger has sent 15,000 GIFs.
- There are 103,447,520 spam emails sent every minute.
- On Skype, there are 154,200 calls.

Consider all of the ways you collect data when you go through your day, now that you have these figures. When you realize how much data you produce as a single person, you can begin to imagine how much data is collectively generated every day in the whole world.

Natural language processing techniques can arrange unstructured data in a structured format and automate tasks like automatic summarization, emotion interpretation, and speech recognition on it.

Understanding the Data for Creditworthiness Assessment

In this paper, the dataset is obtained from Kaggle, i.e. an online dataset provider (Give me some credit) that stores the credit information of a borrower. Although, for getting this information, it appears that one needs to have some credit history. But that problem can be resolved using the digital footprints of the target person. The data represents the credit data that can be generated using the credit history of the person or the digital footprints(using Artificial Intelligence).

The data contains the historical credit data for 250,000 borrowers. It contains 11 Attributes that are explained in Table 1.

Table 1. Attributes used in the dataset

Variable Name	Description
SeriousDlqin2yrs	Person experienced 90 days past due delinquency or worse Y/N
RevolvingUtilizationOfUnsecuredLines	The total balance on credit cards and personal lines of credit except for real estate and no installment debt like car loans divided by the sum of credit limits percentage.
age	Age of borrower in years
NumberOfTime30-59DaysPastDueNotWorse	Number of times the borrower has been 30-59 days past due but not worse in the past 2 years.
DebtRatio	Monthly debt payments, alimony, living costs divided by monthly gross income
MonthlyIncome	Monthly Income of the borrower
NumberOfOpenCreditLinesAndLoans	Number of Open loans (instalment like car loan or mortgage) and Lines of credit (e.g. credit cards)
NumberOfTimes90DaysLate	Number of times borrower has been 90 days or more past due
NumberRealEstateLoansOrLines	Number of mortgage and real estate loans including home equity lines of credit
NumberOfTime60-89DaysPastDueNotWorse	Number of times the borrower has been 60-89 days past due but not worse in the last 2 years.
NumberOfDependents	Number of dependents in family excluding themselves (spouse, children etc.)

EXPLORATORY DATA ANALYSIS

1. Identification and Treatment of Null Values

It can be seen in Table 2, that there are very few missing values in two attributes. Still, these values are needed to be replaced with the mean of respective attributes. Missing value treatment is another area that has so many options but the quickest is replacing it with mean or median (when the missing percentage is really less).

Many of the Machine Learning algorithms do take missing values in their analysis, but it is always a better strategy to treat them before reaching the modeling stage.

Table 2. Null values in the dataset

	Column Name	Missings	Missing Percentages
0	MonthlyIncome	29731	0.2
1	NubmerOfDependents	3924	0.0

2. Default and Non-Default Visualization

We tried to visualize the Defaults and Non-Defaults on a 2axis framework as can be seen in Figure 1, and see how much of the overlap they have. PCA has been used to extract two main components, which are a combination of all variables. This helped us to understand the default and non-default distributions better.

Figure 1. Scatter plot showing defaults and non-defaults in the dataset

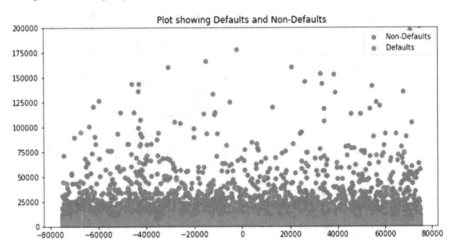

3. Correlations

Correlation (Amit Upadhyay, 2020) explains how one or more variables are related to each other. In our case, these variables are the input data features discussed before which have been used to forecast our target variable i.e. the creditworthiness of the potential borrower.

We checked for two types of correlations:

- To see which variable compares best with the dependent variable, we can use correlation with the dependent variable.
- Correlations between various variables are tested for multi-collinearity.

From Figure 2, we can see that the correlation values for all variables are a little low. There is no association between any of the factors that are greater than 0.5. The dependent variable has the greatest correlation with the variable NumberOfTime30-59DaysPastDueNotWorse.

Correlation as heat map - The correlation heat map shows the correlation values in a multi-color format. The lightest and darkest areas have strong positive and negative correlations.

The heat map showing correlations among different variables is shown in Figure 3.

We can see that variable, 'Number Of Time 60-89Days Past Due Not Worse', 'Number Of Times 90Days Late' & 'Number Of Time 30-59Days Past Due Not Worse' have a high correlation among themselves. To avoid the problem of multi-collinearity, we can eliminate one of the variables and retain the other. This is another example of function engineering in action.

Figure 2. Bar graph of correlation between attributes and target

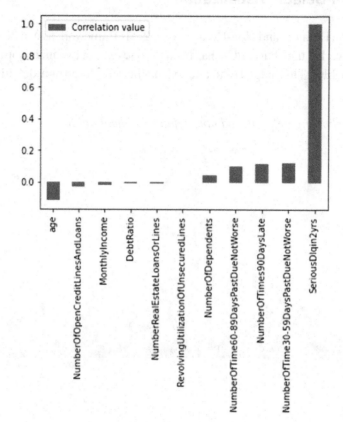

Now, the variable 'Number Of Time 60-89Days Past Due Not Worse', 'Number Of Times 90Days Late' are chosen to be removed as firstly the variable *NumberofTime90DaysLate* is a collection related variable which is heavily used, when an individual is unable to repay a loan and the collection team (which collects the money) contacts the customer to either convince him to pay or face legal action.

RESULTS OF MACHINE LEARNING ALGORITHMS

Different Machine learning algorithms have been used to find the most accurate model for finding the credit score of the target person. This paper focussed on developing the model with various ML algorithms that includes Logistic Regression, Random Forest, Gradient Boosting. Also, although tuning these ML algorithms appears to be easy, it is difficult to refine and tune those algorithms.

In a classifier, we had to use some metrics on which basis we can tune and improve our classification (Purva, Huilgol, 2020). These metrics are:

- **Precision** - The ratio of True Positives to all Positives is known as precision. That will be the indicator of a borrower's creditworthiness that we correctly classify out of all the entries in the dataset for our issue statement. The formula for calculating Precision is shown in Figure 4.

Figure 3. Heat map of correlation between attributes

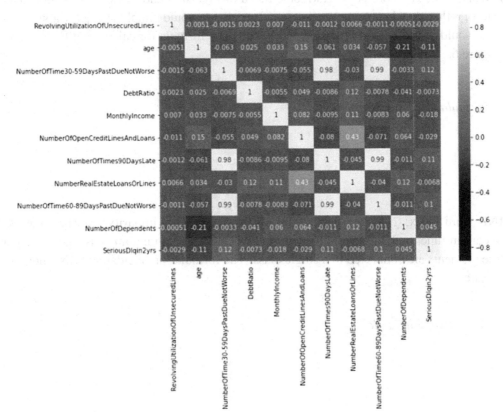

Figure 4. Formula of precision

$$Precision = \frac{True\ Positive(TP)}{True\ Positive(TP) + False\ Positive(FP)}$$

- **Recall -** Recall is a test on how well a model can detect True Positives. As a result, recall shows us how many of the creditors with a good credit outcome we correctly described. The formula for calculating Recall is shown in Figure 5.

Figure 5. Formula of recall

$$Recall = \frac{True\ Positive(TP)}{True\ Positive(TP) + False\ Negative(FN)}$$

- **F1 Score** - The F1-score is the Harmonic mean of Precision and Recall. It is easier to deal with because, rather than balancing precision and recall, we could simply strive for a good F1-score, which would indicate good Precision and Recall. The formula for calculating F1 Score is shown in Figure 6.

Figure 6. Formula of F1 score

$$F1\ Score = 2 * \frac{Precision * Recall}{Precision + Recall}$$

- **GINI** - Gini Index, (Neelam Tyagi, 2020) also known as Gini impurity, measures the likelihood of a certain function being wrongly identified when chosen at random. It is said to be pure if all of the elements are connected to a single class. The formula for calculating GINI Index is shown in Figure 7.

Figure 7. Formula of GINI index

$$Gini\ Index = 1 - \sum_{i=1}^{n} (P_i)^2$$

- **AUC** - Area Under Curve (AUC) is defined as the area bounded by the ROC (Receiver Operating Characteristic Curve) curve and the axes. This is the region that is regarded as a decent model metric. Models with a high AUC are referred to as "qualified" models.

Logistic Regression

Logistic Regression is a classification algorithm that uses a class for building and uses a single multinomial logistic regression model with a single estimator (JET Akinsola, 2017).

The results of the testing data of the classification metrics are given in Table 3.

Table 3. Result metrics of logical regression model

Performance Parameters	Training data	Test data
Accuracy	0.932992	0.933667
F1 Score	0.000249	0.001004
Recall	0.000124	0.000503
Precision	0.142857	0.500000
Gini	0.000071	0.000467
AUC	0.500035	0.500233

The data clearly shows that the Logistic Regression model provides fair accuracy but the F1 Score, GINI Index and Recall are negligible. It is graphically represented in Figure 8.

Figure 8. Graphical representation of performance metrics of logical regression model on training data(left) and test data(right)

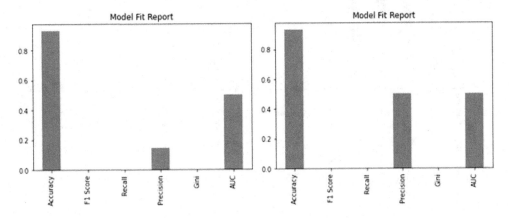

Random Forest

Random forest (Niklas Donges, 2020) is a supervised learning algorithm that builds a "forest" out of a set of decision trees that are typically trained using the "bagging" technique. The fundamental theory of the bagging approach is that incorporating various learning models increases the final result.

The performance metrics of the Random Forest model is given in Table 4.

Table 4. Performance metrics of random forest algorithm on test data

Performance Parameters	Training data	Test data
Accuracy	0.998975	0.880367
F1 Score	0.992395	0.299707
Recall	0.998631	0.385930
Precision	0.986236	0.244976
Gini	0.997631	0.301424
AUC	0.998815	0.650712

It can be seen that Logistic Regression performs very poorly in comparison to Random Forest. Random Forest is performing decently when we see the Train Data Results but if you compare it with test data, it is a clear case of overfitting. It is also known that Random Forest is prone to high variance or overfitting.

The graphical representation of Feature importance for Random Forest algorithm is shown in Figure 9.

Now, Random Forest can't be used as our go-to metric because of this reason. Boosting algorithms needs to be used which are not prone to overfitting and uses a different technique.

Figure 9. Graphical representation of the feature importance of random forest model on training data(left) and test data(right)

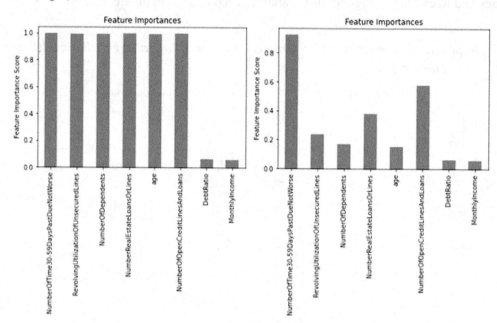

Gradient Boosting

Gradient boosting (Jerome H. Friedman, 2002) builds additive regression models by least-squares fitting a basic parameterized function (base learner) to existing "pseudo"-residuals at each iteration. The gradient of the loss functional being reduced with respect to the model values at each training data point tested at the current level is the pseudo-residuals. The performance metrics of the Gradient Boosting algorithm is shown in Table 5.

Table 5. Performance metrics of gradient boosting algorithm

Performance Parameters	Training data	Test data
Accuracy	0.852567	0.851667
F1 Score	0.317386	0.313483
Recall	0.511822	0.510553
Precision	0.230008	0.226180
Gini	0.388845	0.386454
AUC	0.694422	0.693227

The graphical representation of performance measures of gradient boosting algorithm is shown in Figure 10.

Figure 10. Graphical Representation of Gradient boosting model on training data(left) and test data(right)

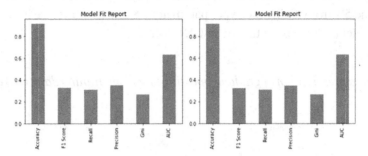

It can be easily seen that the GINI Index of the test data is less than 50%, it is needed to tune it so that better GINI on our Test data could be obtained.

Various hyper parameters of Gradient Boosting are tuned to improve the first cut results.

- n_estimators: The number of trees to be modeled in sequential order. Even though GBM is pretty stable when dealing with a large number of trees, it can also overfit. As a result, CV can be used to tune this for a specific learning rate.
- max_depth: This is the number of maximum depths of the tree. It is used to control over-fitting as higher depth will allow the model to learn relations very specific to a particular sample
- min_samples_split: This is the minimum number of samples (or observations) that must be included in a node before it can be separated.
- min_samples_leaf: This is the minimum samples (rows or observations) required in a terminal node or leaf.
- max_features: While looking for the right split, there are a lot of factors needed to be considered. While fixing the number of functions, we do random sorting to eliminate bias. Over-fitting will occur if the values are too high.
- subsample: The fraction of observations is to be selected for each tree. That selection is done by random sampling.

After combining them together and running them, the performance parameters obtained are shown in Table 6.

Table 6. Performance metrics of gradient boosting algorithm after tuning

Performance Parameters	Training data	Test data
Accuracy	0.893183	0.875200
F1 Score	0.389735	0.309480
Recall	0.509333	0.421608
Precision	0.515623	0.244464
Gini	0.430066	0.329034
AUC	0.715033	0.664517

The graphical representation of the same is shown in Figure 11. It can be seen that there is a lift in GINI Index by around 5% from tuning the hyper parameters. So, in this case, we have been able to reduce the bias from the model by increasing the lift in GINI Index.

Figure 11. Graphical representation of gradient boosting model on training data(left) and test data(right) after tuning

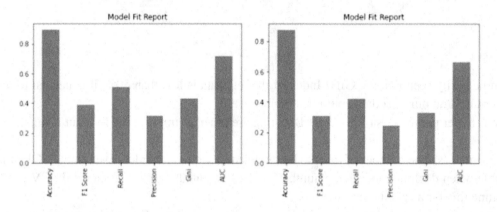

XgBoost Classifier

XGBoost is a gradient boosting-based decision-tree-based ensemble Machine Learning algorithm. XGBoost and Gradient Boosting Machines are both ensemble tree approaches that use the gradient descent architecture to boost slow learners. But, XGBoost enhances the base GBM architecture by algorithmic improvements and device optimization.

The performance metrics obtained using XgBoost classifier is shown in Table. 7 and its graphical representation is shown in Figure 12.

Table 7. Performance metrics of gradient boosting algorithm

Performance Parameters	Training data	Test data
Accuracy	0.866517	0.858500
F1 Score	0.346471	0.317853
Recall	0.528372	0.496985
Precision	0.257739	0.233640
Gini	0.419159	0.81169
AUC	0.709579	0.690585

Figure 12. Graphical representation of XgBoost algorithm on training data(left) and test data(right)

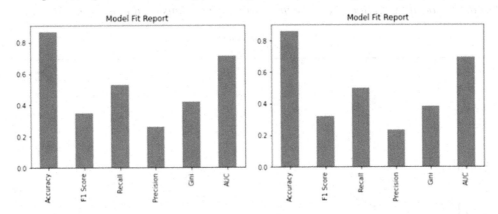

DEEP LEARNING

KERAS (Francois Chollet, 2015) is a Python-based Open Source Neural Network library that uses Theano or Tensorflow as its backend. Keras does not perform low-level programming. Instead, it employs the 'Backend,' which is a separate library. Keras is a high-level API wrapper that can be used with TensorFlow, CNTK, or Theano to access a low-level API.

The Keras API is responsible for determining levels, constructing structures, and configuring different input-output models. At this stage, Keras compiles our model, including the loss and optimizer functions, as well as the training loop with the fit function. Since the "backend" engine handles low-level API like generating a numerical graph, tensors, and other variables, Keras doesn't do them.

Deep learning can be used to predict the norm. Deep Learning is a type of machine learning algorithm that uses neural networks to train the model.

The AUC and GINI index obtained using the deep learning model are:

AUC - 0.7985654979646538
GINI Index - 0.5971309959293076

A comparative study on data obtained by all the machine learning and deep learning models is shown in Figure 13.

Result: As we can clearly see that the Deep Learning model works best on the Test data. It has an AUC score of around 81% which is a good classifier score for a first-second cut version. This can be improved a lot by tuning the Keras model.

Creating a Score from Probability

Next, the probabilities are taken into consideration. Since forecasting a default is the responsibility of a bank's Credit Risk team, we need to convert these odds into a more consumable format, such as a Score, equivalent to a FICO Score, a CIBIL Score, or an Experian Score. These are all Bureau Scores, which can be used to estimate the likelihood of a borrower defaulting on a loan.

Figure 13. A comparative study of all various machine learning algorithms (Logistic Regression, Random Forest, Gradient Boosting, XgBoost) and deep learning algorithms on the basis of AUC values

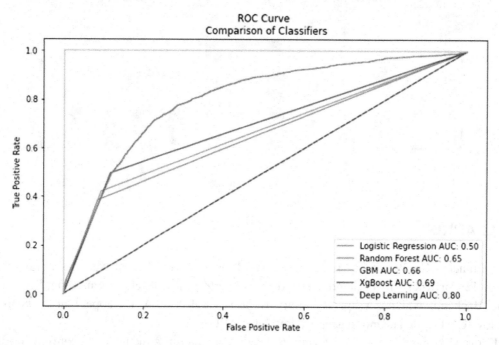

We'll also translate this likelihood into our internal Bank Score, which will be used to determine whether or not a customer qualifies for a loan. Based on the evidence submitted by the user, this is referred to as an Application Score.

Some of the terms which will be used are:

- **Base Score:** For each client, we'll start with this score and then add/subtract points (absolute value) based on his likelihood of defaulting (predicted).
- **PDO (Points to Double Odds):** These are the points that would double the odds. The odds are based on a (Good/Bads) ratio. For example, assume the odds ratio is 300/100 (3) at a score of 620, and if PDO is 100, the odds ratio would be 6 at a score of 720.
- **Goods/Bads:** This is the starting point for the Goods/Bads ratio.

Predicting the Probability for the Full Dataset with the Deep Learning Model

To estimate the likelihood for all customers, the Deep Learning model has been used. The model was put to test using KPIs like GINI and AUC. The score distribution for the complete dataset is shown in Figure 14.

Figure 14. Graphical representation of count of the application scores for the whole testing dataset

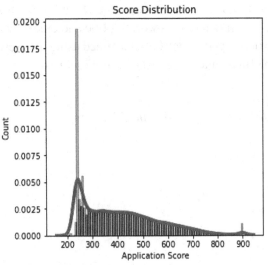

Creating Deciles and Checking Default Rate by Score Bands

This is an ideal exercise that every Credit Risk Manager does to understand if the scores created by him are rank-ordering as per actual defaults. We created 10 groups in the score we have created and then checked the overall defaults and default rates in that particular Score Band.

The Score for different groups is shown in Figure 15.

Figure 15. Variation of scores with respect to different default rate groups

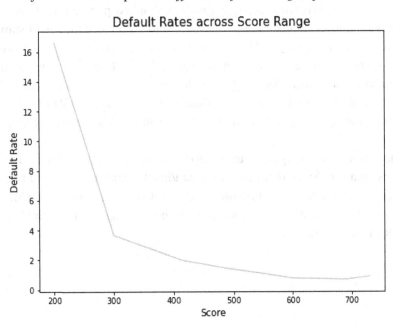

Result: As can be seen in Figure 15, there is no rank-ordering break, which basically shows that the default rate for low score buckets is not lower than the Default rate for high score buckets. Hence it can be deduced that the deep learning model is working fine and credit scores can be obtained from the model. The creditworthiness of any person can be determined using these credit scores. The probabilities representing credit risk in the final database are shown in Figure 16.

Figure 16. Probabilities of different users in the final database

	ID	Probability
0	1	0.230989
1	2	0.216114
2	3	0.164295
3	4	0.368795
4	5	0.441147
...	...	...
101498	101499	0.142472
101499	101500	0.922634
101500	101501	0.056043
101501	101502	0.329716
101502	101503	0.363580

CONCLUSION

In this paper, it has been explored how the creditworthiness of a person can be found and how the obtained credit score can be used for bringing solutions for the unbanked population using Natural Language Processing/ Natural Language Understanding. These techniques involve the use of some machine learning and deep learning algorithms. Since NLP is less intrusive than requiring direct access to a person's entire contact list or a social media site, it is a more equitable way to measure risk while still having the potential to target a larger audience. Although NLP is a recent advancement in the field of technology, there has been a tremendous success to date in various fields that suggests that NLP-based information accessing technologies are proving to leave a huge impact in today's competitively advancing technological environment.

Creditworthiness assessment may prove to be needed in many countries like India where there exists a huge unbanked population. Since there exists no data/insufficient that can lead to an effective credit score of a person, creditworthiness may provide a fair credit score that could help him with credits and loans. This could prove to be an effective solution to all the banking and financial institutions for proving loans/credits to such a population.

REFERENCES

Akinsola, J.E.T. (2017). Supervised Machine Learning Algorithms: Classification and Comparison. *International Journal of Computer Trends and Technology, 48.*

Chen, T., & Guestrin, C. (2016). XGBoost: A Scalable Tree Boosting System. *ACM Digital Library.*

Chollet, F. (2018). *Keras: The Python Deep Learning library.* Astrophysics Source Code Library.

Crouspeyre, C., Alesi, E., & Lespinasse, K. (2019). *From Creditworthiness to Trustworthiness with alternative NLP/NLU approaches.* ACL Anthrology. https://www.aclweb.org/anthology/W19-5516

Domo. (2017). *Data never sleeps 5.0.* https://www.domo.com/learn/infographic/data-never-sleeps-5

Donges, N. (2020). *A complete guide to random forest algorithm.* https://builtin.com/data-science/random-forest-algorithm

Finezza. (2020). *How Digital Footprint Data is Shaping the Future of Credit Scoring?* Retrieved from https://finezza.in/blog/digital-footprint-data-credit-scoring/

Friedman, J. H. (2002) Stochastic Gradient Boosting. In Computational Statistics and Data Analysis (CSDA). International Association for Statistical Computing (IASC).

Hirschberg, J., & Manning, C. D. (2015). *Advances in natural language processing.* American Association for the Advancement of Science (AAAS).

Huilgol, P. (2020). *Precision vs. Recall – An Intuitive Guide for Every Machine Learning Person.* https://www.analyticsvidhya.com/blog/2020/09/precision-recall-machine-learning/

Marr, B. (2018). *How Much Data Do We Create Every Day? The Mind-Blowing Stats Everyone Should Read.* Forbes. https://www.forbes.com/sites/bernardmarr/2018/05/21/how-much-data-do-we-create-every-day-the-mind-blowing-stats-everyone-should-read/?sh=316adc3360ba

Mejia, N. (2019). *AI for Credit Scoring – An Overview of Startups and Innovation.* https://emerj.com/ai-sector-overviews/ai-for-credit-scoring-an-overview-of-startups-and-innovation/

Netzer, O., Lemaire, A., & Herzenstein, M. (2018). *When words sweat: Identifying signals for loan default in the text of loan applications.* Columbia Business School Research Paper.

Tripathi, C. (2020). *Important use cases of Natural Language Processing.* https://ashutoshtripathi.com/2019/05/30/examples-nlp-natural-language-processing/

Tyagi, N. (2020). *Understanding the GINI index.* Medium. https://medium.com/analytics-steps/understanding-the-gini-index-and-information-gain-in-decision-trees-ab4720518ba8

Upadhyay, A. (2020). *What is correlation in Machine Learning.* Medium. https://medium.com/analytics-vidhya/what-is-correlation-4fe0c6fbed47

Chapter 8

NLP for Chatbot Application:
Tools and Techniques Used for Chatbot Application, NLP Techniques for Chatbot, Implementation

Shyamala Devi Nithyanandam
VISTAS, India

Sharmila Kasinathan
VISTAS, India

Devi Radhakrishnan
VISTAS, India

Jebathangam Jebapandian
VISTAS, India

ABSTRACT

The chatbot is one of the increasing number applications in the era of conversational series. It is a virtual application that can efficiently interact with any human being using the deep natural language processing skills. In NLP, for chatbot application, the various techniques needed for chatbot using NLTK tool are explained and implemented. The process of converting the text to numerical value is called text embedding. In NLTK tool, various text embedding tools are available such as TF-IDF vectorization and bag of words. Deep NLP is an efficient way to implement the chatbot. Thus the chatbot is implemented with sequence-to-sequence networks.

DOI: 10.4018/978-1-7998-7728-8.ch008

INTRODUCTION

The Chatbot's are one of the applications which are growing in the era of conversational series. It is a virtual application which can efficiently interact with any human being using the Deep Natural language processing skills. The reality of Chatbots is the integration of machine learning technique where the data is trained to build a relatable model. The proficiency with chatbots is its ability to understand the queries to provide quick and relevant response to the users. Its instantaneous adroitness pertaining to messaging framework augments the efficiency of service multifariously. The construction of a chatbot application can be easily implemented due to its autonomist nature that accelerates quick responses. The natural language processing is categorised into classical and deep learning models, where the former is a set of tools and techniques which enable the computer machine to learn and understand the natural linguistic language such as text and voice of the humans. The tools and techniques that are used are machine translation, text summarization, information retrieval and multilingual cross language information retrieval etc. but there is certain limitation in the classical natural language processing system, where it will not train huge amount of online social media data for chatbot application. Thus, the classical natural language processing system is taking a backseat, with more migrative utilization towards the Deep Natural language processing system. Deep Neural network which has multiple hidden layers aids in training the deep expressive data and renders good result. The deep NLP is the combination of deep learning and Natural language processing system where the former comprises of if-else rules, Audio frequency component analysis (Speech recognition), Bag of words of model (Classification) and Convolution neural network for text recognition (text classification).

The deep NLP holds an end-to-end deep learning model, and applies the deep neural network architecture with various deep learning algorithms for classifying the text-based inputs from the neural network. Some of the stratifications of these algorithms are logistic regression, linear regression, Naïve Bayes, random forest, support vector machine and passive aggressive classifier.

The deep NLP is categorised into different word embedding techniques for converting the words or text in to Numerical vector The word or text which is generated by the human being can be converted to a numerical vector space, to be subsequently fed into the deep neural network architecture. Once the completion of text vectorization is done, the weighted data is applied to deep neural network. Some of the models used in this process are Bag of words, binary encoding, TF-IDF vectorization.

The various deep neural network frameworks are elaborately detailed through the recurrent neural network architecture, sequence to sequence architecture, convolution neural network architecture, gated recurrent neural network and contextual LSTM architecture. Recurrent Neural Network (RNN) is a family of neural networks,that generates the output of the previous layer to be passed as input to the current layer. Sequence to sequence model is a derivation of the RNN. Convolution neural network is a most efficient model to recognize the image of the text, and gated neural network allows the network to find the increment of layers. The Contextual LSTM is used to learn the context of text and to understand the sematic of the text entailed.

All the above content which gives an explanation to implement the Chatbot application hold lesser reference to the data pre-processing techniques for developing the chatbot application. Thus, some of the techniques that requires further exploration for adequate cognizance to effectively delve into the chatbot data pre-processing are tokenization, lemmatization, stemming and stop word removal. The sequence-to-sequence model is a dialog and machine translation system which comprises of two recurrent neural network, encoder and a decoder, with the encoder taking the sequence of text as input and then processing a single text in a given time to convert them into fixed size feature vectors.

The data which is pre-processed with the NLP technique, is then developed with the sequence-to-sequence model, with the code implemented in the Tensorflow framework integrated with python.

The various techniques for adjusting the weights in a deep neural network are detailed more explicitly, and categorized using the gradient descent, stochastic gradient descent and Back propagation methods. The gradient descent is a brute force approach, and is used to adjust the weight of the neural network to yield best results. Stochastic gradient descent is an approach, which is more efficient than the former, with each iteration consisting of one row of neural network being chosen for weight adjustment. It is more relevant and adaptable in helping the user to understand the problems behind the network layers. Finally, back propagation is a process where the weight of the neural network is adjusted after the forward propagation is implemented. The output thus obtained may hold significant errors, which is further iteratively back propagated until the weight of the neural network is adjusted to yield the efficient output.

The LSTM is defined as long short-term memory, and it is a type of RNN drop-out technique that is used for regularization of neural network. It can help in learning and preventing over-fitting of data, and thus holds relative significance with the development of code for a chatbot application.

The beam search decoder is efficient, and consists of an encoder which accepts inputs, and a decoder that generates the relevant output. It is a fast algorithm used to decode the deep neural network content to a final text translation, and is implemented in python for effective construction of a chatbot application. Thus, from the above discussed neural network models, the chatbot application is implemented in deep neural network Natural language processing (Csaky, 2019).

TOOLS AND TECHNIQUES USED FOR CHATBOT APPLICATION

The tools and techniques used for Chatbot Application are:

Spyder: The Scientific Python Development

The Spyder IDE is used for developing the chatbot application which consists of different building blocks they are

- **Editor**
- **IPython console**
- **Variable Explorer**

Editor

The Spyder editor consist of Multi-Lingual editor which has a horizontal and vertical splitting of the platform. The code cell in Spyder consists of block of lines which is executed using the **IPython Console** as depicted in the diagram below (Gerlach, 2020).

Figure 1. Spyder IDE

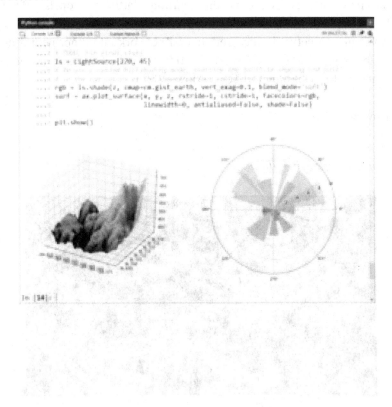

IPython Console

The IPython console allow the user to execute the python code and also helps in data visualization. The IPython interpreter can be used to execute selected or a whole snippet from the editor. Each console can be used to terminate the execution, restart the terminal and interrupt the execution at any given time. The image of the Ipython console is displayed below (Gerlach, 2020).

Figure 2. Ipython console

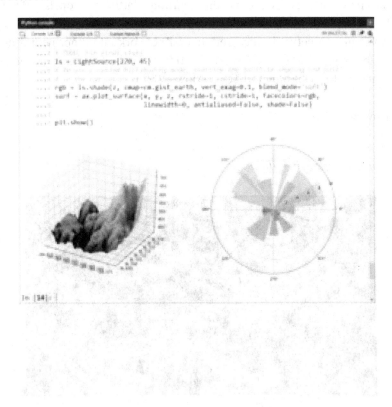

Variable Explorer

The variable explorer is used to interact with the objects generated while running the code. It gives information such as size, name, size and type of the data generated after the execution of the code. It is used to edit the strings, dictionaries, arrays and data frame, and can be potentially used to plot data and visualize them in a click. The figurative representation is as given below (Gerlach, 2020).

Figure 3. Spyder- variable explorer

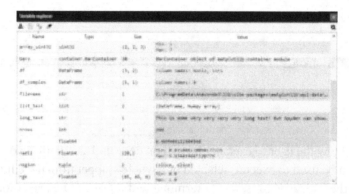

Tensorflow

The Tensorflow is an open-source end to end machine learning platform. It consists of a flexible ecosystem that can build a flexible model. Tensor flow is used to train and run the deep learning neural network such as sequence-to-sequence network, recurrent neural network and other neural network models as well. To create a chatbot application the Tensorflow 1.0.0 is installed in the Anaconda prompt as shown in figure 4. The command for installing the Tensorflow 1.0.0 is

pip install Tensorflow ==1.0.0.

Figure 4. Console for tensorflow installation

NLP TECHNIQUES FOR CHAT BOT

NLP (Natural language processing) is based on the deep learning. To create a chatbot, the NLP must amalgamate with deep learning to form a concept of Deep NLP. There are various techniques used in NLP for developing a chatbot application. They are:

Name Entity Recognition

Named entity recognition is based on the grammar rules and supervised machine learning. The entity can be data, fields, place, date, time, location, description, synonym and information about the object. It is used for chatbot identification of additional attributes given by the user. Figure 5, demonstrates a sample program implemented for the named recognition of a simple text.

Figure 5. Code for named entity recognition

Figure 6. Output of named entity recognition

Vocabulary Identification

The NLP technique helps the chatbot to identify the synonym of different words and execute a reply based on the synonym of matching words in the dictionary. The code in python is implemented for the identification of meaning of different words. The program executed in spyder and the output is given below.

Figure 7. Code for vocabulary identification

Figure 8. Output for vocabulary identification

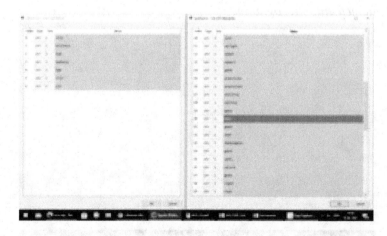

Part-of-Speech (POS)

Part-of-speech is all about tagging, reading the text in a certain language and assigning a tokens of word that can be nouns, verbs or adjectives from the given word. It labels the individual word in a sentence with the speech tagging. In NLTK tool kit there is special function to define the parts of speech. The below code explains this in a Spyder console.

Figure 9. Code for part of speech tagging

Stop Word Removal

The important thing in the chatbot application is to understand the message from the user input with different typo errors, message short cuts, misspelled words, thereby establishing a process to remove noise from the message. In the NLP tool kit, there is an inbuilt method to remove the Stop words, and is illustrated as below.

Figure 10. Code for stop word removal

Figure 11. Output of stop word removal

Text Embedding Technique for Chatbot

Word embedding or text embedding is the process of converting a text into vectors of dimensional space. There are various word embedding techniques in NLTK tool which is used for the creation of chatbot application, and they are:

TF-IDF Vectorizer

TF-IDF Vectorizer is termed as Term Frequency – Inverse Document Frequency. It is process of transforming the text into numbers that can be used in machine learning algorithm for prediction. It generally determines the weight of each text in a document. The term frequency, measures the number of words frequently occurring in a document. IDF is an inverse document frequency that is a process of calculating common terms and rare term words in a given document. IDF result is obtained by the total number of document divided by the number document containing the term (Ndukwe, 2019).

TF-IDF = TF(t, d) X IDF(t)

Where, *TF = Number of times term t appears in the document.*

$$IDF = Log(1 + \frac{Total\ documents}{Documents\ with\ Keyword})$$

To create a chatbot application, the conversion of a text to numerical vector needs to be done, thus the TF-IDF Vectorizer is implemented using NLTK tool kit which is illustrated in the below snippet, and the output given in figure 12 and 13 subsequently.

```
import nltk
import re
import heapq
import numpy as np
```

```
paragraph = """The current situation along LAC is a bit delicate  and serious
But we are thinking about it For our security we had undertaken some precau-
tionary
 steps and we are assured that situation will remain unchanged We have taken
steps
 we will help us he said The current situation along LAC is a bit delicate
 and serious But we are thinking about it. For our security we had undertaken
 some precautionary steps and we are assured that situation will remain un-
changed.
 We have taken steps we will help us he said.
After reaching Leh yesterday, I went to different places an
On the night of August 29-30,
the Indian Army"""
sentences = nltk.sent_tokenize(paragraph)
for i in range(len(sentences)):
    sentences[i] = sentences[i].lower()
    sentences[i] = re.sub(r'\W',' ',sentences[i])
    sentences[i] = re.sub(r'\s+', ' ',sentences[i])


  #creating a histogram
    word2count = {}
    for data in sentences:
        words = nltk.word_tokenize(data)
        for word in words:
            if word not in word2count.keys():
                word2count[word] = 1
            else:
                word2count[word] += 1

freq_words = heapq.nlargest(100,word2count,key = word2count.get)
#IDF MATRIX
word_idfs = {}
for word in freq_words:
    doc_count = 0
    for data in sentences:
        if word in nltk.word_tokenize(data):
            doc_count += 1
    word_idfs[word] = np.log((len(sentences)/doc_count)+1)
#tf matrix
tf_matrix = {}
for word in freq_words:
    doc_tf = []
    for data in sentences:
        frequency=0
```

```
        for w in nltk.word_tokenize(data):
            if w == word:
                frequency +=1
        tf_word = frequency/len(nltk.word_tokenize(data))
        doc_tf.append(tf_word)
    tf_matrix[word] = doc_tf
#idf matrix
tfidf_matrix =[]
for word in tf_matrix.keys():
    tfidf = []
    for value in tf_matrix[word]:
        score = value * word_idfs[word]
        tfidf.append(score)
    tfidf_matrix.append(tfidf)
X = np.asarray(tfidf_matrix)
X = np.transpose(X)
```

Figure 12. Output in variable explorer

Figure 13. Output of tfidf_matrix

Bag of Words

The Bag of words is a process of converting a text into equivalent vector number. It keeps a total count of frequent word occurrences. In other word it is a process of extracting a feature from the text document and uses these for feeding data into a machine learning algorithm. The bag of words technique can be incorporated with a NLP technique and is implemented using a NLTK library.

```
import nltk
import re
import heapq
import numpy as np
paragraph = """The current situation along LAC is a bit delicate and serious
But we are thinking about it For our security we had undertaken some precau-
tionary steps and we are assured that situation will remain unchanged We have
taken steps we will help us he said The current situation along LAC is a bit
delicate  and serious But we are thinking about it. For our security we had
undertaken some precautionary steps and we are assured that situation will
remain unchanged. We have taken steps we will help us he said .After reaching
Leh yesterday, I went to different places an On the night of August 29-30, the
Indian Army"""
sentences = nltk.sent_tokenize(paragraph)
for i in range(len(sentences)):
    sentences[i] = sentences[i].lower()
    sentences[i] = re.sub(r'\W',' ',sentences[i])
    sentences[i] = re.sub(r'\s+', ' ',sentences[i])

    word2count = {}
    for data in sentences:
        words = nltk.word_tokenize(data)
        for word in words:
            if word not in word2count.keys():
                word2count[word] = 1
            else:
                word2count[word] += 1
freq_words = heapq.nlargest(100,word2count,key = word2count.get)
X = []
for data in sentences:
    vector = []
    for word in freq_words:
        if word in nltk.word_tokenize(data):
            vector.append(1)
        else:
```

```
        vector.append(0)
    X.append(vector)
    X = np.asarray(X)
```

Figure 14. Output of variables in variable explorer

Figure 15. Output for bag of words

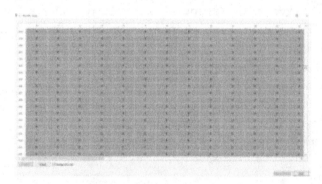

CLASSICAL NATURAL LANGUAGE PROCESSING VS. DEEP NATURAL LANGUAGE PROCESSING

The **classical natural language processing** aims to convert the unstructured data information to machine readable format. Machine learning complex algorithms are used for breaking the text to extract the sematic information. In classical NLP the syntactic and sematic extraction is obtained from the textual data to find the text pattern.

In syntactic analysis, the various machine learning algorithm are used to follow the grammatical rules to unsheathe the meaning of the text. The most generally used syntactic technique are lemmatization, stemming, tokenization POS tagging etc.

In Sematic analysis, the various technique such as named entity recognition, text classification and sentiment analysis are popularly entailed for processing.

Figure 16. Classical NLP

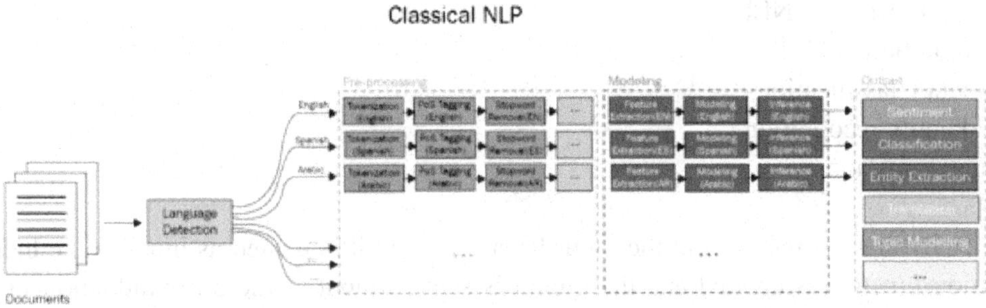

Classical NLP

The Deep natural language processing is the combination of classical NLP and deep learning algorithm. The Deep learning is subset of machine learning which comprises lot of algorithms which works on neural network. It resembles a human brain, and learns information from large amount of data. In Figure 17, the deep learning model illustrated, that evinces the large neural network which consist of multiple layer such as input layer, hidden layer and output layer.

Figure 17. Deep learning-based NLP

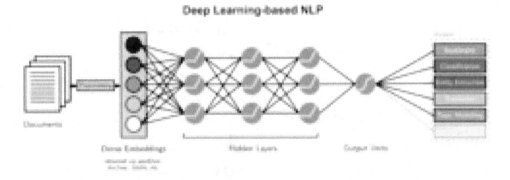

Deep Learning-based NLP

In the chatbot application the end-to-end deep learning model is applied to analyse the question and to search the result using the if-else rule. The various Deep NLP techniques such as sequence to sequence network, recurrent neural network and attention mechanism is used for building the chatbot model (Thanaki, 2021).

RECURRENT NEURAL NETWORK

Recurrent neural (RNN) is a machine learning algorithm which emphasis on integrated system that manipulates the refactoring of layer into loops which iterates the concatenation of two loops. RNN performs well in sequence prediction of text data such as

- Sequencing labelling of dataset
- Text classification in NLP
- Text prediction in NLP.
- Sentiment Classification
- Named entity recognition
- Machine translation

In deep RNN input is received in the input layer and then it is passed as input to the hidden layer then activation function is applied and the output is sent as input to the other hidden layer and then successive activation function is applied to the layer to produce the final output .Each hidden layer as its separate weight and bias. (Note in the **Figure 18** w is weight, b is a bias, FC is activation functions (Bahdanau et al., 2016).

Figure 18. Weights of neural networks

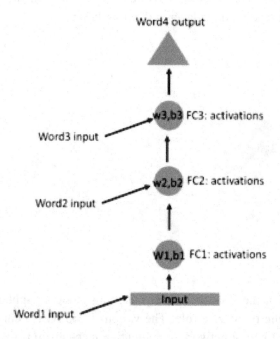

SEQUENCE TO SEQUENCE NETWORK

The Sequence to Sequence architecture consist of encoder and decoder which helps to model data with varying length and with attention mechanism (Haoa et al., 2019). The sequence to sequence network is special recurrent neural network, it is used for the purpose of machine translation, text summarisation, text prediction etc. For various applications, there are a wide range of structures of RNN models they are one to one RNN model where it has one input x^1 and one output y^1, in one to many RNN it consist of one input sequence x^1 and many output sequence y^{1-ty} and in many-to-many RNN where the length of the input sequence T_x and the length of the output sequence T_y are same, appeared in **Figure 19** In many-to-many model, the RNN/LSTM layers filter input sequence from x_1 to x_t based on that it compute

y_t .In single layer RNN models while at times stacking various layers to fabricate a more profound RNN model would be useful to learn more intricate capacities (Mattmann, 2021).In google Multi-lingual architecture they have used three interesting cases of mapping the language such as many to one, one to many and many to many techniques (Johnson et al., 2017) .

Figure 19. Different types of sequence to sequence network

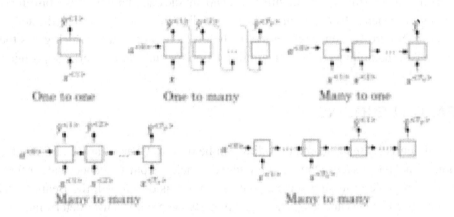

The sequence to sequence network consist of Encoder and decoder LSTM model on **Figure 20**. The encoder architecture is present on the right side of the model and the decoder architecture present on the left side of the model. The encoder accepts the input and encode to fixed size vector representation. The decoder network which is likewise worked as a RNN/LSTM model will disentangle the encoding portrayal and produce the yield grouping. During the time spent translating, the setting vector from encoding will be utilized as the underlying concealed condition of the decoder organization, and the yield an incentive from the last time step will likewise be taken care of into next RNN/LSTM unit as contribution to dynamically make forecasts.

Figure 20. Encoder and decoder

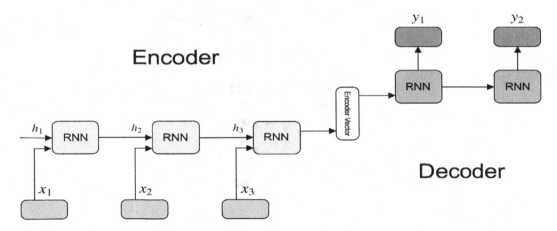

ATTENTION MECHANISM

One of the limits of sequence to sequence structure is that the whole data in the input sentence ought to be encoded into a fixed length vector, setting. As the length of the arrangement gets bigger, we begin losing extensive measure of data. This is the reason the fundamental seq2seq model doesn't function admirably in interpreting huge sequence .It permits the decoder to specifically take a gander at the information grouping while at the same time interpreting. This eases the heat off the encoder to encode each valuable data from the information. In attention mechanism the encoder which as a bi-directional LSTM can accept the input sequence from forward to backward direction and to calculate the activation of both the forward and backward sequence which yields the prediction of output which gives the amount of attention mechanism should pay on the activation function for encoder network (Sojasingarayar, 2020).

BEAM SEARCH DECODING

The well-known heuristic Beam search decoding can be used to Chatbot application that develops the insatiable inquiry and returns a rundown of undoubtedly yield output sequence. Rather than covetously picking the most probable following stage as the succession is developed, the Beam search grows all conceivable subsequent stages and keeps the k doubtlessly, where k is a user determined boundary and controls the quantity of pillars or equal ventures through the sequence of probabilities. Bigger Beam widths bring about better execution of a model as the numerous competitor sequence improve the probability of better coordinating an objective arrangement. This expanded exhibition brings about a reduction in interpreting speed. At the given **Figure 21** given below the decoder yield a decision as what word come next in the sequence and the decision of the beam decoder is greedy so it will find out the most likely word at each sequence (Brownlee, 2018). The Conventional shaft search is an uncommon instance of our proposed approach with one cluster where K-mean clustering is used for decode (Tam, 2020).

Figure 21. Beam search encoding

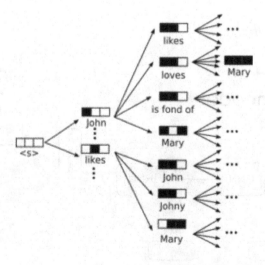

IMPLEMENTATION OF CHATBOT USING DEEP NLP

The Chatbot is implemented with the Movie dataset conversation using deep Natural language processing technique. Initially for the implementation we need to import basic header files such as tensorflow, numpy, re and time. After importing the header file the dataset should be read from the external text document. The text in the document is pre-processed using re library the text is cleaned then the question and answers are separated from the document then every text data is converted to integers. The sequence to sequence model is built with tensorflow placeholder after that the data is pre-processed in both left side and right side of sequence. Encoder RNN is built with LSTM model then the user input is passed in to the encoder and decoder rnn training set function is defined for training and test of decoder is defined. After that epoch training a data with supported hyper parameter is initialized .The splitting of question and answer for training and validation is obtained. Finally the sequence to sequence model for Chatbot application is trained and checkpoint is created. Hence the output for Chatbot is executed for the sequence to sequence to model.

Text Pre-Processing

Text Preprocessing and Question Mapping, where phonetic NLP and rule-based NLP are applied, individually. The Figure shows that given an information sentence (i.e., an inquiry) presented on our chatbot model, the Text Preprocessing stage executes semantic strategies such as Spell Checking, NER and POS (Part-Of-Speech) undertakings, Lemmatization, and Stopwords expulsion, in this manner acquiring a rundown of elements and tokens that address the significant piece of the sentence. The substances and tokens are given as contribution to the following preparing stage, Question Mapping, which applies a bunch of rules for questioning explicit information tables and track down the required data.

The variable short_questions, short_answers, clean_questions and clean_answers variable is declared .The questions and answers are fetched through the variable and the word count of question and answer is calculated if the answers and question is too long or too small is filtered using the threshold value.

Figure 22. Code for chatbot NLP

Figure 23. Code for text pre-processing

Figure 24. Code for chatbot NLP

Figure 25.Code for creating threshold value and variable

Figure 26. Code for creating a variable and looping for chatbot NLP

CREATING A PLACEHOLDER FOR MODEL INPUT

A placeholder is a variable in tensorflow using the import tensorflow as tf and inputs = tf.placeholder(tf. int32, [None,None], name = 'inputs') that will initialized a data for later data it is used for the data inputting operations and inputs used to build the computational graph. The data can be feed in the graph through the placeholder and it is processed using tensorflow is given in the below code (Jha et al., 2021).

In preprocess_targets function uses tf.fill which creates tensor filled with the scalar value, tf.strided_ slice which extract slice value of tensor and tf.concat will concatenate the tensor along single dimension.

Figure 27. Code for creating placeholder

CREATING A DECODER AND ENCODER

Recurrent neural network like LSTM and GRU are incredible arrangement models. I will disclose how to make intermittent organizations in TensorFlow and use them for succession characterization and naming assignments.

The decoder and encoder function is created using rnn(recurrent neural network) where encoder_ rnn,decoder_rnn,decoder_training set, decoder_test set is defined for encoder and decoder operation .In encoder rnn and decoder rnn the tf.contrib.BasicLSTMCell(rnn_size) which creates LSTM layer and is used to initialize the variables of all inputs, tf.contrib.rnn.DropoutWrapper operator is used to add input and output for the given cell.The tf.contrib.rnn.MultiRNNcell is used to build the bidirectional mulilayer recurrent neural network.

The decoder training set and decoder test uses various tensorflow operator such as tf.zeros, tf.contrib. seq2seq.attention_decoder_fn_train,tf.contrib.seq2seq.attention_decoder_fn_inferen-ce,tf.contrib.se-q2seq.dynamic_rnn_decoder, tf.nn.dropout is processed and returns the output functions and test_predictions (Brownlee, 2018).

Figure 28. Code for creating decoder and encoder function

Figure 29. Code for creating decode_test_set

Figure 30. Code for creating decoder_rnn

BUILDING SEQUENCE TO SEQUENCE MODEL

The sequence to sequence model is built for chatbot application which implements tf.contrib.layers. embed_sequence,tf,Variable, tf.nn.embedding_lookup is applied and returns the training predictions and test predictions.

After building the sequence to sequence model the epoch,batch_size,rnn_size encoding_embedding size,encoding_embedding size,learning rate,learning rate decay and keep probability is initialized with the threshold value for the process of validation then the checkpoint is created for the program thus the program is executed.

Figure 31. Code for creating building sequence to sequence model

Figure 32. Code for creating building sequence to sequence model

Figure 33. Code for creating apply_padding function

Figure 34. Code for creating checkpoint and looping for Epoch

Figure 35. Code for calculating the training and learning rate of chatbot NLP

Figure 36. Code for getting input from the user in chatbot

Program executed and the training is running.

Figure 37. Output of the chatbot application

The Chatbot Conversational displaying can straightforwardly profit by this plan since it requires planning among questions and responses. Because of the intricacy of this planning, conversational demonstrating has recently been intended to be very limited in area, with a significant endeavour on include designing. In this work, we explore different avenues regarding the discussion displaying task by projecting it to an assignment of foreseeing the next succession given the past grouping or arrangements utilizing intermittent organizations (Sutskever et al., 2014). We find that this methodology can excel on producing familiar and precise answers to discussions (Vinyals et al., 2015).

RECENT AND RELATED STUDIES

ELIZA is one of the first ever chatbot programs composed (Weizenbaum, 1966). It utilizes shrewd written by hand layouts to produce answers that take after the client's info expressions. From that point forward, endless hand-coded, rule-based chatbots have been created (Ramesh, 2017).

The Golden period of conversational man-made consciousness (AI) is here. Conversational bots or just put chatbots have applications that reach from client confronting AI collaborators, support chatbots, expertise chatbots, right hand bots, and value-based bots. The premium of business in this section is wild with the gigantic interests in this arising innovation by governments, medical care foundations, producing ventures, etc.

Conversational Chatbots are utilizing the force of conversational AI to improve their client experience, and accordingly increment the investor returns.

The modern Chatbots are classified based on Artificial intelligence and Conversational intelligence. They are voice based interface and text based interface.

Customer Support Chatbot

The part of conversational AI is changing as are the bots that force it. From noting basic questions to understanding complex solicitations expect chatbots to be found in each space of current undertakings.

For example, Generali, the third-biggest insurance agency on the planet, saved million in its first year of organization of a client confronting intellectual colleague. This chatbot use NLP (common language preparing) to change over client voice inquiries to message questions, taking care of and noting the underlying inquiries about home and collision protection approaches and claims.

Agent Based Chatbot

In the coming occasions, AI aides upheld by Conversational AI stages will help human client care specialists with inner help while they interface with clients. A genuine model would be found in the BFSI business where chatbots would help bank experts to open a client's record by asking the specialists to physically satisfy all the AOP necessities like KYC checks, and gathering evidence of address and pay subtleties.

Conversational Chatbot

In the future, anticipate that AI technologies should be conveyed in basic lifesaving capacities that incorporate older consideration, aiding life-saving tasks and assisting with catastrophe the executives. Anticipate a drawn out fellowship among people and Conversational AI Platforms to cooperate for the advancement of business and humankind.

In a core, Conversational AI is still at its early stage and is ready to assume an essential part in the advancement of how people will connect with machines in the energizing occasions ahead. The improvement of NLP and Deep learning will open a range of chances for the chatbot stages to interface and become another face of advancement for the advancement of the world (Mnasri, 2019).

Scope of Chatbot Application

The Chatbot Application is used for various industries such as

1. E- commerce industry which provides customer support such as phone calls, emails etc
2. Chatbot is used in medicine industry it synergy front office health care support and which answers to lot of patients query.
3. Chatbot in human resource is used to most internal factors such as identifying the employee performance and answers lot of employee query.
4. Chatbot application for travel industry which helps to answer the query about travelling information to customer.
5. Chatbot application in the Banking industry helps to answer the various query related banking plans and scheme.

Thus lot of industry are using the Chatbot application for their organization customer support.

CONCLUSION

The NLP for Chatbot application have explained about the different NLTK Techniques needed for Chatbot is discussed and implemented with the help of Sypder IDE. Deep learning techniques such as recurrent neural network and sequence to sequence network is built on Tensorflow with Spyder IDE then the Chatbot is trained and tested.

REFERENCES

Bahdanau, D., Cho, K., & Bengio, Y. (2016). Neural Machine Translation by Jointly Learning to Align and Translate. *Proceedings of 3rd International Conference on Learning Representations, (ICLR 2015).* https://arxiv.org/abs/1409.0473

Brownlee, J. (2018). *Deep Learning for Natural Language Processing.* https://machinelearningmastery.com/beam-search-decoder-natural-language-processing/

Csaky, R. K. (2019). Deep Learning Based Chatbot Models. *Scientific Students Associations Report.* https://arxiv.org/pdf/1908.08835.pdf

Gerlach, C. A. M. (2020). *MIT and others SpyderIDE.* http://docs.spyder-ide.org/current/panes/editor.html

Haoa, S., & Lee, D.-H. (2019). Sequence to sequence learning with attention mechanism for short term passenger flow prediction in large-scale metro system. Transportation Research Part C: Emerging Technologies, 107, 287-300.

Jha, R. Prakash, & Kanagachidambaresan. (2021). Tensorflow Basics. In Programming with Tensorflow (pp. 5-13). EAI/Springer Innovations in Communication and Computing.

Johnson, M., Schuster, M., Le, Q. V., Krikun, M., Wu, Y., Chen, Z., Thorat, N., Viégas, F., Wattenberg, M., Corrado, G., & Hughes, M. (2017). *Zero-Shot Translation with Google's Multilingual Neural Machine Translation System.* https://direct.mit.edu/tacl/article/doi/10.1162/tacl_a_00065/43400/Google-s-Multilingual-Neural-Machine-Translation

Mattmann, C. (2021). Sequence-to-sequence models for chatbots. In *Machine Learning with TensorFlow* 2e. Manning. https://livebook.manning.com/book/machine-learning-with-tensorflow-second-edition/chapter-18/

Mnasri. (2019). *Recent advances in conversational NLP: Towards the standardization of Chatbot building.* https://arxiv.org/abs/1903.09025

Ndukwe, I. G., Daniel, B. K., & Amadi, C. E. (2019). A Machine Learning Grading System Using Chatbots. *International Conference on Artificial Intelligence in Education (AIED 2019): Artificial Intelligence in Education,* 365-368. https://link.springer.com/chapter/10.1007/978-3-030-23207-8_67

Ramesh, K., Ravishankaran, S., & Joshi, A. (2017). A Survey of Design Techniques for Conversational Agents. In *International Conference on Information, Communication and Computing Technology (ICICCT 2017): Information, Communication and Computing Technology* (pp 336-350). Springer. 10.1007/978-981-10-6544-6_31

Sojasingarayar, A. (2020). *Seq2Seq AI Chatbot with Attention Mechanism Artificial Intelligence.* IAS-chool/University, Boulogne-Billancourt, France. https://arxiv.org/ftp/arxiv/papers/2006/2006.02767.pdf

Sutskever, I., Vinyals, O., & Le, Q. V. (2014). Sequence to sequence learning with neural networks. NIPS.

Tam, Y.-C. (2020). Cluster-based beam search for pointer-generator Chatbot grounded by knowledge. *Computer Speech & Language, 64,* 101094. doi:10.1016/j.csl.2020.101094

Thanaki, J. (2021). *Python Natural Language Processing.* O'Reilly. https://www.oreilly.com/library/view/python-natural-language/9781787121423/6f015f49-58e9-4dd1-8045-b11e7f8bf2c8.xhtml

Vinyals, O., & Le, Q. V. (2015). A Neural Conversational Model, *Proceedings of the 31st International Conference on Machine Learning, 37)* https://arxiv.org/abs/1506.05869

Weizenbaum, W. J. (1966). Eliza—A computer program for the study of natural language communication between man and machine. *Communications of the ACM, 9*(1), 36–45. doi:10.1145/365153.365168

Chapter 9
Significance of Natural Language Processing in Data Analysis Using Business Intelligence

Jayashree Rajesh
School of Computing Sciences, VISTAS, India

Priya Chitti Babu
School of Computing Sciences, VISTAS, India

ABSTRACT

In the current machine-centric world, humans expect a lot from machines right from waking us up. We expect them to do activities like reminding us on traffic, tracking of appointments, etc. The smart devices we have with us are creating a constructive impact on our day-to-day lives. Many of us have not thought about the communication between ourselves and the devices we have and the language we use for communication. Natural language processing runs behind all these activities and is currently playing a vital role with respect to the communication with humans with the use of virtual assistants like Alexa, Siri, and search engines like Bing, Google, etc. This implies that we are talking with the machines as if they are human. The advanced natural language processing techniques have drastically modified the way to discover and interact with data. In the recent world, the same advanced techniques are primarily used in the data analysis using NLP in business intelligence tools. This chapter elaborates the significance of natural language processing in business intelligence.

INTRODUCTION

Natural Language Processing is being referred as the AI based technology which qualifies the machines/computers in understanding, interpretating and manipulating the human natural language. It enables the computer systems in reading the characters in text, speech recognition and interpretating it. It is derived

DOI: 10.4018/978-1-7998-7728-8.ch009

from a variety of disciplines like computer science and linguistics computation and tries to remove the gap between communications with computer and with humans. The terminologies involved with NLP are given in Figure 1.

Figure 1. NLP terminologies
Ref: https://www.blumeglobal.com/learning/natural-language-processing/

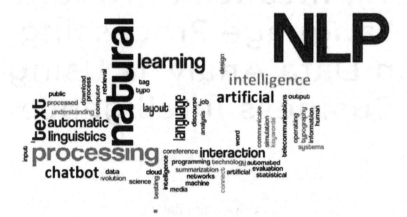

CHRONICLE OF NATURAL LANGUAGE PROCESSING

- Georgetown, 1954 —-An Experiment from IBM – A programmed computer was designed that translates 60 statements from Russian into English by assigning specific rules and steps to specific words.
- LISP, 1958 -- John McCarthy released the Locator/Identifier Separation Protocol, one of the computer programming language still being used in the current world.
- STUDENT, 1964 – Daniel Bobrow, as part of his Ph.D. thesis work, developed an program based on AI named STUDENT created in specific to read and resolve word problems on algebra.
- ELIZA, 1964– A program developed at MIT, which deemed to be first of kind Chatbots, creates the simulation of conversations using the substitution methods and pattern-match methodology.
- ALPAC, 1964 – NRC, United States National Research Council developed ALPAC (Automatic Language Processing Advisory Committee) to evaluate the development of research work on Natural Language Processing.
- SHRDLU, 1970 – Terry Winograd created a computer strategy named SHRDLU, which can understand NLP and considered to be the first of kind program that can understand the context, in which the user provides several programming directions to shift several blocks in disparate ways.
- LADDER/ LIFER, 1978 – An NLP database system which utilized a connotative syntax to analyse questions and inquiry any distribute database to provide solution questions regarding the US Naval ships.
- MACHINE LEARNING, 1980 – Machine Learning algorithms gathered significance by replacing the traditional complex and handwritten rules used in NLP systems. Few of the ML algorithms like Decision Trees provided the systems with traditional rules which were handwritten but many

research activities arose which pivot on statistics based models which are capable enough to produce probability based decisions of which IBM was the major contributor in developing many complicated and successful models with statistics..

- N-Grams, 1990 – Statistics based NLP model to recognize and track linguistic data in a numerical way.
- LSTM/RNN, 1997 -- Recurrent Neural n Network models entered in their way for text and voice processing.
- AskJeeves, 1997 –Search engine evokes users to raise queries with their natural languages.
- Watson, 2006 – A software combination of Artificial Intelligence and Analytics, was created by IBM to address the queries on hazard on a typical question-answering model of machine.
- Hummingbird, 2013 –Google product which updated its query mechanism to anchor on the intention of the searcher rather than merely understanding the query type of the search.
- 2011 – Till Date – Alexa, Google Assistant and Siri have become the Virtual assistants like Siri, Alexa, and Google Assistant become the most quality tool out of NLP, being used in almost all smart gadgets.

SCHOLARLY REVISIT

Bafna & Parkhe, on their paper proposes a predictive analysis on Business Intelligence. The proposed application also enables the users to raise queries in natural language. As part of the proposed architecture, the queries were classified as Regression/Cluster/Classification, etc. and different algorithms are applied and compared for evaluation on parameters like precision, accuracy, etc. The viable algorithm will then be used to arrive the final prediction model. Apache Spark and Mongo DB were used for building the model.

Kate and Kamble, on their paper proposed an automatic approach to convert SQL queries into Natural language queries. This will enable the users who are not aware of any technical query writing to get the required data in a much easier way. As part of the proposed approach, users can raise their queries through voice as well. The systems automatically convert the voice into text. The user entered input query was tokenized and selected tokens were used to form the syntax to be entered in database. The final query formed was verified by issued against the database.

Reshma & Remya, on their paper, proposes architecture and prototype for different NLIDBs (Natural language interfaces to databases) which converts natural language text into Database SQL queries to get the output from the relational databases. The underlying issue of the domain dependency with the NLIDB was resolved by the appliance of Natural language interface which could take away the language barriers and could easily convert the text into SQL query.

Saini, on his paper proposed the Machine learning model using Python which identifies and extracts the language used in any social media post using Natural Language Process techniques. The model also used linguistics and several other prediction approaches for identifying the language. According to the author, detection of Code Mix is the first and foremost step in identifying the language in a post to do any NLP based task in social media.

TASK OVER SOCIAL MEDIA

Characteristics of Natural Language Processing

NLP algorithm splits down the lingo into very short, with more fundamental sections, named Tokens (Periods, Words, etc.), and venture to identify the relationships between the tokens (Reshma and Remya, 2019), using some of the features like

- **Content / Material Categorization**: Summary of a semantic document containing the alerts, detection of duplicates, indexing and search of the given content.
- **Topic Detection and Designing**: Encapsulates the different themes as well as the meanings of text clusters and solicits advanced analytic programming methods into the text.
- **Extraction of Context**: Automatic pull to extract constructed data from text-form origins.
- **Sentiment Analytics**: Discovers the common mood, subjective point of views, maintained in huge collection of text. Used mainly for opinion-mining.
- **Conversion of Speech-to-Text & Text-to-Speech**: Converts the vocal commands into simple text, and vice versa.
- **Document Encapsulation**: Automatic creation of synopsis by liquidizing huge amount of text.
- **Machine Translation**: Automatic translation of speech or text of any language into the other language.

APPLICATIONS OF NATURAL LANGUAGE PROCESSING

NLP has been widely used across many fields in the recent days for better and quick response and resolution to the problems. Some of the vital applications are as follows:

In Voice Assistants

Voice Assistants like Apple Siri, Amazon Alexa & Google Assistant, became admired with the recent technology advancements. They use NLP, Speech synthesis & Voice recognition are being used by them for communication between human beings. (Saini, 2019) They accomplish many activities like creating calls, answer for questions, playing specialized songs, look for anything on the web, etc.

Customer Behavioural Research

Several organizations started performing Sentimental Analysis using NLP to understand the buying behaviour of customers, their interest areas, categorization of their comments into positive and negative, etc. Meaningful cognizance arises when we understand about customers. Depending on customer's behavioural pattern, Marketing and Sales decisions can be made by business effectively.

Classification of Emails

In the current world, NLP functions are used by many Email contributors for understanding the timbre of every email as well the segregation of inbox. Automatic categorization of emails as Spam and are sent automatically to the Spam folder using NLP based algorithms (Joshi et.al., 2018). A plenty of human energy and time can be saved by the auto-segregation of emails. Email providers like Yahoo and Gmail uses these techniques instead of the manual scanning of every email.

Financial Analysis

NLP performs analysis individual user comments and point of views related to a specific subject and renders meaningful knowledge to Finance trade users and other finance-based companies. NLP is used in these places for tracking the daily global circumstances which in turn will provide the relevant data to enhance the business profit.

Detection of False Information

With the advent of social media consumption, Fraud news became a quite major issue across the globe (Asur & Huberman 2010) nowadays. The issue was looked as a substantial issue and produces unwanted worries and strain between people. Algorithms of NLP analyses the lingo and inspect whether it is reliable or not. This information helps in critical times like a natural disaster or a pandemic.

Spell Check and Syntax

Syntax is cardinal for blog writing and sending emails. An engrossing mail or a post makes a noticeable difference with the person who reads the post. During earlier days, people manually checked the word spell and grammar checks as there was no automatic mechanism for checking was available. NLP is used currently for automatic spell check and grammar correction as it is robust and precise and as well influential while writing lengthy essays or articles as well for sending vital emails. "Grammarly" is one such automatic utility for Grammar checks.

Automated Messenger Bots

Majority of the internet websites have started using the Chatbots for maintaining faster and reliable communication with customers. An ideal example would be the delivery operators who provides the delivery of food based on the discussions with customers using Chatbots. Bots provide more user-friendly communication (Thejaswini & Indupriya, 2019) and provides many options to customers in a short span of time so that the customers will have enough options to choose from.

Autocomplete Property in Search

While searching for a specific search through search engines, we can identify that auto complete property is running. This will be helpful in search, as we do not want to type the complete search word. A catalogue of suggestions would be provided for the user to select as per his likes which is possible with the use of NLP algorithms.

BUSINESS INTELLIGENCE – AN INTRODUCTION

Business Intelligence (BI), a primary data-driven Decision Support System, consists of the list of practices, technologies and applications that performs the analysis, integration, presentation and collection of business data to render assistance for business decision-making strategies. BI systems provide different views (predictive / historical / current) (Bollen, Mao & Zeng, 2011) about the business operational activities mostly with the data from Datawarehouse or from a Datamart and at times from the operational business information. Supporting software tools (elements) provide visualization, management reporting (Adhoc / dashboard), pivot tables (used to analyse the information in slice-and-dice manner) (Jayashree & Priya 2019). and statistics-based data mining Applications tackle sales, production, financial, and many other sources of business data for purposes that include business performance management. Information is often gathered about other companies in the same industry which is known as benchmarking.

Quite recently, organizations commenced to view both content and data not to be treated as disparate entities of Information Management, rather to be observed in a combined approach at enterprise level. EIM (Enterprise Information Management) presents both BI and ECM (Enterprise Content Management) at once. Organizations have slowly getting moved towards Operational BI, that is not being challenged by any vendors so far. Conventionally, BI vendors targeted the top-level pyramid however the model is getting shifted towards moving the Business Intelligence to the bottom pyramid focusing self-service BI.

SSBI (Self-service Business Intelligence) provides customers with the access to organization data and their business applications/systems via tool-based data analysis, thereby providing detailed analytics on the company data without involving the organization's IT department. It provides the end-users, the capability to do and play with data neglecting the technical capability which could help them to make better decisions on data.

Using the Business Intelligence Tools, a user can hunt through with the information on a similar note of searching through any search engine like Google, with the use of NLP. Data analysis can be expanded in BI, depending on the raw data (Jayashree & Priya, 2020) and its user interactions, that seems to be a quite cumbersome task to handle with because of the defending nature of the human languages with their syntax rules, semantics and tone.

DEMAND OF NLP IN BUSINESS INTELLIGENCE

It has been estimated that an individual on the world can create around 1.7 MB data every second. Right from buying a cappuccino, or reading a book or blog, like a video, a steady flow of 0s and 1s discharging from people all-time and businesses tries to catch the data for continuous improvement of the business.

They collect these customer and business data for identifying better insights, and provides insights on sales openings, marketing blueprints, stock planning, etc. Organizations will be able to extract and investigate on the key performance indicators whenever required based on the ad-hoc demand and at frequent intervals can largely improve the performance, efficiency of the company and drives eventually for the growth. However, the information is collected from several distinct data structures which are complex and sensitive by nature. Huge efforts are required for the collection, organize and report on these data.

Business Intelligence services collects the key performance indicators of business and output them in a graphical way using graphs/charts/dashboards. Reporting solutions with ad-hoc (or On-demand) capabilities can help the user for navigating into the collected metrics (Jayashree & Priya 2019) and can dig deep in the information for answering any noticeable questions.

However, not all of the Business Intelligence services are easy to work with as many of them need sound technical knowledge on the BI tool to be use and also should know how to write the queries in database to fetch the required data output. This means that the organization may need a set of skilled people (E.g. A Data scientist) who knows the knowledge of how to create the reports and analyse the data based on the report output. Hence the focus in the current BI industry has been shifted from the traditional reporting needs to creation of simplified and easiest user experience for which natural language processing a key step to move forward.

ASSOCIATION OF NLP WITH UNSTRUCTURED DATA

A huge amount of data is being captured by the Organizations to make them sensible for business reporting needs. For many decades, the companies have chosen to neglect the semi-structured and unstructured information as the due available tools during the course of time were not flexible and involves complex procedures (Singh & Solanki 2016) to derive the meaningful insights. They were using the manual entry of data or through a template for gathering the unstructured data for analysis.

The usage of BI was limited due to the reason that the user needs to know and write the database queries which is a combination of one or more entities available in the relational database and should know the proper way of interaction with the Business Intelligence products to obtain the required results. Data analysis has become user-friendly by using NLP as the translation of the queries on natural language to the required language happens automatically. Currently, enormous amount of non-structured data (social media, online review, etc.) can be made for analysis with the help of NLP.

NLP performs the understanding of human languages, identifying the insights of conversations of customer and categorization of the insights into appropriate business metric. This helps in recognizing the sentiment present on a specific subject, which helps to change the relevance on a product, through their regular marketing campaigns.

The unique solicitation of NLP in the healthcare zone in which it is used as a tool to analyse the sensitive medical data. There was a huge amount of non-structured data exist in the healthcare section which are very essential for accurate and fulfilled quality measurement analysis. Several health organizations frequently can leave out the important patient details due to the constraints of applying free content (text) in data analytics. An ideal instance would be: The 'drinking status' of a patient could be marked as "drank in the past" or "drinking 2 liquor bottles per day", or, "Reduced to 1 liquor bottle per day." NLP identifies the qualitative descriptions inside the patient record and obtains the synonyms for categorization of phrases into well-organized findings like, "is a dipsomaniac," "ex- dipsomaniac," or "not a dipsomaniac." The organizations would be able to withdraw such information from the free content that helps the physicians for prescribing the ideal medication availabilities and therapies.

DOMINANCE OF NLP FOR BUSINESS INTELLIGENCE

Democratization of Information

The most important benefit of data analysis with NLP is the accessibility of difficult business details using natural language. By which the need for a data scientist requirement in an organization for analysing data can be eliminated as everyone will eventually turn into a data scientist.

For instance, a typical business user may rise the below requirement

I need the comparison of the turn-over rate of the inventory with the last quarter and the current quarter.

Figure 2. Quarter-wise comparison of inventory turn-over rate
Ref: https://www.izenda.com/natural-language-processing-business-intelligence

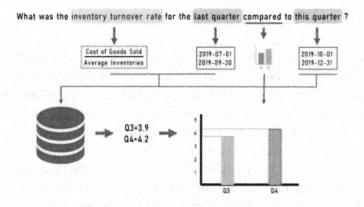

Business Intelligence tool investigates the question, search the database using database queries, and provide the data in the well-suited visualization format. These kind of use cases will always have a strong impact on decision-making.

Workable Perceptions

Empowering users to manipulate and explore information for identifying better insights, will provide the business organizations to arrive at better business conclusions. These decisions will help to increase revenue and improve the execution efficiency.

Keep Resources and Time

Organizations need not spend their resources and time to learn about how to raise data-related questions. Instead, it will be automatically taken care by NLP as it authorises a user irrespective of his skills (technical / non-technical) to No longer will businesses need to spend time and resources learning how to ask a data question. Natural Language Processing empowers every user, regardless of technical skill, to execute difficult queries by just raising a question in simple English.

IMPLEMENTING NLP IN BUSINESS INTELLIGENCE

Natural Language Processing is used by the search engines like Google that transforms the questions in natural language into database queries and obtains the relevant information from enterprise data warehouses. The similar approach is followed in BI tools as well. A user can speak and raise their clarifications to tools which in turn will be converted into SQL (Kumar & Goyal 2016) or any other type of queries with different technical language with the help of NLP and obtain the needed information from the relational database. There will be a combination of queries that fetches the information from disparate sources. The process is made simpler by NLP by just asking the question through a virtual assistant app. Tableau and Power BI of Microsoft have introduced the feature and is running effectively.

NLP IMPLEMENTATION IN POWER BI – AN INVESTIGATION LEARNING

Power BI is a Business Intelligence service from Microsoft, primarily used for data visualization using the scalable and integrated self-service platform for Enterprise BI (Business Intelligence) to obtain deep data cognizance. It consists of several applications, software and connectors, which collaborates together to obtain the conversion of non-related data source into immersive and interactive insights. Data source could be a simple Excel spreadsheet, or a list of on-premise/cloud hybrid data warehouses. Power BI can connect, model, visualize, create meaningful reports with your data with the custom KPIs. It can also provide AI-powered responses to any business question when raising with spoken language and hence bridging the space between decision making and data.

The way in which the Topic Modelling is applied in Power BI using PyCaret will be elaborated in detail here., The implementation of Natural Language Processing in Power BI will also be discussed with a case study.

Topic Modelling

Topic model is a statistics-based model, falling below the unsupervised machine learning, is being primarily used in the Natural Language Processing and Machine Learning algorithms to identify the theoretical topics which exist in a set of documents. It is also used in the text-mining to determine the isolated lingual architecture in the body of a text. A well-structured document talks about specific topic in consideration and thus it is expected that several words appearing in the document more frequently. The document thus has several topics appearing across in distinct proportions.

Gathering of comparable and similar words are produced by Topic model techniques. The model entraps this divination using a mathematical structure, that explores the document collection and identifies the distinct topics based on the word statistics and the topics' balance across the document.

Topic model can also be mentioned as probability-based topic model, which utilizes statistic algorithms for determining the semantic architecture from the text body. In the current era of information, we deal with enormous amount of the written/collected material which is far away from our operating magnitude. They assist in organizing and provide insights to study on collections of un-structured text bodies. They were also used in detecting informative structures like networks, genetics and images and have their footprints in computer vision and bioinformatics.

Topic Modelling is predominantly in the following use-cases:

- **Text Summarization**: Summarize large texts data by topics' specific classification of documents.
- **Empirical Data Analytics**: Gain knowledge on data like survey outcomes, customer product reviews from websites, feedback forms, etc customer feedback forms
- **Feature Engineering**: Creation of relevant features required for supervised ML experiments like regression or classification.

Algorithms of Topic Modelling:

Many algorithms are being used specifically for Topic Modelling. Popular ones are given below.

- LDA - Latent Dirichlet Allocation
- LSA - Latent Semantic Analysis
- NMF - Non-Negative Matrix Factorization

However, LDA (Latent Dirichlet Allocation) is primarily used with BI while working with the NLP modules of the BI software.

TOPIC MODELLING WITH NLP IN BUSINESS INTELLIGENCE – AN INVESTIGATION STUDY USING POWER BI

The below case study will elaborate in detail, on how the NLP modules are being used in Business Intelligence Software with a case study. Microsoft Power BI is being taken for this exploratory analysis along with open source libraries from PyCaret.

PyCaret is the primary low code ML Python library which is open-source in nature provides the automation of Machine Learning venture. It provides a complete machine learning models development model management tool which eventually speeds up the investigation cycle exponentially to reduce our development efforts and increase the productivity.

Text data should be pre-processed before it gets fed into any algorithm to obtain meaningful insights from topic models which is a common task while using NLP. This text pre-processing differs from the traditional pre-processing methods used in the Machine Learning world, when handling the data with rows and columns (structured).

There are about 15 techniques being used by PyCaret for the automatic pre-processing of text data. The techniques include lemmatization, extraction of bi-gram/tri-gram, tokenization, removal of stop words, etc

Below are the high-level steps involved in the Power BI based Topic Model.

1. Setting up the environment for Power BI and PyCaret
2. Get Source Data

3. Train the model in Power BI using Python
4. Verify the output

Setting the Environment

Below steps to be carried out to set the Power BI and Python environments.

1. Create the anaconda environment by executing the below code in anaconda environment.
```
conda create --name powerbitest python=3.7
```
2. Install PyCaret
   Execute the below code in Anaconda prompt.
```
pip install pycaret
```
3. Map the Python Directory
   The environment created above should be mapped with Power BI in order to use.
   The below path to be used for any modifications to the Power BI settings.
   File → Options → Global → Python scripting
4. Install the required Language Model. This is required for performing NLP tasks.
```
conda activate powerbitest
python -m spacy download en_core_web_sm
python -m textblob.download_corpora
```

Get Source Data

The dataset from Github will be used for the case study purpose. A non-profit organization called Kiva, who wants to expand their financial data access to under privileged people and help them to thrive. The dataset from Kiva will be used to test the NLP function in Power BI. The dataset contains the loan information like amount, gender, country along with some textual data of the borrower which is abstracted from the application form of the borrowers for which the loan is approved. A snapshot of the loan data is given in Figure 3.

The objective is to examine the textual data present in column 'en' to obtain the isolated topics and further to appraise the consequence of specific topics (in this case, specific loan types) on the basic rate.

Import the dataset into Power BI desktop using the web connector in the below path. The same is also shown in Figure 4.

Power BI Desktop -> Get Data -> Other -> Web

The data from Github will be downloaded in the form of a .csv file using the below link.

https://raw.githubusercontent.com/pycaret/pycaret/master/datasets/kiva.csv

Figure 3. Snapshot of loan data
Ref: https://raw.githubusercontent.com/pycaret/pycaret/master

country	en	gender	loan	nonpay	sector	status
Dominican Republic	"Banco Esperanza" is a group of 10 women looking to receive a small loan. Each of them has taken out a very small loan already, so this would be their second. With this loan the group is going to try and expand their small businesses and start generating more income. <P> Eduviges is the group representative and leader of the group. Eduviges has a lot on the line because she has 6 children that she has to take care of. She told me that those children are the	F	1225	partner	Retail	0
Dominican Republic	"Caminemos Hacia Adelante" or "Walking Forward" is a group of ten entrepreneurs seeking their second loan from Esperanza International. The groups past loan has been successfully repaid and the group hopes to use additional loan funds for further business expansion. Estella is one of the coordinators for this group in Santiago. Estella sells undergarments to her community and neighboring communities. Estella used her first loan, which has now been completely repaid, to buy additional products and Estela was able to increase the return on her	F	1975	lender	Clothing	0
Dominican Republic	"Creciendo Por La Union" is a group of 10 people hoping to start their own businesses. This group is looking to receive loans to either start a small business or to try and increase their business. Everyone in this group is living in extreme poverty, and they see this as a chance to improve their lives and the lives of their families.	F	2175	partner	Clothing	0
Dominican Republic	"Cristo Vive" ("Christ lives" is a group of 10 women who are looking to receive their first loans. Thi	F	1425	partner	Clothing	0
Dominican Republic	"Cristo Vive" is a large group of 35 people, 20 of which are hoping to take out a loan. For many of	F	4025	partner	Food	0
Dominican Republic	"Dios con nosotros" is a large group of Esperanza borrowers. In this group, ten members are hoping to receive a loan. This group has all been very successful and some are receiving their sixth loan! <p> Lorenza is the group representative and chosen leader, and for good reason. Lorenza is a very hard worker and a very responsible person. She is the mother of two young children and does everything with her children in mind. She owns a small store and hopes to keep increasing business. She is a great success story because she went from having no income to owning her	F	2700	partner	Food	0

Figure 4. Dataset import in power BI with web connector
Ref: https://towardsdatascience.com/topic-modeling-in-power-bi-using-pycaret-54422b4e36d6

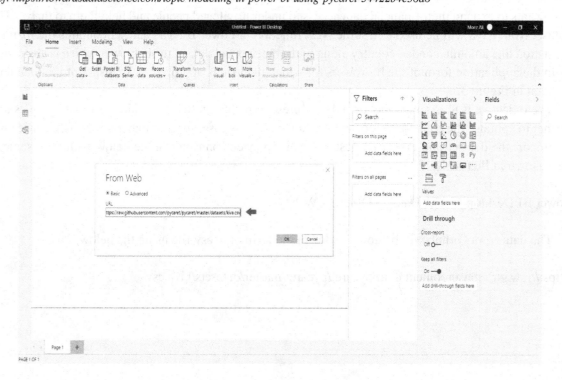

Train the Model in Power BI

Execute the below Python code in Power BI. The code to be executed from the following path. The same is also illustrated in Figure 5.

Power Query Editor → Transform → Run python script

```
from pycaret.nlp import *
dataset = get_topics(dataset, text='en')
```

Figure 5. Python script execution from editor
Ref: https://towardsdatascience.com/topic-modeling-in-power-bi-using-pycaret-54422b4e36d6

The code imports the NLP libraries into Power BI and identifies the set of topics from the given data. In our case, it is from Kiva's Loan documents. The model will then be trained using the LDA (Latent Dirichlet Allocation) model with 4 topics. This can be changed and customized per requirements as below.

- Model type can be changed by modifying the *"model"* parameter inside the **get_topics**() function.
- Number of topics can be changed, using the parmeter *"num_topics"*.

Example code given below with 6 model topics for a Non-Negative Matrix Factorization (NMF)

```
from pycaret.nlp import *
dataset = get_topics(dataset, text='en', model='nmf',
num_topics=6)
```

Output

The dataset along with its distinct topics will then be imported into Power BI using the Dataset icon from the Palette as given in Figure 6.

Figure 6. Result from model after python code execution
Ref: https://towardsdatascience.com/topic-modeling-in-power-bi-using-pycaret-54422b4e36d6

Once the dataset is imported, the distinct topics along with their weightage are included along with the original dataset once the table is clicked as given in Figure 7.

The columns containing the topic weights are now attached with original dataset. The final output in Power BI after applying the query is illustrated in Figure 8.

Data Visualization

The Power BI output data can be visualized in different ways for easy understanding. Some of the noticeable visualizations of loan data against several topics are as follows.

- Topic Categorization
- Topic wise Default Rate set
- Distribution of Topics by Sector
- Gender count across Topics

Figure 7. Topics with weightage
Ref: https://towardsdatascience.com/topic-modeling-in-power-bi-using-pycaret-54422b4e36d6

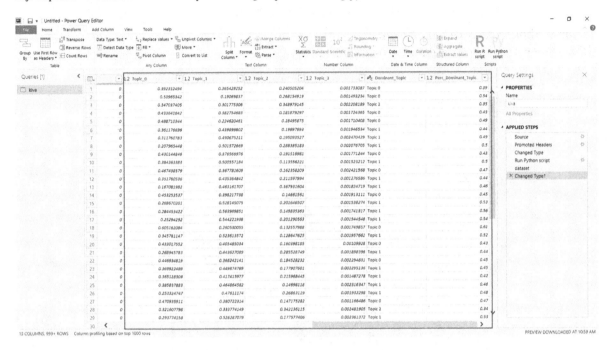

Figure 8. Final output in power BI after applying the query
Ref: https://towardsdatascience.com/topic-modeling-in-power-bi-using-pycaret-54422b4e36d6

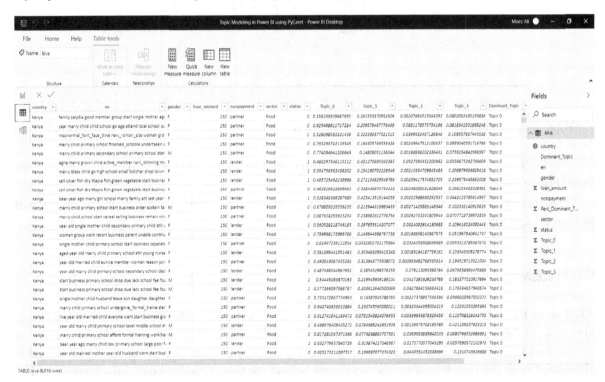

Topic Categorization: The categorization of words against every topic is illustrated in Figure 9.

Figure 9. Topic categorization of words
Ref: https://raw.githubusercontent.com/pycaret/pycaret/master

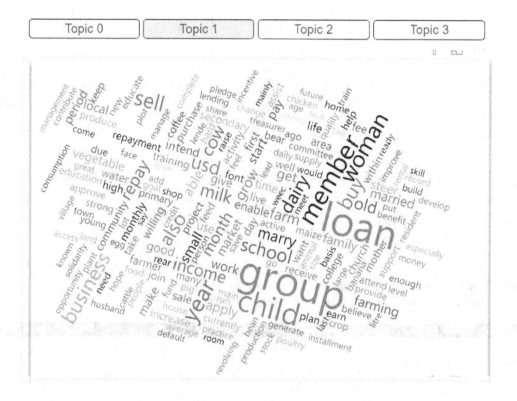

Topic wise Default Rate Set: The rate set that can be set for every topic is explained visually in Figure 10 as below.

Distribution of Topics by Sector: Sector-wise distribution of topics can be viewed for detailed analysis using Figure 11 as follows.

Gender count across Topics: Aggregated count of gender against distinct topics is illustrated in detail in Figure 12 as follows.

CHALLENGES WITH NLP

Vitality of Human Languages: Leveraging the space between the human and machine languages is always a cumbersome activity. It is always difficult to understand the grammatical rules of the search question for a person who is not aware of programming languages. If the interpretation of the context is eliminated from the search queries, the synonyms behind the words can be easily mis-interpreted as the basic words alone will only be left out.

Figure 10. Default rate by topic
Ref:https://towardsdatascience.com/topic-modeling-in-power-bi-using-pycaret-54422b4e36d6

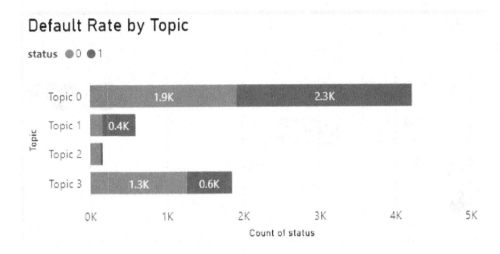

Figure 11. Distribution of topics by sector
Ref: https://towardsdatascience.com/topic-modeling-in-power-bi-using-pycaret-54422b4e36d6

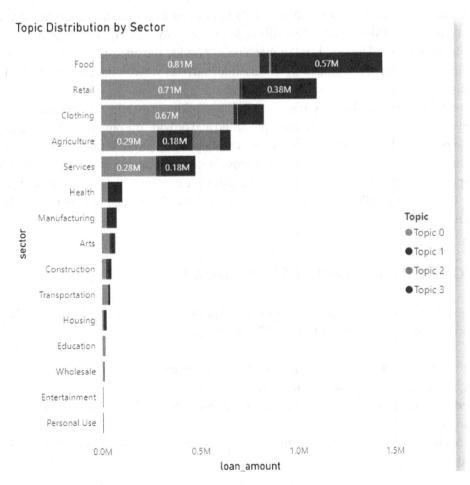

Figure 12. Gender count across topics
Ref: https://towardsdatascience.com/topic-modeling-in-power-bi-using-pycaret-54422b4e36d6

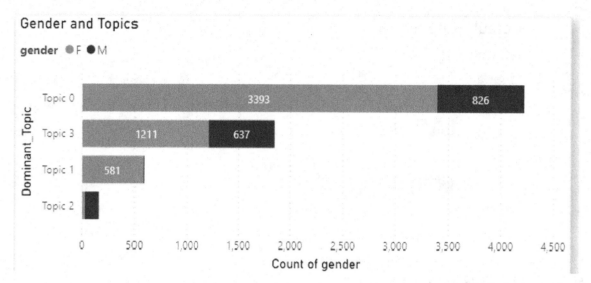

Emotion and Context. The AI-based server should be capable enough to decrypt the variance between, "Can Apple be transform into a Quadrillion dollar company?" & "Will the export company which exports apple work in San Diego?" For the machine to provide the appropriate response, it should be able to differentiate the order of phrase/word variation, suffixes which converts one portion of speech to other, inflection, etc.

Equipment Limitations: The compound neural networking capability of computers were able to analyse the variables (in millions) in a fraction of second and provide the output with the storing capacity and compute power of the modern computers. Humans depend on physical and emotional relationships associated to other humans. A unique word can provide disparate things at disparate times. Machines were not capable enough to put in the identical meaning of the context to the non-structured information. Refinement of sarcasm, Intelligence, anger are some emotions which machines are not able to today are unable to get hold.

LIMITATIONS WITH NLP IMPLEMENTATION IN BI

For NLP to work with a BI tool, there are some prerequisites should be met. Below are the requisites should be present in the tool in order to have NLP working.

- **Single Repertory**: Base business data on which the intelligence needs to be applied should be preserved in the same repertory or repository.
- **Nomenclature**: The conventions of names in databases and tables should reprint the natural spoken language.
- **Data Model**: The data model capable of adapting the NLP assumptions with an interface is needed.

THE FUTURE OF BI

In the recent times, many organizations started collecting information both in structured and unstructured forms. Due to this, the necessity for better user-friendly Business intelligence software has increased. The existence of Big data has become crucial (Gupta & Siddiqui 2014) and became more meaningful and complex because of eCommerce and social media. BI tool needs to be strong enough to carry out the more and more businesses collect vast amounts of structured and unstructured data, the demand for more user-friendly Business Intelligence tools will grow. Big data (Mohd Ali. et.al., 2016) has become even more complex (and valuable) due to social media, eCommerce, and more. BI software will not only need to be powerful enough to perform compound analytics like customer behaviour and sentimental analyses in a user- friendly platform.

CONCLUSION

Data is not useful if it is not been able to properly obtain meaningful insights by appropriate collection, exploration and manipulation. The capabilities, however, lies with the user and not with the tool. NLP is the integral part of this data exploration in the recent times.

REFERENCES

Asur, S., & Huberman, B. (2010). Predicting the future with social media. In *2010 IEEE/WIC/ACM International Conference on Web Intelligence and Intelligent Agent Technology*, (pp. 492–499). IEEE.

Bafna, A., Parkh, A., Iyer, A., & Halbe, A. (2019). A Novel approach to Data Visualization by supporting Ad-hoc Query and Predictive analysis. *Proceedings of the International Conference on Intelligent Computing and Control Systems ICICCS 2019.*

Bollen, J., Mao, H., & Zeng, X. (2011). Twitter mood predicts the stock market. *Journal of Computational Science.*

Gupta, D., & Siddiqui, S. (2014). Big Data Implementation and Visualization. *IEEE International Conference on Advances in Engineering & Technology Research, ICAETR - 2014.*

Jayashree, G. & Priya, C. (2019). *Design of Visibility for Order Lifecycle using Datawarehouse.* DOI: .F9171.088619 doi:10.35940/IJEAT

Jayashree, G., & Priya, C. (2019). Comprehensive Guide to Implementation of Datawarehouse in Education. *Proceedings of ICTIDS 2019.*

Jayashree, G., & Priya, C. (2020). Data Integration with XML ETL Processing. *Proceedings of ICCSEA 2020.*

Kate, A., Kamble, S., Bodke, A., & Joshi, M. (2018). Conversion of Natural Language Query to SQL Query. *IEEE Second International Conference on Electronics, Communication and Aerospace Technology, ICECA - 2018.*

Kumar, O., & Goyal, A. (2016). Visualization: A novel approach for big data analytics. *Second International Conference on Computational Intelligence & Communication Technology*.

Mohd Ali, S., Gupta, N., Nayak, G. K., & Lenka, R. (2016). Big data visualization: Tools and challenges. *IEEE-2nd International Conference on Contemporary Computing and Informatics, IC3I 2016*.

Reshma, E. U., & Remya, P. C. (2017). A Review of Different Approaches in Natural Language Interfaces to Databases. *Proceedings of the International Conference on Intelligent Sustainable Systems ICISS 2017*.

Saini, A. (2019). A Novel Code-Switching Behaviour Analysis in Social Media Discussions Natural Language Processing. *2019 IEEE International Conference on Big Data*.

Singh, G., & Solanki, A. (2016). An algorithm to transform natural language into SQL queries for relational databases. *International Academy of Ecology and Environmental Sciences (IAEES) Selforganizology, 3*(3), 100–116.

Thejaswini, S., & Indupriya, C. (2019). Big Data Security Issues and Natural Language Processing. *Proceedings of the Third International Conference on Trends in Electronics and Informatics ICOEI 2019*.

Chapter 10
Deep NLP in the Healthcare Industry:
Applied Machine Learning and Artificial Intelligence in Rheumatoid Arthritis

Krishnachalitha K. C.
Department of Computer Science, VISTAS, India

C. Priya
VISTAS, India

ABSTRACT

A reliable provocative issue which impacts the joints by harming the body's tissue is called rheumatoid arthritis. The ID of rheumatoid arthritis by hand, particularly during its unanticipated turn of events or pre-expressive stages, requires an extraordinary construction analysis. The standard end technique for rheumatoid arthritis (RA) calls for the assessment of hands and feet radiographs. Still, for clinical experts, it winds up being an unconventional endeavor considering the way that regularly the right completion of the disease relies on the exposure of unfathomably subtle changes for the typical eye. In this work, the authors built a design using convolutional neural networks (CNN) and reinforcement learning technique for detecting RA from hand and wrist MRI. For this, they took 564 cases (real information) which provided a precision of 100%. Compared to the existing system, the system showed a high performance with very good results. This model is highly recommended to detect rheumatoid arthritis automatically without human intervention.

Artificial neural network is intended by the style within which the natural neural framework works for instance however the brain measures knowledge. Artificial intelligence and Machine learning is being tested for a scope of examination and medical aid utilizes, together with recognition of various type of infection, the board of chronic(persistent) conditions, conveyance and revelation of well being administrations, and medicine severally. Rheumatic infections are a lot of traditional than another type of

DOI: 10.4018/978-1-7998-7728-8.ch010

sicknesses, rheumatism or we are able to say the system pain that influences the existence's everyday exercises. it's vital to investigate patients that are a lot of defenseless against rheumatic diseases as so much as life quality. It focuses on all ages but it's a lot of traditional in women. This illness has various facet effects like completely different diseases. Hence, it's extraordinarily tough to acknowledge. to boot, the demonstrative tools are unpredictable and uneconomical. inflammatory disease is Associate in Nursing current, Associate in Nursing system infection which can influence in various basic medical problems in patients. From the previous couple of years, the amount of patients experiencing inflammatory disease are quickly intensifying. As of shortly past there's no precise treatment found for this uncommon illness. The chapter talks concerning the various AI ways in early discovery of inflammatory disease in order that, early conclusion will assist the patients with recognizing/fix the illness.

AI as a field of computing is more and more applied in medication to assist patients and doctors. Developing datasets provides a sound premise that to use AI techniques that gain from past encounters. This review explains the fundamentals of machine learning and its subfields of supervised learning, unattended learning, reinforcement learning and deep learning. We offer an summary of current machine learning applications in medicine, primarily supervised learning strategies for e-diagnosis, malady detection and medical image analysis. Later on, AI can in all probability facilitate rheumatologists in foreseeing the course of the infection and distinctive vital unhealthiness factors. significantly a lot of curiously, AI can presumably have the choice to create treatment suggestions and gauge their traditional advantage (for example by reinforcement learning). on these lines, in future, common dynamic will not simply incorporate the patient's opinion and also the rheumatologist's empirical and proof based mostly insight, nonetheless it'll likewise be wedged by machine-learned proof. Over the previous decade, there has been a modification in outlook in however clinical info area unit gathered, handled and used. Machine learning and computing, crammed by forward leaps in superior registering, info accessibility and algorithmic developments, area unit preparing to viable examinations of big, multi-dimensional assortments of patient chronicles, centre outcomes, therapies, and results. within the new amount of AI and discerning examination, the impact on clinical dynamic in each clinical region, together with medicine, are going to be outstanding.

To forestall chronicity of arthritis (RA) by early medical aid, recognizing provocative signs in an exceedingly starting stage is basic. Since resonance Imaging (MRI) of the wrist joint, hand and foot will distinguish irritation before it's clinically perceivable, this technique could assume a big half in accomplishing early determinations. By gathering heaps of tomography data from solid controls and patients with hurting dubious for movement to RA, examples will be thought-about that are typically express for early improvement of RA. Besides, tomography will be used as result boundary for randomised pretend treatment controlled preliminaries on early RA medical aid, by characteristic invisible changes in image powers ranging from common movement or treatment impacts. extraordinarily heaps of tomography data, yet, create manual analysis illogical and therefore the coarse scale used in visual rating frameworks (for example entire qualities somewhere within the vary of zero and 3) restricts its affectability to spot changes that are likely to be extraordinarily retiring in quite an starting stage. Lately, propels in computing and significantly 'deep learning' in deciphering clinical photos have indicated that - in express regions a mechanized investigation will beat human spectators. later, analysis has been started into applying these computing ways to the analysis of early RA from tomography data. during this section, a review is given on the inspiration and history of computing, with Associate in Nursing exceptional spotlight on late enhancements in 'deep learning', and the way these ways may well be applied to acknowledge invisible provocative changes in tomography data.

INTRODUCTION

Most rheumatic diseases have fluctuating, progressing courses including complex pathophysiology which tangles their treatment. Notwithstanding the event to centered brand name also, arranged cures, kept up diminishing of rheumatoid joint exacerbation (RA) is really evolved during a minority of patients. for a couple of other rheumatic sicknesses, similar to osteoarthritis (OA), lupus, or Sjögren's condition, controlled clinical starters for pristine medications are thoroughly puzzling a delayed consequence of fluctuated ailment totals. Given the information expanded examines basic for find the most straightforward treatment frameworks for particular patients, (AI) can include a fundamental effect inside the advancement of redo drug. Especially machine learning (ML), a subfield of AI, can make patch up treatment by engaging PCs to get for a reality without rules unequivocally showed up by individuals. The potential for ML in drug is enormous and, meandered from standard experiences, ML offers a lot of most recent possible results. While there's an essential cover in techniques among encounters and ML, expressly the machine goals and adaptability of courses of action is throughout extraordinary. Standard encounters includes a solid work in exact frameworks of information tests, understanding veritable relationship among factors, and correctly assessing individuals limits; the standard target of most ML techniques, on the contrary hand, is prudent execution on unpretentious information. Additionally, ML assessments can ordinarily learn strong information portrayals, and administer varying kinds of information, e.g., patient accessories, clinical pictures and hereditary data. Along these lines, ML fills a fundamental opening for learning from clinical experience. In a perfect world, it makes an interpretation of the information acquired into clinical proof with PCs being ready for predicting clinical results, seeing illness plans, recognizing infection joins, and refreshing treatment frameworks.

Deep learning, despite called hierarchical learning or deep planned learning, is such a machine learning that utilizes a layered algorithmic anxious to research information. In deep learning models, information is separated through a course of different layers, with each reformist layer utilizing the yield from the past one to illuminate its outcomes. Deep learning models can end up being intensely more particular as they measure more information, basically learning from past outcomes to refine their capacity to shape affiliations and affiliations. Deep learning is for the preeminent part gotten settled travel typical neurons interface with one another to administer data inside the characters of creatures. actually like the comportment during which electrical signs cross the phones of living makes, each subsequent layer of focuses is begun when it gets upgrades from its accomplice neurons. In artificial neural affiliations (ANNs), the motivation behind see in deep learning models, each layer could likewise be given out a chose piece of a change errand, and information may investigate the layers on different occasions to refine and revive a whole yield.

ARTIFICIAL INTELLIGENCE AND MACHINE LEARNING

Artificial Intelligence (AI) might be a subfield of PC programming, committed to furnishing PCs with limits concerning competent fundamental sense, for example to influence complex issues such a great deal that we should seriously think about as clever. These cutoff focuses join arranging, thinking, data or learning . Machine Learning, a subfield of AI, gives counts (developments of all around portrayed PC headings that deal with a particular issue) that structure mathematical models snared in to explored data. These mathematical models (called limits) map input data to required yields. Wellsprings of information are frequently pictures and an optional game plan of numerical or unflinching data. The picked inputs are henceforth indicated as data features. Decision trees(tree model), Support vector machines(SVM),Random forest re some of the models used.

SVMs are discovered to find the easiest section of shifted depictions by changing a great deal of polynomial cutoff focuses. Another technique, called k-nearest neighbor approach, packs tests by a lion's offer vote, submitting the classification customarily standard among the k models with the preeminent in every practical sense, undefined features.

Data wont to plan ML structures is generally valid data. ML plans can in like manner be discovered with artificial data gathered from test structures, where moves are frequently made tentatively to search two or three arrangements concerning different outcomes. inside the fields of bleeding edge mechanics, games or free driving, test frameworks are frequently used to open ML ways of thinking to a colossal number of most recent situations during getting ready. In drug, ML systems are on a significant level engineered and surveyed on chronicled datasets. In cases showing convincing execution, they may then have the determination to be explored on legitimate benchmark packs using genuine achievement mindful advances and ideally as a controlled clinical foundation.

The subfields of ML are supervised learning, unsupervised learning and Reinforcement learning and Deep learning.

WORK DONE ON REAL DATA SET: A NOVEL APPROACH FOR THE EARLY DETECTION OF RHEUMATOID ARTHRITIS ON HAND AND WRIST USING CONVOLUTIONAL REINFORCEMENT LEARNING TECHNIQUES

A reliable provocative issue which impacts the joints by harming the body's tissue is called as Rheumatoid arthritis . As needs be, the ID and ID of rheumatoid arthritis by hand, particularly during its unanticipated turn of events or pre-expressive stages, requires an extraordinary construction analysis. The standard end technique for Rheumatoid Arthritis (RA) recalls for the assessment of hands and feet radiographs. Notwithstanding, still for clinical experts it winds up being an unconventional endeavor considering the way that regularly the right completion of the disease relies on the exposure of unfathomably subtle changes for the typical eye. In this work, we built up a design using Convolutional Neural Networks (CNN) and Reinforcement Learning Technique for detecting RA from hand and wrist MRI. For this we took 564 cases(real information) which provided a precision of 100%. Compared to the existing system, the system showed a high performance with very good results. This model is highly recommended to detect Rheumatoid arthritis automatically, without human intervention.

In around 1% of the world population, Rheumatoid arthritis is an unobtrusively common disease(Krishnachalitha.K.C, et.al, 2021) Rheumatoid arthritis is a persistent incendiary problem which will influence very your joints. In certain individuals, the skin, eyes, lungs, heart and veins can be affected. An immune system sickness, rheumatoid arthritis happens when your framework erroneously assaults your own body's tissues. Rheumatoid arthritis influences the liner of your joints, causing a difficult expanding which will in the long run end in bone disintegration and joint disfigurement. The aggravation identified with rheumatoid arthritis is the thing that can harm different pieces of the body additionally . While new kinds of prescriptions have improved treatment alternatives significantly, extreme rheumatoid arthritis can in any case cause actual handicaps(Mate G.S,et.al, 2020)

Fundamentals that may develop your risk of rheumatoid arthritis include:

- Your sex- Ladies are almost certain than men to create rheumatoid arthritis.
- Age- Rheumatoid arthritis can happen at whatever stage in life, on the other hand it usually starts in middle age.
- Family ancestry- On the off chance that if your relative has rheumatoid arthritis, you perhaps will have a long-drawn-out risk of the sickness.
- Smoking- Cigarette smoking forms your threat of making rheumatoid arthritis, above all in case you have an inborn inclination for developing the ailment. Smoking moreover has all the reserves of being connected with more imperative ailment reality.
- Environmental Exposure- Rheumatoid arthritis hazard increments with word related openness to material residue. Also, word related residue openness is moreover connected to a danger of creating antibodies to rheumatoid arthritis, accordingly conceivably accelerating movement of the sickness.
- Obesity- People — especially women age 55 and more youthful — who are overweight or hefty have all the earmarks of being at a fairly higher danger of creating rheumatoid arthritis.

Figure1 shows the MRI of a patient with the affliction.

Figure 1. A) axial plane; B) coronal plane: synovitis, disintegrations and incendiary growths in the radio-carpal, midcarpal, carpo-metacarpal and metacarpophalangeal joints

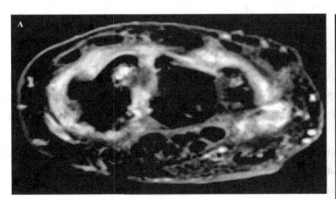
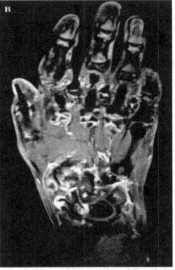

Various joints are covered with a covering called the synovium, which oils up the joint so it moves much more with no issue. Precisely when you have rheumatoid arthritis, the synovium gets energized, thickens, and passes on an overabundance of joint fluid. This is known as synovitis. That additional fluid — close by the strongly hot designed substances passed on by the protected framework — causes creating, harms ligament, and smooth the bone inside the joint (Schett G, 2012) The swollen tissue may expand the including tendons, accomplishing disfigurement and shakiness, as shown by the American Society for Surgery of the Hand.(Czaplicka K, et.al, 2015) The aggravation may moreover disable and harm ligaments(Aizenberg E,et.al,2019) Tendons are connective tissues that join two bones; ligaments are connective issues that join muscle to bone.

Right when RA strikes the hand, it is by and large norm in the wrist (Mette Klarlund, et.al, 1999) and finger knuckles — considerably more explicitly the MCP (metacarpophalangeal) joint, or the tremendous knuckle where the fingers and thumb meet the hand, and the center knuckle or PIP (proximal interphalangeal) joint. Rheumatoid arthritis (RA) impacts joints on the various sides of the body, like two hands, the two wrists, or the two knees. This harmony assists with disengaging it from different sorts of arthritis. The confirmation of rheumatoid arthritis depends from a general point of view on the 1987 adjusted models of the American College of Rheumatology (earlier, the American Rheumatism Association), including clinical, biologic, and radiologic divulgences. The joints of the hands are among the first to be influenced in rheumatoid arthritis, and they are astoundingly persuading in the appraisal of patients with suspected early rheumatoid arthritis (Maria Hügle., et.al, 2020) X-shaft has been demonstrated to be more delicate than radiography at seeing bone disintegrations in the hands and wrists of patients with rheumatoid arthritis (McQueen FM, et.al, 1998). In like manner, MRI (Mette Klarlund, et.al, 1999) can give depiction of edema, hyperemia, and joint radiation, identically as perspective on synovial pannus with the usage of IV gadolinium (Boesen M, et.al, .2012) implantation .Advances in AI, especially CNN and Reinforcement Learning have opened extra open entrances in the field of drug, making structures for seeing dermatological debasements lung pathologies, breaks and bone damage, among others, to tie the space for give and take in clinical finding and attracting an early revelation of illnesses.

ASSOCIATED WORKS

The finish of Periarticular Osteoporosis (one of the consequences of RA) was tried in the evaluation coordinated by Murakami et al.(Murakami S, et.al, 2018) .Thickness characteristics of hand X-transmits utilizing histogram assessment, co-occasion frameworks, fourier changes and extraction of line parts were chosen by the structure .

A changed assurance plan of RA from hand radiographs, utilizing a couple of electronic picture taking care of figuring for feature extraction and a neural association for its strategy was proposed by Chokkalingam and Komathy (Chokkalingam, SP, et.al, 2014). Twenty three pictures were used for setting up the model in any case no underwriting tests were performed, along these lines its precision is dull.

Considering the area of bone deterioration, Murakami et al.(Murakami S, et.al, 2017) executed a system for diagnosing RA by using 129 radiograph pictures. In this evaluation, a division assessment and a CNN were used to remove the region of the phalanges and for perceiving the presence of the pathology . The underwriting was performed with 30 cases with RA, obtaining a real sure speed of 80.5% and a counterfeit positive speed of 0.84%, in any case the fake positive number of the division calculation was 3.3 per case.

The existing systems present restricted results, with high slip up rates and low hypothesis to detect RA. Made on Convolutional Neural Network, works on retrained model with less number of images, detects simply finger joint deteriorations and it fail to recognize intercarpaljoints. Sensitivity for deteriorations was unmistakably low. Their unflinching quality should improve to be used as an end mechanical gathering in the clinical environment, which has no protection from botches in light of the regular meaning of this assignment.

METHODOLOGY

For the improvement of this work, we used Convolutional Reinforcement Learing Technique to perceive Rheumatoid Arthritis from hand and wrist MRI, considering Feature Extraction, Deep learning and Reinforcement learning methodology to distinguish RA(Rheumatoid Arthritis) to diminish human dependence and takes most choices naturally.

i. Imagedataset

The pictures utilized in this examination came from Dr Kirubanadan, Radiologist,Noble scan centre,Vaniyambadi,Tamil Nadu, associated with Apollo Hospitals and Central labs, Thrissur Kerala with the assistance of DrHari, Rheumatologist,Kottayam Medical College,Kerala.They comprise of 564 gray scale MRI of both hands and wrist of the patients between the age 30 to 60, utilized by clinical expert in their analysis of RA. The properties of dataset is displayed in Table 1.

ii. Ethics

It is not possible to expect to relate the patient's name to the MRI.They are anonymous .Keeping all rules of confidentiality, they were just utilized to build the model .

Table 1. Image database characteristics.

Total cases	564
RA-affected	282
RA-not affected	282
Resolution of Image	1378 x 654 pixels
Format- Image	DICOM
Bit depth	32 bits

iii. Software Tools

For the ease, speed and control during the arrangement of complex networks, we used Python, Tensorflow and Keras. OpenCV, sklearn, imutils,matplotlib,and Numpy modules were used to manage and quantify the photos.

iv. Algorithm

KCP Algorithm

- Required import statements for packages: This characterizes all the significant packages for picture pre handling, preparing system, data wrangling and directory storage.

- Dataset of 282 Images of RA influenced and another 282 pictures of Normal pictures are stacked in the 'yes' and 'no' indexes separately.
- Using the ImageDataGenerator capacity of cv2 (opencv) for making more pictures utilizing picture augmentation, the outcome is increased in addition to the ordinary images.(6200 pictures after augmentation)

These augmented images are utilized to identify the contours of the images for cropping of the image, aka edges of the image. This uses erode and dilate. When the shapes are done, the example picture and the cropped picture is shown.

- These pictures are given as 3 dimensional, and the influenced and ordinary pictures are plotted for review of the augmented pictures.
- Data is part utilizing train test split into 3 phases – train, approve and test. 70% for preparing, 15% for validation and another 15% for testing.The state of the pictures, for all x_train, x_val and x_test seen and showed.
- The model is planned with (input layer + zeropadding layer + convolutional layer+ maxpooling layers + flatten layer). This is a binary classifier with 1 as Affected and 0 as Normal.
- The synopsis of the model, is brought with the state of the dev network made. The tensorboard is instated.
- The models is prepared for 30 epochs, the callbacks are utilized for each age which stores the validation accuracy and the age for each model made.
- The trained network details are utilized with history which stores all the loss, accuracy and f1 score subtleties of all train, validation and test clumps. The loss and accuracy plots are plotted
- The best model is picked from the maximum validation accuracy from the ages, and the measurements are assessed with the hyper parameters.
- Finally the after effects of the accuracy, exactness and f1 score are determined for test and validation datasets in the confusion matrix.
- Use Deep Reinforcement learning to anticipate and just as train the framework.

Figure 2. Deep Reinforcement learning architecture

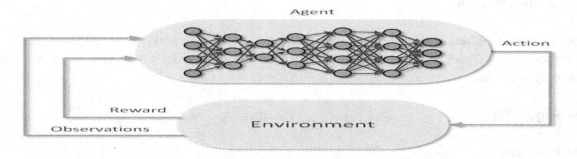

v. Data Augmentation for Rheumatoid Arthritis Detection

The dataset contains 2 organizers: yes and no which contains 564 Hand MRI Images. The folder 'yes' contains 282 Hand MRI Images that are RA influenced and the organizer 'no' contains 282 Hand MRI Images that are Normal.As this is a little dataset, We have utilized information augmentation utilizing ImageDataGenerator to make more pictures on the fly.It is very difficult to train a model with limited data. To overcome this, we did augmentation of the images.by ransforming the MRI with a random combination of rotation, width shift, height shift, shear, brightness, horizontal flip,vertical flip and fill mode .Since the training examples got incremented, it helped us to improve the classification results of the arcghitecture.The progressions applied, granted the networks to become familiar with these changes in various points and sizes without having influence on the visual highlights in little locales of the primary pictures

vi. Preprocessing and Segmentation

The dataset contains 2 organizers: yes and no which contains 564 Hand MRI Images. The folder 'yes' contains 282 Hand MRI Images that are RA influenced and the organizer no contains 282 Hand MRI Images that are Normal. After augmentation we have a sum of 6200 Images for the identification.

Figure 3. Original Image and Cropped Image

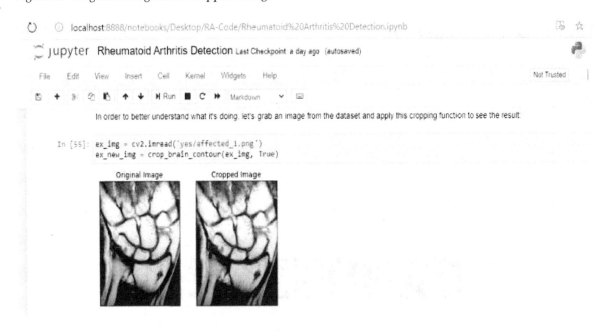

vii. Load Data

• The following function takes two arguments, the first is a rundown of directory paths for the folders 'yes' and 'no' that contain the picture information and the subsequent argument is the picture size, and for each picture in the two directories and does the accompanying:

- Read the picture.
- Crop the piece of the picture addressing just the hand and wrist..

Resize the picture (in light of the fact that the pictures in the dataset come in various sizes (which means width, height and # of channels). Along these lines, we need the entirety of our pictures to be (240, 240, 3) to take care of it as a contribution to the neural organization.

- Apply standardization since we need pixel esteems to be scaled to the reach 0-1.
- Append the picture to X and its mark to y.
- After that, Shuffle X and y, on the grounds that the information is requested (which means the exhibits contains the initial segment having a place with one class and the subsequent part having a place with the other class, and we don't need that).

At long last, Return X and y.

Figure 4. Plot Sample Images For RA

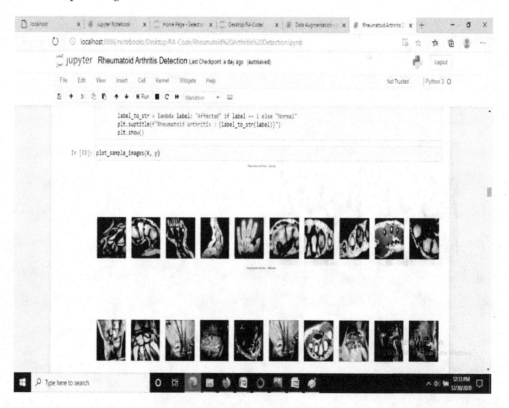

viii. Data Set Division

We used the following way to split:

- 70% of the data for training.
- 15% of the data for validation.
- 15% of the data for testing.

RESULTS AND DISCUSSIONS

i. Build the Model

There are 9 layers in the model

Table 2. Number of parameters

Total Parameters	11137
Trainable Parameters	11073
Non Trainable Parameters	64

Figure 5. Number of layers in the Serialization Model

```
model.summary()

Model: "Rheumatoid_Arthritis_Detection_Model"
_____
Layer (type)                 Output Shape              Param #
=================================================================
input_4 (InputLayer)         [(None, 240, 240, 3)]     0

zero_padding2d_3 (ZeroPaddin (None, 244, 244, 3)       0

conv0 (Conv2D)               (None, 238, 238, 32)      4736

bn0 (BatchNormalization)     (None, 238, 238, 32)      128

activation_3 (Activation)    (None, 238, 238, 32)      0

max_pool0 (MaxPooling2D)     (None, 59, 59, 32)        0

max_pool1 (MaxPooling2D)     (None, 14, 14, 32)        0

flatten_3 (Flatten)          (None, 6272)              0

fc (Dense)                   (None, 1)                 6273
=================================================================
Total params: 11,137
Trainable params: 11,073
Non-trainable params: 64
```

Figure 6. Convolutional Reinforcement Learning Network Architecture for RA Detection

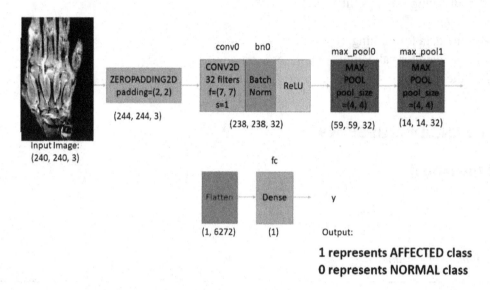

CNN ARCHITECTURE

ii. Train the Model

For the determination of the optimization algorithm Adam was thought of, contrasting their outcomes after 30 epochs of preparing. Adam was picked for having the quickest combination result.We used Serializing Model which is the best model for industry organization as it decrease measure and improve performance. Figure 7 shows the plot of loss and accuracy.

iii. Load The Best Model

After training we evaluated the best model on the testing data by using pretrained model.

Table 3. Accuracy of the best model on testing data

Test Loss	0.5157854557037354
Test Accuracy	0.7935484051704407

Figure 7. Plot Loss & Accuracy

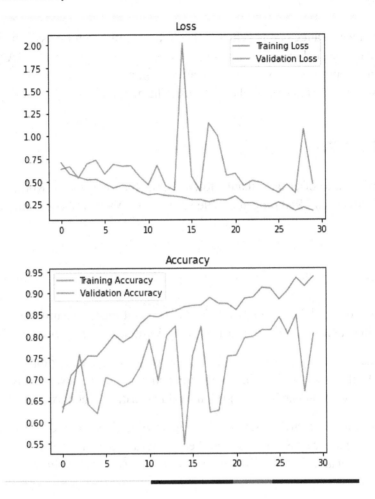

RESULT

Table 4. Result Interpretation

	Training Data	**Validation Data**	**Testing Data**
No: of Examples	4340	930	930
No: of positive examples	2184	441	474
Percentage of positive examples	50.32258064516129%	47.41935483870968%	50.96774193548387%
No: of negative examples	2156	489	456
Percentage of negative examples	49.67741935483871%	52.58064516129032%	49.03225806451613%

CONCLUSION

In this examination we arranged and evaluated the certified enlightening assortment with Convolution Reinforcement Learning Techniques. We propose this system that recognizes RA from hand and wrist MRI without broad preprocessing or excellent features, simply using rough pixel regards and achieving favored exactnesses over near models of the front line. The major results show the ability of this structure.

ACKNOWLEDGMENT

The authors might want to offer their thanks to Dr. Hari, Rheumatologist, Kottayam Medical College, Kerala and Dr. Kirubanadan, Radiologist, Noble scan centre, Vaniyambadi, Tamil Nadu for supporting this examination.

REFERENCES

Aizenberg, E., Shamonin, D. P., & Reijnierse, M. (2019). Automatic quantification of tenosynovitis on MRI of the wrist in patients with early arthritis: A feasibility study. *European Radiology*.

Boesen, M., Kubassova, O., & Bouert, R. (2012). Correlation between computer-aided dynamic gadolinium-enhanced MRI assessment of inflammation and semi-quantitative synovitis and bone marrow oedema scores of the wrist in patients with rheumatoid arthritis—a cohort stud. *Rheumatology*.

Chokkalingam, S.P., & Komathy, K. (2014). Intelligent Assistive Methods for Diagnosis of Rheumatoid Arthritis Using Histogram Smoothing and Feature Extraction of Bone Images. *World Academy of Science, Engineering and Technology International Journal of Computer, Information, Systems and Control Engineering*.

Czaplicka, K., Wojciechowski, W., & Włodarczyk, J. (2015). Automated assessment of synovitis in 0.2T magnetic resonance images of the wrist. *Computers in Biology and Medicine*.

Hügle. (2020). *Applied machine learning and artificial intelligence in rheumatology*. Rheumatol Adv Pract.

Krishnachalitha & Priya. (2021). A Novel Approach for the Early Detection of Rheumatoid Arthritis on Hand and Wrist Using Convolutional Reinforcement Learning Techniques. *Annals of the Romanian Society for Cell Biology*.

Mate & Kureshi (2020). Understanding CNN to Automatically Diagnose Rheumatoid Arthritis using Hand Radiographs. *International Journal of Advanced Science and Technology*.

Table 5. F1 Score For The Best Model On The Testing Data & Validation Set

Data Set	Validation Set	Test Set
Accuracy	80%	79%
F1 Score	0.76	0.76

McQueen, F. M., Stewart, N., & Crabbe, J. (1998). Magnetic resonance imaging of the wrist in early rheumatoid arthritis reveals a high prevalence of erosions at four months after symptom onset. *Annals of the Rheumatic Diseases*.

Mette Klarlund, M. (1999). Wrist and Finger Joint MR Imaging in Rheumatoid Arthritis. *Acta Radiologica*.

Murakami, Hatano, Tan, Kim, & Aoki. (2017). Automatic identification of bone erosions in rheumatoid arthritis from hand radiographs based on deep convolutional neural network. *Multimed. Tools Appl.*

Murakami, S., Hatano, K., & Tan, J. (2018). Automatic identification of bone erosions in rheumatoid arthritis from hand radiographs based on deep convolutional neural network. *Multimed Tools Appl.*

Schett, G. (2012). Synovitis an inflammation of joints destroying the bone. *Swiss Medical Weekly*.

Chapter 11
Information Retrieval in Business Industry Using Blockchain Technology and Artificial Intelligence

Sheela K.

Department of Computer Science, VISTAS, Chennai, India

Priya C.

Department of Computer Science, VISTAS, Chennai, India

ABSTRACT

Industry 5.0 promotes automation in an optimized way. Collaboration with blockchain technology and artificial intelligence helps to enrich Industry 5.0 with its quantifiers and qualifiers. In the business industry, information plays an iconic role. When we consider the issues of storage and retrieval, we need to think about blockchain technology where the data will be stored and shared in a secure way. Here, the data will be distributed across the network in an encrypted format; hence, the original data can be viewed only by the owner of the data. Blockchain stores the information in the form of blocks. Every block has three sections. The first section holds the hash value of the previous block, the second one holds the information to be stored in a block, and the third one holds the hash value of an upcoming block. It does not allow an intruder to hack or modify the data without user's knowledge as these blocks are interconnected on both the sides with their hashes. This synergy of technologies brings supremacy in the field of business industries which will be discussed in this chapter.

INTRODUCTION

Industry 5.0 is a new construction model where the cornerstone lies on the interactivity between the human and machine. This interaction must resolve the manufacturing complexity of the future in tackling the growing customization through an enhanced robotized production. We can strongly believe that,

DOI: 10.4018/978-1-7998-7728-8.ch011

machines will take over all the tedious and repetitive tasks whereas human will be handling the creative portion of a task along with the responsibility of supervising machines to lift the quality of production across the globe (Melnyk et al., 2019). In many cases, we come across situation where the personal data are getting hacked and misused or finding trouble with a central server. In order to avoid such circumstances, the authors are advising to store the confidential records in a blockchain based platform. This can also be termed as decentralized cloud which promotes data access from anywhere in the world. As the transactions are stored as blocks, each block contains certain storage potentials. All these blocks are chained together in a corresponding order. When it gets filled in, it reaches another block. The generated hash values are entirely different for different data. Even a small change in the original data will reflect a drastic difference in the hash value. This makes the intruders more difficult to identify the original data. Hence, authors define it as "all the blockchains are databases but not all the databases are blockchains". Usage and collaboration of blockchain technology and Artificial Intelligence, brings out the best in business industry.

Section I presents a detailed view about this chapter. In section II, authors briefly explain about industry 5.0 and its advantages. In section III and IV, let us understand about the technologies like Blockchain and Artificial Intelligence. Integration of Blockchain and AI can be seen in section V. Benefits of merging these technologies in information retrieval can be focused in section VI. Finally, conclusion will be presented in section VII along with the benefits of synergizing technologies like Blockchain, AI and Internet of Things.

INDUSTRY 5.0 AND ITS ADVANTAGES

Industry 5.0 is an insurgence in which human and machine reconcile and realizes the ways to work together to refine the effectiveness of the production. Few people believe that this industry 5.0 might replace humans in all the industrial activities in our near future. But the truth is, it reduces the difficulties that human face in their day-to-day life. It provides a complete background support in order to make the task simpler to the human beings. Industry 5.0 also helps in doing repetitive task for many numbers of times. Industry 4.0 highly promotes digitization and automation with certain drawbacks like complex and overpriced software, replacement of people's job by machine, experts for robotic communication and so on. All these are resolved in Industry 5.0 to bridge the technical gap between the common people. It also advocates zero-waste production by reducing the waste material expenses and waste management fare. Also, it highly relies on personalization from mass customization.

Industry 5.0 will reach its peak when the 5G network is coupled with technologies like IoT-Internet of Things (including Industrial IoT), Artificial Intelligence (AI) increases the level of automated production (Bryndin, 2020). Also, integrating with Big data, blockchain technology, cloud and fog computing takes the industry into further reach by promoting automation.

The following are the advantages of imposing Industry 5.0(Digitalya, n.d.).

Highly Focused Maintenance Plan: So far, we have applies preventive maintenance in prior revolutions whereas industry 5.0 works in predictive maintenance.

Sustainability: It manages the resources in a well-organized manner based upon a current need. The partnership between human and machine power leads to resilient business models. Also, overproduction will be eliminated.

Productivity and Human Competence: This new technology brings back people to the center of production. Complex repetitive tasks can be managed by machines instead of being carried out by human beings.

Contexture Control Inside an Organization: Smartly interconnected sensors and personalized software gives real-time and predictive outline of humidity, energy consumption, climate and temperature. Having knowledge on, what to anticipate and where to arbitrate prevents severe loss in production.

Estimating Line Production Efficiency: Every process can be adjusted according to their parameters without wasting the resources. This occurs through the flexibility of smartly connected sensor based devices.

ARTIFICIAL INTELLIGENCE

AI is termed as Artificial Intelligence which can be defined as an intelligence that is artificially constructed. It has created a huge impact in our digital environment. AI is termed to reproduce human intelligence in machines that are programmed and designed to think and imitate their actions. Many algorithms have been proposed for estimating missing data elements, general analysis, economics and robotics. As per the major goals of AI, it focuses to create expert system in all the domains and to implement human intelligence in machines. Basically, Intelligence is composed of (i) Reasoning (which provides us the baseline for judgement and prediction) (ii) Learning (pursuit of acquiring knowledge) (iii) Problem solving (iv) Perception (v) Linguistic intelligence

Natural Language Processing (NLP) is one of the five major application areas of artificial intelligence among expert system, neural networks, robotics and fuzzy logic. NLP is used for communication with intelligent systems with our natural language (most commonly English). It is one of the sub-division of Data Science which includes systematic processes for understanding, analyzing, and deriving information for text data in an elegant and efficient way. With the help of NLP and its components, we can easily organize huge chunk of text data to perform number of automated functionalities and decode broad span of complications like machine translation, automatic summarization, inter-relation extraction, named entity recognition, speech recognition, topic segmentation, emotion analysis and so on. Text is the most commonly considered unstructured data among the available formats. They need to be preprocessed as there are chances for different kinds of noise to occur. Text preprocessing consists of three steps as follows: (i) Noise removal, (ii) Lexicon normalization, (iii) Object Standardization (Analytics Vidhya, 2017)

Noise Removal- The process of removing unnecessary data from the given text is known as noise removal. For example, is, am, the, in, punctuators, URLs (links), hash-tags, etc.,

Lexicon Normalization – It is used to avoid multiple representation of a single word. For example, dance, dancer, dancing. This normalization can be done by following two methods.

1. **Stemming**: It is an elementary rule based process of looting out the suffixes like 'ly', 'ing', 'er', 's', etc.
2. **Lemmatization**: It is an algorithmic process of acquiring the root word from the given word

Figure 1. Flow of acquiring clean text

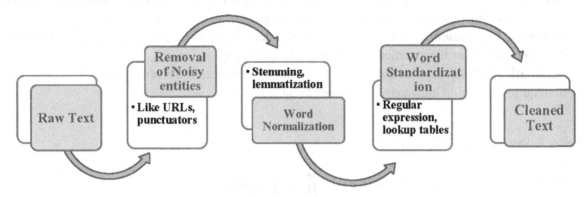

Object Standardization- Text data frequently holds clauses or words which will not be available in any standard lexical dictionaries. Hence these words are not commonly recognized search engines. For example, colloquial slang of the user will not be mentioned in dictionaries ('dm' for direct message, 'awsm' for awesome, 'gud' for good and so on).

Word Clouds- Word Cloud is also known as Tag Cloud. It is a data visualization technique where we can view the text in the chart based on its importance. More essential words will be displayed in bigger font and the least important words will be written in small fonts or sometimes it will not be displayed at all.

Extraction of Keywords- It provides us different ways for uprooting the most essential words and clauses from the given collection of texts. This process will be helpful for us to organize, store, search and retrieve the content in a well-organized way. We have more number of keyword extraction algorithms with different kinds of concepts and principles.

Named Entity Recognition (NER)- It is responsible for identifying entities in an unstructured text and assigning to the record of predefined categories like person, date, place, etc. It includes 2 steps as identification and classification of NER.

Knowledge Graph- It is highly meant for storing information in the form of triples, a subject, a predicate and an object. It belongs to the technique called Information Retrieval (procuring structured data from an unstructured text). (Programmer Backpack, n.d.)

The input and output of this kind of systems will require both audio and visual effects. NLP has two major components like NLU- Natural Language Understanding (Mapping an input into the required representation and analyzing various aspects of languages) and NLG – Natural Language Generation (it involves text planning, sentence planning and text realization).

Steps in NLP

When we discuss about Natural Language Processing, we need to consider these five basic steps for implementation.

Lexical Analysis: It involves the process of recognizing and examining the structure of words. It splits up the whole block of text into words, sentence and paragraphs.

Syntactic Analysis: It considers proper arrangement of words where we can seek relationship among the words in a sentence. For example, "Temple went to Sara"

Semantic Analysis: It extracts absolute meaning from the given text. Each text will be checked for meaningfulness. This semantic analyzer ignores sentences like "pleasant tragedy".

Disclosure Integration: Significance of a sentence depends upon the meaning of a prior sentence. It also supports to know the significance of forthwith succeeding sentence.

Pragmatic Analysis: It promotes re-interpretation of a sentence on the same aspect of its meaning. It also requires real world knowledge. (Tutorials Point, n.d.)

Figure 2. Steps in NLP

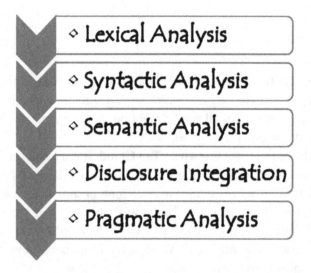

- ◇ Lexical Analysis
- ◇ Syntactic Analysis
- ◇ Semantic Analysis
- ◇ Disclosure Integration
- ◇ Pragmatic Analysis

Applications of NLP

NLP plays a vital role in communication which will be different for different kinds of people. After understanding the potentials of NLP, here we will discuss about the applications of Natural Language Processing.

Financial Trading: NLP has a significant place in the field of commerce where sentiment analysis effectively analyses the flow of the business and predict the next move. For example, consider a game where the interested audience will have a keen focus on the game and predict the upcoming move with their intelligence. These kinds of prediction have been a game changer in stock market in many cases which can be made possible through NLP. Also, analyzing the sentence or words will be done to identify the spam and filtering emails. We can also avail virtual assistance which responds to customer's queries in the formats like, text, speech, audio, and video.

E-Governance: It is completely relied on the infrastructure of information and communication technology. With NLP, we can promote communication between the citizen and government sector people using an e-governance platform. Though it is difficult to filter and format huge data, it can be procedurally done by Natural Language Processing using AI and ML techniques. E-Governance highly encourages the participation of both the officers and common people of a city to uplift our society by effectively following the government policies.

Healthcare: According to the survey taken in recent times, it is proven that NLP can improve automated registry reporting, clinical documentation, medical coding. It also provides clinical decision support, trial matching and does risk adjustments. It improves interaction between the patients and healthcare professionals by providing high quality healthcare (Intech Open, n.d.).

Education: NLP supports education sector by analyzing the needs of students, teachers and researchers. It magnifies the teaching by concentrating on reading, writing and speaking. Chatbots can also be integrated with education sector to encourage active learner environment in an e-learning context. It grabs the attention of the students by providing innovative media features.

Creditworthiness Assessment: With a utilization of NLP, many banking sectors in developing countries have started to assess the creditworthiness of the clients with practically zero financial records. Algorithm of NLP helps to examine the social media activity, geo-location information in order to infer their quality of relationships, habits and peer systems. The data will be kept confidential and analyses the trustworthiness of the clients.

Advertising: Text analytics plays an essential role in advertising and audience analysis. It is very common for the people to discuss about their favorite TV shows in social media along with their colleagues. These texts can be analyzed and reviewed for the betterment of the show as per audience desire. This also provides way for the sponsors to insert effective advertisements in between the show. They may also make the artist of the show as their model in-order to enrich their business level. These kinds of analysis can be done with the techniques of NLP (Analytics Insight, n.d.).

BLOCKCHAIN TECHNOLOGY

A blockchain is a distributed, decentralized and public digital ledger which is used to track the transactions across many computers called nodes. It is essential for a business industry to store every data in a confidential way. Unlike cloud computing, there is no single point of failure in this technology. Hence, the machines connected to blockchain will never suffer from failure in central access. Every data gets hashed and stored in multiple nodes connected with each other. In blockchain, data will be stored in blocks and each block will be connected with each other in the form of chain. Initial block of the chain in termed as genesis block (Guru99, n.d.). Every new block in the chain will be connected with the previous block. They are immutable and tamperproof as alteration is not permitted in blockchain platform. This can be implemented by following three major concepts, namely, hashing, decentralization and utilization of consensus protocol In order to build a secure platform, blockchain uses hash function.

Hashing

It is the process of returning a fixed length string for a given input string of any length. Many numbers of hashing algorithms are being used to provide a fixed length output which hides the original text and stores the content in a secure way. Some of the cryptographic hash functions are SHA2, SHA3, SHA256 (developed by National Security Agency), KECCAK-256 (developed by ethereum), MD5, BLAKE2 and so on. The basic architecture of blockchain technology is shown in figure (c)

Figure 3. Blocks with hash values

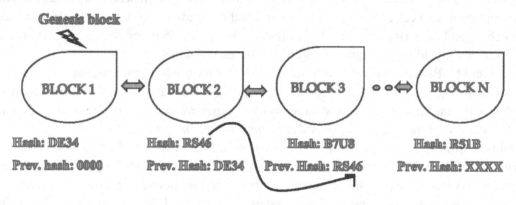

Figure 3 depicts the connection between each node. Every node carries the hash value of previous node in order to maintain the continuity between blocks. It is not possible for an intruder to alter the data as it directly affects the hash values by changing it in an unpredictable manner. We can see that each node is connected with another node using the previous hash value (as shown in the figure, block 2 has the hash value as RS46 and the same will be reflected in the next block). If the change was made to the original data, it automatically alters the hash of that data. This can be easily tracked by other nodes in the chain and denies the process in case of witnessing unauthorized changes. Each of these transactions is digitally signed with their own "digital signature". To understand the concept of digital signature, let us consider an example. Suppose we need to send few ethers to *A1*. Then, we will cryptographically hash our message with a private key and send the hash along with the address of *A1*.

Now everyone in the network will be able to view the transaction and can validate them using the public key, but only *A1* will be able to add those ethers in his wallet. Therefore, it is clear that, everyone can see the transaction but no one can steal it.

A hashing algorithm is a mathematical function that condenses data to a fixed size. So, for example, if we took the sentence, "Collaboration of Artificial Intelligence and Blockchain" we can find the difference in their hash value in the given figure. The result produced is known as hash or hash value. Occasionally, this hash value will be termed as one-way encryption. In fig 4 and fig 5, we can clearly notice that even a small change in the text is changing the entire hash value. Here drastic change in the hash value has been seen for the case of case sensitiveness in the text. In this example, the authors have used Keccak-256 algorithm of ethereum.

Decentralization

Since blockchain as a technology is decentralized in nature it does not rely on one central point of control. It is a digital ledger of transactions with every computer having a complete copy of the data. Lack of a single authority makes the system fairer and considerably more secure. Instead of depending on a central authority to securely transact with other users, blockchain utilizes innovative consensus protocols across the network of nodes, to validate transactions and to record the data to make it incorruptible. Blockchain forms a chain of trusted nodes by authenticating using Public Key Infrastructure (PKI). Any node can request to access the ledger but only the authorized, trusted node will gain access to the chain (Hirtan et al., 2019). As blockchain holds a ledger of information, it is extremely important to observe that the information being stored is honest and accurate. Since the data is saved on multiple computers, it is extremely secured even if one or two computers malfunction. Hence, we can say that decentralization allows for a single version of the truth but no single point of failure.

Figure 4. Generated hash value for the text "Collaboration of Artificial Intelligence and Blockchain"

Keccak-256

Keccak-256 online hash function

Collaboration of Artificial Intelligence and Blockchain

Input type [Text ∨]

Hash ☑ Auto Update

9790bb3129865340ea3de75ed311c4120061c64303fb77d89c64ef612c3c6c6c

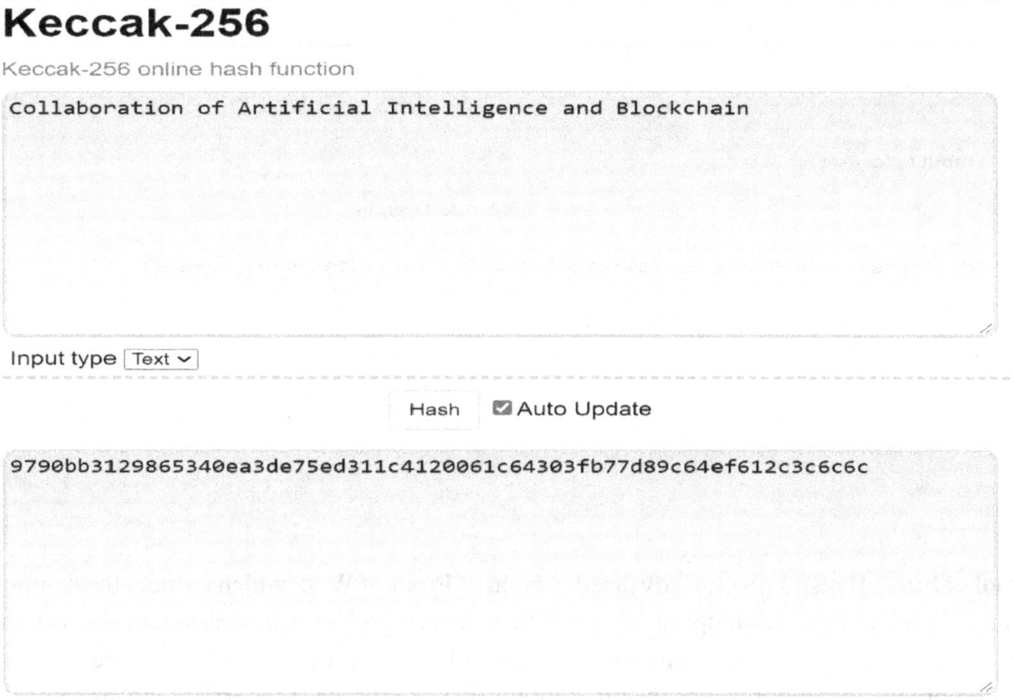

Consensus Protocol

The consensus protocol is an agreement for the majority of participants of a network regarding the validity of a transaction. A single miner validates the transaction while the entire network can confirm the credibility of the validator by checking the Proof-of-Work (PoW), Proof-of-Stake (PoS), Proof-of-Burn (PoB), Directed Acyclic Graph (DAG), Distributed P2P network and so on. So, even if there are few malicious participants in the network, they can be easily weeded out and their opinion never matters. These fundamental properties form the trifecta of security that integrates into blockchain and discourages any kind of foul play. It includes two nodes namely, user node and miner node. User node is the one which performs only its transactions whereas miner node can create new blocks, validate transactions and also it can be a normal node by performing transactions.

Proof of Work [PoW]: PoW usually slows down the process of creating new blocks. If the user needs to add a new block to the chain, he is supposed to come across proof of work by resolving a computational problem which requires certain effort (Sgantzos & Grigg, 2019). If an intruder wants to alter the data in a single block, he must compute PoW for all the upcoming blocks too. This is how PoW makes blockchain tamperproof.

Figure 5. Generated hash value for the text "collaboration of Artificial Intelligence and Blockchain"

Keccak-256

Keccak-256 online hash function

collaboration of Artificial Intelligence and Blockchain

Input type [Text ⌄]

Hash ☑ Auto Update

d1111bfa6376f6d5d713a93af55c358090984af282f90ae529c993909a2bb752

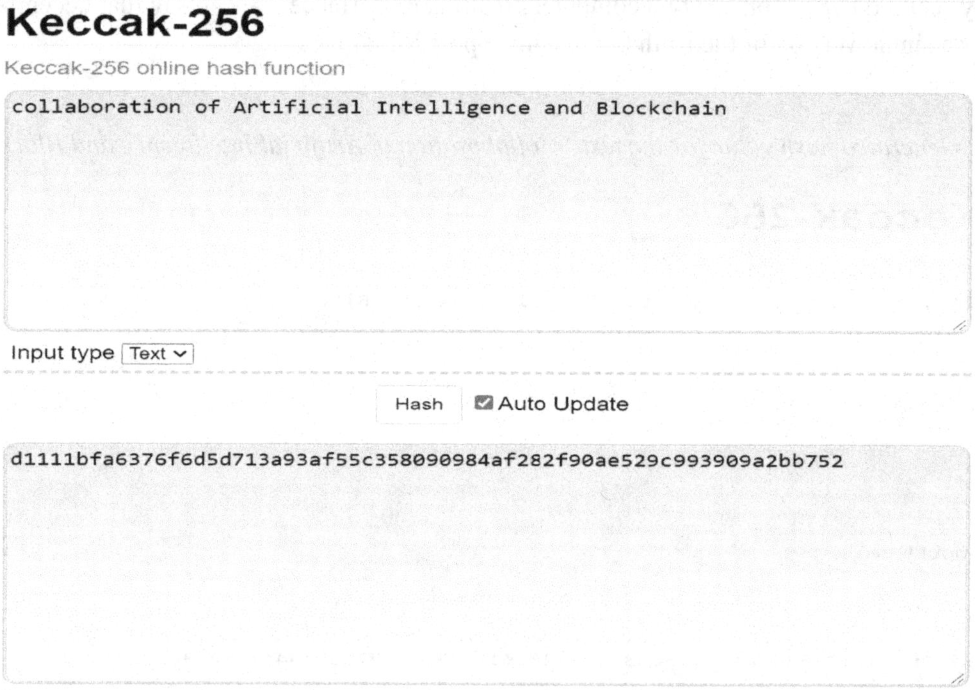

Proof of Stake [PoS]: PoS is an advanced version of Proof of Work which reduces the computational requirements and energy consumption. Proof of Stake considers the stake grasped by the user as digital tokens in blockchain. Participant with huge stake and holding time has higher chance to get selected for mining process. Ouroboros, Chains-Of-Activity (CoA), Casper, Tendermint are some of the stake based protocols.

DAG: Directed Acyclic Graph (DAG) is a web of individual transactions associated with various other transactions. Every transaction is validated and inserted into the group of existing validated blocks. Simply, DAG can be referred as another form of Distributed Ledger Technology (DLT). Nano determined three types of nodes: **historical**- to maintain entire history of all the transaction, **current**- holds only the head of account-chains, **light**- will not maintain any centralization to conserve the user's hardware. In order to reduce the size of a ledger, pruning technique will be implemented (Bencic et al., 2018). If we consider blockchain as a linked list, then we can assume DAG as a tree which spreads out its branches from one transaction to another.

Distributed Peer to Peer Network: In general, people rely on the central authority to manage the network chain. Instead of doing that, blockchain uses distributed peer to peer network which allows every data to get stored in all the systems. The computers connected with the network are known as nodes. If any nodes are need to be added, it must be agreed by all the other nodes. As per the consensus, it might undergo any algorithm like PoW, PoS, PoC or 51% attack to proceed with the work.

Smart Contract: Smart contract is process of self-executing lines of code with pre-established terms and conditions between the parties which will be automatically executed when the situation permits (Sheela & Priya, 2020). It encourages trusted transactions. It includes necessary details along with the timestamp of the transaction.

Varients of Blockchain

Blockchain is classified into three basic types, namely private, public and consortium which will be discussed further.

Private Blockchain: It can also be termed as permissioned blockchain. It will be restricted for the users as it is a closed chain. Comparatively, private blockchain is more efficient and quicker than the public ones. It can be used in intra-business communication where the nodes will be limited inside the office. Also, validation and adding new blocks will be done only by the limited people in the network.

Public Blockchain: It is a native form of distributed ledger technology. It is completely distributed where any number of nodes can be added into the transaction. It is open for anybody in the network. People can transfer and receive transactions from anywhere in the world. Every transaction must be validated by all the authorized nodes through the consensus mechanisms. Conservation of huge data leads to great energy consumption. This stands as a huge disadvantage of public blockchain (BMC, n.d.).

Consortium: This blockchain variant can only be administered by pre-authorized nodes. Hence only a selected group of people can validate and add a transaction. Generally, it will be utilized in cross-organizations. It can either be open or restricted to the groups.

INTEGRATION OF BC AND AI

Blockchain and Artificial Intelligence are demonstrated to be a robust combination in the industries wherever it gets implemented. These two technologies have got synergized to uplift everything from food supply chain to financial security. This collaboration provides various benefits like **globalized verification system, improved business data models, sharp-witted finance, unambiguous governance, smart predictive analysis** and so on.

Technical augmentation that Artificial Intelligence could empower is as follows:

Security: With an application of AI in blockchain, future deployments have become hassle-free. Increased development in AI's decision making algorithms enhances the efficiency and usage of blockchain technology. It also reduces the threat of "double spending" and "51% attack" using its intelligence. Confidentiality is strongly maintained as the transaction will be encrypted and it can be decrypted only by the authenticated user. Plain text are encrypted using any encryption algorithm (like symmetric key cryptography, RSA algorithm, Diffie Hellman key exchange algorithm and so on) to prevent malicious activities (Javed et al., 2020).

Privacy: As blockchain is secured, we can strongly believe that it provides privacy for its users. To enrich the level of privacy, we can proceed with the algorithms of "Homomorphic encryption" which directly performed on an encrypted text instead of performing in a plain text. This process enhances the privacy level.

Efficiency: AI supports to improve the calculations to reduce the network load which results in the speed of the transaction. It reduces the miner's load. Also, AI machines can replace miners by mining each transaction which makes the process faster and consuming the energy spent by the miners. We can also ignore unnecessary data using data pruning algorithm.

Storage: Blockchain itself provides a reliable platform to store the sensitive and private data. This when elegantly processed with Artificial Intelligence, increases its value and comforts the users.

Management: When we discuss about a repetitive task done by the human beings, it will be hard to repeat the same for several days. Hence these can be intelligently replaced by incorporating AI in blockchain to maintain and manage the workflow of the routine work. We can also accomplish risky factors (like fire brigade) by utilizing robots instead of human beings which saves human life.

Figure 6. Beneficial areas of blockchain and AI collaboration

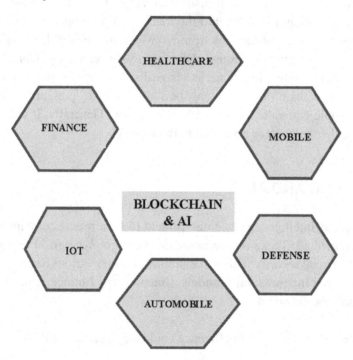

Trust: Entire data maintained in a secure platform can be utilized by the authorized user at their required time. By integrating with AI, we promote machine to machine relationship in-order to interact with each other by sharing the required data in a secure way. This also supports bots to perform effectively (Geeks for Geeks, n.d.).

The collaboration of AI and blockchain provides huge benefits in almost all the sectors in its own way. Figure (f) depicts few areas where this integration can shine and support for the betterment of our society. This integration promotes the development of smart city with completely automated and validated transactions. Smart city includes efficient management of crash prevention, transport services, tourism, healthcare records, defense areas, Traffic management, goods and services and so on(Singh et al., 2020).

ADVANTAGES OF INTEGRATING BLOCKCHAIN AND AI

Here we have listed certain reasons why do we need to include blockchain technology with our existing technologies.

Fraud Prevention: Frauds can be classified into many types out of which identity fraud, financial fraud and supply-chain fraud are the most commonly occurring fraud. This can be sorted out with blockchain's distributed ledger technology and consensus algorithms (ESDS, n.d.).

Reliability: Blockchain verifies and validates the identities of fascinated parties which speeds up the transaction and removes dual records. These transactions cannot be modified even by the authorized users. They can only be updated with the permission of another nodes in the network.

Resilience: Due to its decentralized nature, blockchain does not suffer from central point of failure. Hence, it has the capacity to spring back its original data even in the case of any clash with the current system.

Time Reduction: It is not necessary for the miners to verify the blocks each time. Once it is added to the network, the users can use it any number of times.

Transparency: Public blockchain provides at most transparency. Any changes made in one node will be automatically reflected in all the other nodes in an encrypted format.

Decentralization: It guarantees that every transaction is validated and added one after the other. It improves stability and services of the technology by storing the data in all the available nodes in the network.

Collaboration: Blockchain encourages direct communication between the users without losing their privacy. It also promotes collaboration with other technologies to effectively satisfy the requirements of the people.

INVOLVEMENT OF TECHNOLOGY IN INFORMATION RETREIVAL

Blockchain is a platform which stores the information in a more secure way. Every data accumulated by the blockchain must be retrieved efficiently. With the help of artificial intelligence, data can be segregated as per the situations and retrieved accordingly. Every data must be given access control to the authenticated users. Access control is classified into three types as follows.

Role Based Access Control: In this model, control will be provided based on the given role. Based on the role of the user, limitations of access are designed.

Rule Based Access Control: It provides access based on the rules framed earlier. These rules are framed by considering the external parameters like geographical location, date, time, etc,.

Attribute Based Access Control: It is more relevant to rule based access control. Here, the rules are framed by the attributes used by the users (Samaniego et al., n.d.).

The process of building information management is an essential method to provide an efficient information retrieval system. It requires Architecture, Engineering and Construction (AEC) as a basic platform building the information management system which makes the process of retrieval simple (Liu et al., 2021). In the case of business, ensuring the quality of the product can be analyzed by the algorithms of artificial intelligence and the history of the product will be tracked using blockchain. As the complete chain, from the scratch to the end product is maintained in the supply chain management, it shows the result based on authorized request. Hence, fraudulent activities are clearly impossible. When we discuss about storage, it is essential to consider QoS (Quality of Service) to anticipate the performance of a system by analyzing the reliability, cost, elasticity, execution time, etc.,(Gill et al., 2019) Usually the parameters of QoS are designed by the Service Level Agreement (SLA) which is an agreement signed by the users to store the information in a blockchain platform at the time of mining. While retrieving the information, search query plays a key role to retrieve the desired information. Search can be done by following certain strategies.

Short-Term History: It describes the past recent interaction between the user and the system in search query.

Long-Term History: It considers all the historical information based on the user's queries placed in web search session.

Situational Context: This strategy completely focuses on the current request to search by ignoring the history of it without considering the location, date and time.

Relevance Feedback: It is a kind of searching based on pseudo relevance strategy where the implicit or explicit relevance will be analyzed for searching. It encourages the retrieval performance (Guoa et al., 2019).

For accessing and sorting the contents like data, file, websites, images, we can use Interplanetary File System (IPFS) which is in a peer to peer distributed format. Each file has unique identifier depending on their cryptographic hash value (Kumar et al., 2020). Every transaction is needed to be supervised when working with the departments of government. Different degrees of transparency are maintained with the supervision department as per their levels (country level, state level, district level, etc) (Miao et al., 2020). Mostly essentially, data transparency and end to end process tracking with automation and verification stands as a major aspect in implementing this technology in many application areas including smart city and business industries. When the authors think about a city with smart features, they need to consider about the durable environment (to ensure robustness for smart cities), interactivity and elasticity with intelligent infrastructure where we can monitor its behavioral process, secure framework with scalability for stabilized procedural working of smart cities and so on (Hacioglu, n.d.).

Augmented Data Security: Storing secure data in a disk-less environment.

Upgraded Trust on Robotic Decisions: Involvement of third party will be reduced, as the decisions are automated with AI algorithms.

Collective Decision Making: Decisions must be taken in a coordinated manner to achieve the assigned goal.

High Efficiency: Storage of information and its retrieval are efficiently managed with the collaborated technologies (Salah, 2018).

These features illustrate the basic essentials and morals of integrating the technologies.

CONCLUSION

It is necessary to consider the issues like sustainability, scalability, security, privacy, efficiency, proper utilization of hardware and so on while synergizing artificial intelligence with blockchain technology. It can mainly focus on finance sector with robotic task automation by promoting human-robot interaction in a consortium. It can overpass the physical and digital world through global network. This secure storage of information also provides marketing for this technology. Also, this combined technology takes the supply chain management to the next level where each product will have a transparent history from the scratch to the final consumer. This avoids the presence of unnecessary intermediaries and encourages direct communication between the producer (source) and the consumer (destination) in a sealed method. It also increases the business performance and transforms the Society of Human Resource Management (SHRM) from traditional to digital platform. The concept of smart contract in blockchain technology which is similar to traditional contract enables secure communication between two parties. Authors are also considering the benefits of aggregating blockchain and AI with IoT and Big Data to use and manage the information more efficiently. Also it offers various kinds of data-based information to number of companies. Information retrieval is usually done with several phases of indexing in order to obtain information using a reference key. Indexing, querying, comparison and feedback are the distinct phases of information retrieval to proceed with an efficient searching. This retrieval mostly uses probabilistic method and Self Organizing Map (SOM) where we have to gain information from raw data and also in an unsupervised classification. By including the features of blockchain technology like consensus, hashing, authentication, encryption/decryption, etc., with artificial intelligence lifts up this information retrieval to next level. Major desire of industry 5.0 is to upgrade the machine-to-human interaction which renders lofty benefits. We can hardly ignore blockchain and Artificial Intelligence in Industry 5.0. It is necessary for us to understand and promote the benefits of this combined technology.

REFERENCES

Analytics Insight. (n.d.). Available at https://www.analyticsinsight.net/potentials-of-nlp-techniques-industry-implementation-and-global-market-outline/

Analytics Vidhya. (2017). Available at https://www.analyticsvidhya.com/blog/2017/01/ultimate-guide-to-understand-implement-natural-language-processing-codes-in-python/

Bencic, F. M., Zarko, I. P., & Technology, D. L. (2018). *Blockchain Compared to Directed Acyclic Graph*. arXiv:1804.10013v1

BMC. (n.d.). Available at https://www.bmc.com/blogs/public-vs-private-blockchain/

Bryndin, E. (2020). *Formation and Management of Industry 5.0 by Systems with Artificial Intelligence and Technological Singularity*. SciencePG.

Digitalya. (n.d.). Available at https://digitalya.co/blog/industry-5-opportunities-and-challenges/#:~:text=The%20advantages%20of%20Industry%205.0,offer%20a%20better%20work%20environment.&text=Industry%205.0%20moves%20from%20mass%20customization%20to%20personalization

ESDS. (n.d.). Available at https://www.esds.co.in/blog/blockchain-and-fraud-detection/#sthash.7nsj1xU4.dpbs

Geeks for Geeks. (n.d.). Available at https://www.geeksforgeeks.org/integration-of-blockchain-and-ai/#:~:text=AI%20and%20blockchain%20are%20proving,media%20royalties%20and%20financial%20security

Gill, S. S., Tuli, S., Xu, M., Singh, I., Singh, K. V., Lindsay, D., Tuli, S., Smirnova, D., Singh, M., Jain, U., Pervaiz, H., Sehgal, B., Kaila, S. S., Misra, S., Aslanpour, M. S., Mehta, H., Stankovski, V., & Garraghan, P. (2019). *Transformative Effects of IoT, Blockchain and Artificial Intelligence on Cloud Computing: Evolution*. Vision, Trends and Open Challenges, Internet of Things.

Guoa, J., Fana, Y., Liang, P., Yang, L., Ai, Q., Zamani, H., & Wua, C. (2019). A Deep Look into Neural Ranking Models for Information Retrieval. *Journal of Information Processing and Management.*

Guru99. (n.d.). Available at https://www.guru99.com/blockchain-tutorial.html

Hacioglu. (n.d.). *Digital Business Strategies in Blockchain Ecosystems-Transformational Design and Future of Global Business*. Springer.

Hirtan, L., Dobre, C., Krawiec, P., & Batalla, J. M. (2019). *Blockchain-based approach for e-health data access management with privacy protection*. IEEE. doi:10.1109/CAMAD.2019.8858469

Intech Open. (n.d.). Available at https://www.intechopen.com/online-first/natural-language-processing-applications-in-business

Javed, M. U., Rehman, M., Javaid, N., Aldegheishem, A., Alrajeh, N., & Tahir, M. (2020). *Blockchain-Based Secure Data Storage for Distributed Vehicular Networks*. MDPI. doi:10.3390/app10062011

Kumar, Wang, Kumar, Yang, Khan, Ali, & Ali. (2020). *An Integration of Blockchain and AI for Secure Data Sharing and Detection of CT images for the Hospitals*. Academic Press.

Liu, Z., Chi, Z., Osmani, M., & Demian, P. (2021). *Blockchain and Building Information Management (BIM) for Sustainable Building Development within the Context of Smart Cities*. MDPI.

Melnyk, L., Kubatko, O., Dehtyarova, I., Matsenko, O., & Rozhko, O. (2019). The effect of industrial revolutions on the transformation of social and economic systems. *Problems and Perspectives in Management, 17*(4), 381–391. doi:10.21511/ppm.17(4).2019.31

Miao, Y., Song, J., Wang, H., Hu, L., Hassan, M. M., & Chen, M. (2020). *Smart Micro-GaS: A Cognitive Micro Natural Gas Industrial Ecosystem Based on Mixed Blockchain and Edge Computing*. IEEE Xplore.

Programmer Backpack. (n.d.). Available at https://programmerbackpack.com/top-natural-language-processing-nlp-algorithms-and-techniques-for-beginners/

Salah. (2018). *Blockchain for AI: Review and Open Research Challenges*. IEEE.

Samaniego, Kassani, Espana, & Deters. (n.d.). *Access Control Management for Computer-Aided Diagnosis Systems using Blockchain*. Academic Press.

Sgantzos, K., & Grigg, I. (2019). *Artificial Intelligence Implementations on the Blockchain. Use Cases and Future Applications*. MDPI. doi:10.3390/fi11080170

Sheela & Priya. (2020). *Enabling the efficiency of Blockchain Technology in Tele-Healthcare with Enhanced EMR*. IEEE Explore.

Singh, S., Sharma, P. K., Yoon, B., Shojafar, M., Cho, G. H., & Ra, I.-H. (2020). *Convergence of Blockchain and Artificial Intelligence in IoT Network for the Sustainable Smart City*. Elsevier.

Tutorials Point. (n.d.). Available at https://www.tutorialspoint.com/artificial_intelligence/artificial_intelligence_natural_language_processing.htm

Compilation of References

Agarwal, A., Xie, B., Vovsha, I., Rambow, O., & Passonneau, R. J. (2011, June). Sentiment analysis of twitter data. In *Proceedings of the workshop on language in social media (LSM 2011)* (pp. 30-38). Academic Press.

Agarwal, S., & Varshney, L. R. (2019). *Limits of deepfake detection: A robust estimation viewpoint.* arXiv preprint: arXiv:1905.03493

Aizenberg, E., Shamonin, D. P., & Reijnierse, M. (2019). Automatic quantification of tenosynovitis on MRI of the wrist in patients with early arthritis: A feasibility study. *European Radiology.*

Akhondi, S. A., Singh, B., & van der Host, E. (2013). A dictionary-and grammar-based chemical named entity recognizer. BioCreative Challenge Evaluation Workshop, 2, 113.

Akinsola, J.E.T. (2017). Supervised Machine Learning Algorithms: Classification and Comparison. *International Journal of Computer Trends and Technology, 48.*

Amengol-Estapé, J., Soares, F., Marimon, M., & Krallinger, M. (2019). PharmacoNER Tagger: A deep learning-based tool for automatically finding chemicals and drugs in Spanish medical texts. *Genomics & Informatics, 17*(2), e15. doi:10.5808/GI.2019.17.2.e15 PMID:31307130

Analytics Insight. (n.d.). Available at https://www.analyticsinsight.net/potentials-of-nlp-techniques-industry-implementation-and-global-market-outline/

Analytics Vidhya. (2017). Available at https://www.analyticsvidhya.com/blog/2017/01/ultimate-guide-to-understand-implement-natural-language-processing-codes-in-python/

Anber, H., Salah, A., & Abd El-Aziz, A. A. (2016). A literature review on twitter data analysis. *International Journal of Computer and Electrical Engineering, 8*(3), 241–249. doi:10.17706/IJCEE.2016.8.3.241-249

Antonakaki, D., Fragopoulou, P., & Ioannidis, S. (2021). A survey of Twitter research: Data model, graph structure, sentiment analysis and attacks. *Expert Systems with Applications, 164.* Advance online publication. doi:10.1016/j.eswa.2020.114006

Article. (2016, January 4). *Nucleic Acids Research, 44*(Database issue), D1202–D1213. PMID:26400175

Asif, M., Ishtiaq, A., Ahmad, H., Aljuaid, H., & Shah, J. (2020). Sentiment analysis of extremism in social media from textual information. Telematics and Informatics. *Journal Telematics and Informatics, Telematics and Informatics, 48.*

Asur, S., & Huberman, B. (2010). Predicting the future with social media. In *2010 IEEE/WIC/ACM International Conference on Web Intelligence and Intelligent Agent Technology*, (pp. 492–499). IEEE.

Avatarify: Avatars for Zoom Skype and Other Video-Conferencing Apps. (2020). Available at: https://github.com/alievk/avatarify

Azzouza, N., Akli-Astouati, K., Oussalah, A., & Bachir, S. A. (2017, June). A real-time Twitter sentiment analysis using an unsupervised method. In *Proceedings of the 7th International Conference on Web Intelligence, Mining and Semantics* (pp. 1-10). Academic Press.

Badrinarayanan, V., Kendall, A., & Cipolla, R. (2017). SegNet: A deep convolutional encoder-decoder architecture for image segmentation. *IEEE Transactions on Pattern Analysis and Machine Intelligence*, *39*(12), 2481–2495. doi:10.1109/TPAMI.2016.2644615 PMID:28060704

Bafna, A., Parkh, A., Iyer, A., & Halbe, A. (2019). A Novel approach to Data Visualization by supporting Ad-hoc Query and Predictive analysis. *Proceedings of the International Conference on Intelligent Computing and Control Systems ICICCS 2019.*

Bahdanau, D., Cho, K., & Bengio, Y. (2016). Neural Machine Translation by Jointly Learning to Align and Translate. *Proceedings of 3rd International Conference on Learning Representations, (ICLR 2015)*. https://arxiv.org/abs/1409.0473

Baldi, P. (2017). Article. *Data Mining and Knowledge Discovery*, 1–13.

Baron, K. (2019). *Digital Doubles: The Deepfake Tech Nourishing new wave Retail.* https://www.forbes.com/sites/katiebaron/2019/07/29/digital-doubles-the-deepfake-tech-nourishing-new-wave-retail/?sh=1e1f74654cc7

Bencic, F. M., Zarko, I. P., & Technology, D. L. (2018). *Blockchain Compared to Directed Acyclic Graph.* arXiv:1804.10013v1

Bengio, Y., Courville, A., & Vincent, P. (2013). Representation Learning: A Review and New Perspectives. *IEEE Transactions on Pattern Analysis and Machine Intelligence*, *35*(8), 1798–1828. doi:10.1109/TPAMI.2013.50 PMID:23787338

Berger. (n.d.). *Drug and Chemical Compound Named Entity Recognition using Convolutional Networks.* Academic Press.

Berthelot, D., Milanfar, P., & Goodfellow, I. (2020). *Creating High Resolution Images with a Latent Adversarial Generator.* arXiv preprint:arXiv:2003.02365v1.

Bikel, D. M., Schwartz, R., & Weischedel, R. M. (1999). An algorithm that learns what's in a name. *Machine Learning*, *34*(1/3), 211–231. doi:10.1023/A:1007558221122

Bloomberg. (2018). *How faking videos became easy and why that's so scary.* https://fortune.com/2018/09/11/deepfakes-obama-video/

BMC. (n.d.). Available at https://www.bmc.com/blogs/public-vs-private-blockchain/

Boesen, M., Kubassova, O., & Bouert, R. (2012). Correlation between computer-aided dynamic gadolinium-enhanced MRI assessment of inflammation and semi-quantitative synovitis and bone marrow oedema scores of the wrist in patients with rheumatoid arthritis—a cohort stud. *Rheumatology.*

Bollen, J., Mao, H., & Zeng, X. (2011). Twitter mood predicts the stock market. *Journal of Computational Science.*

Borthwick, A. (1999). *A maximum Entropy Approach to Named Entity Recognition* (Ph.D. thesis). New York University.

Boukkouri. (2018). *Text classification the first step Toward NLP Mastery.* medium.com

Brownlee, J. (2018). *Deep Learning for Natural Language Processing.* https://machinelearningmastery.com/beam-search-decoder-natural-language-processing/

Brownlee, J. (2019). *A Gentle Introduction to Generative Adversarial Networks (GANs).* https://machinelearningmastery.com/what-are-generative-adversarial-networks-gans/

Bryndin, E. (2020). *Formation and Management of Industry 5.0 by Systems with Artificial Intelligence and Technological Singularity.* SciencePG.

Buttcher, S. a. (2016). *Information retrieval: Implementing and evaluating search engines.* MIT Press.

Caprotti, O. a. (1999). OpenMath and MathML: semantic markup for mathematics. *XRDS: Crossroads. The ACM Magazine for Students, 6*(2), 11–14.

Castillo, C., Mendoza, M., & Poblete, B. (2011, March). Information credibility on twitter. In *Proceedings of the 20th international conference on World wide web* (pp. 675-684). 10.1145/1963405.1963500

Centre for International Governance Innovation (CIGI). (2019). *86 percent of internet users admit being duped by fake news: survey.* https://phys.org/news/2019-06-percent-internet-users-duped-fake.html

ChemSpider: An Online Chemical Information Resource. (2010). *Journal of Chemical Education, 87*(11). doi:10.1021/ed100697w

Chen, T., & Guestrin, C. (2016). XGBoost: A Scalable Tree Boosting System. *ACM Digital Library.*

Chieu, H. L., & Ng, H. T. (2002). Named entity recognition: a maximum entropy approach using global information. *Proceedings of the 19th International Conference on Computational Linguistics, 1,* 1–7. 10.3115/1072228.1072253

Choi, Kim, Cho, Lee, & Lee. (n.d.). *A corpus for plant-chemical relationships in the biomedical domain.* Academic Press.

Chokkalingam, S.P., & Komathy, K. (2014). Intelligent Assistive Methods for Diagnosis of Rheumatoid Arthritis Using Histogram Smoothing and Feature Extraction of Bone Images. *World Academy of Science, Engineering and Technology International Journal of Computer, Information, Systems and Control Engineering.*

Chollet, F. (2018). *Keras: The Python Deep Learning library.* Astrophysics Source Code Library.

Christopher, N. (2020). *We've Just Seen the First Use of Deepfakes in an Indian Election Campaign.* https://www.vice.com/en/article/jgedjb/the-first-use-of-deepfakes-in-indian-election-by-bjp

Citron & Chesney. (2019). Deep Fakes: A Looming Challenge for Privacy, Democracy, Democracy, and National Security. *California Law Review, 107,* 1753.

Clement, J. (2020). *Global digital population as of October 2020.* https://www.statista.com/statistics/617136/digital-population worldwide/#:~:text=Almost%204.66%20billion%20people%20were,percent%20of%20the%20global%20population

Corbett, P., Batchelor, C., & Teufel, S. (2007). Annotation of Chemical Named Entities. *BioNLP 2007. Biological, translational, and clinical language processing,* 57–64.

Crouspeyre, C., Alesi, E., & Lespinasse, K. (2019). *From Creditworthiness to Trustworthiness with alternative NLP/NLU approaches.* ACL Anthology. https://www.aclweb.org/anthology/W19-5516

Csaky, R. K. (2019). Deep Learning Based Chatbot Models. *Scientific Students Associations Report.* https://arxiv.org/pdf/1908.08835.pdf

Czaplicka, K., Wojciechowski, W., & Włodarczyk, J. (2015). Automated assessment of synovitis in 0.2T magnetic resonance images of the wrist. *Computers in Biology and Medicine.*

Dadure, P. a. (2020). An Analysis of Variable-Size Vector Based Approach for Formula Searching. *CLEF 2020 Working Notes Working Notes of CLEF 2020 – Conference and Labs of the Evaluation Forum Thessaloniki, 2696.*

Dadure, P. a. (2019). An empirical analysis on retrieval of math information from the scientific documents. In *International Conference on Communication and Intelligent Systems* (pp. 301-308). Springer.

Dahl, G. E., Yu, D., Deng, L., & Acero, A. (2012). Context-dependent pre-trained deep neural networks for large-vocabulary speech recognition. *IEEE Transactions on Audio, Speech, and Language Processing*, 20(1), 30–42. doi:10.1109/TASL.2011.2134090

Darius, A., Vincent, N., Junichi, Y., & Isao, E. (2018). *MesoNet: a Compact Facial Video Forgery Detection Network*. IEEE. doi:10.1109/WIFS.2018.8630761

Davydova, O. (2018). *Text Preprocessing in Python: Steps, Tools, and Examples*. Data Monsters.

Dean, B. (2020). *Social Network Usage & Growth Statistics: How Many People Use Social Media in 2020*. https://backlinko.com/social-media-users#how-many-people-use-social-media

Degtyarenko, Hastings, de Matos, & Ennis. (2009). ChEBI: An open bioinformatics and cheminformatics resource. *Curr Protoc Bioinformatics*. doi:10.1002/0471250953.bi1409s26

Degtyarenko, K., De Matos, P., Ennis, M., Hastings, J., Zbinden, M., McNaught, A., Alcantara, R., Darsow, M., Guedj, M., & Ashburner, M. (2008). ChEBI: A database and ontology for chemical entities of biological interest. *Nucleic Acids Research*, 36(Database), D344–D350. doi:10.1093/nar/gkm791 PMID:17932057

Dhar, S., & Roy, S. (2019). Mathematical document retrieval system based on signature hashing. *Aptikom Journal on Computer Science and Information Technologies*, 4(1), 45–56. doi:10.11591/APTIKOM.J.CSIT.135

Digitalya. (n.d.). Available at https://digitalya.co/blog/industry-5-opportunities-and-challenges/#:~:text=The%20advantages%20of%20Industry%205.0,offer%20a%20better%20work%20environment.&text=Industry%205.0%20moves%20from%20mass%20customization%20to%20personalization

Dimensions. (2021). https://app.dimensions.ai/discover/data_set?search_mode=content&search_text=deepfakes&search_type=kws&search_field=full_search

Dirik. (2020). *Why it's time to change the conversation around synthetic media*. https://venturebeat.com/2020/08/12/why-its-time-to-change-the-conversation-around-synthetic-media

Dolhansky, B., Bitton, J., Ben Pflaum, J. L., Howes, R., Wang, M., & Ferrer, C. C. (2020). *The deepfakes Detection Challenge (DFDC) Dataset*. arXiv preprint: arXiv:2006.07397v4.

Dollarhide. (2020). *Social Media Definition*. https://www.investopedia.com/terms/s/social-media.asp

Domo. (2017). *Data never sleeps 5.0*. https://www.domo.com/learn/infographic/data-never-sleeps-5

Donges, N. (2020). *A complete guide to random forest algorithm*. https://builtin.com/data-science/random-forest-algorithm

Eddy, S. R. (1996). Hidden Markov models. *Current Opinion in Structural Biology*, 6(3), 361–365. doi:10.1016/S0959-440X(96)80056-X PMID:8804822

Eltyeb, S., & Salim, N. (2014). Chemical named entities recognition: A review on approaches and applications. *Journal of Cheminformatics*, 6(1), 17. doi:10.1186/1758-2946-6-17 PMID:24834132

ESDS. (n.d.). Available at https://www.esds.co.in/blog/blockchain-and-fraud-detection/#sthash.7nsj1xU4.dpbs

Faceswap: Deepfakes software for all. (2017). https://github.com/deepfakes/faceswap

Ferreira, D. a. (2020). *Natural language premise selection: Finding supporting statements for mathematical text*. arXiv preprint arXiv:2004.14959.

Files, I. (2020). *deep fakes: part-1 A-creative-perspective*. https://www.vfxvoice.com/deep-fakes-part-1-a-creative-perspective/

Finezza. (2020). *How Digital Footprint Data is Shaping the Future of Credit Scoring?* Retrieved from https://finezza. in/blog/digital-footprint-data-credit-scoring/

Fooshee, D., Mood, A., Gutman, E., Tavakoli, M., Urban, G., Liu, F., Huynh, N., Van Vranken, D., & Baldi, P. (2018). Deep learning for chemical reaction prediction. *Molecular Systems Design & Engineering, 3*(3), 442–452. doi:10.1039/C7ME00107J

Friedman, J. H. (2002) Stochastic Gradient Boosting. In Computational Statistics and Data Analysis (CSDA). International Association for Statistical Computing (IASC).

Friedrich, Revillion, Hofmann, & Fluck. (2006). Biomedical and Chemical Named Entity Recognition with Conditional Random Fields: The Advantage of Dictionary Features. *Proceedings of the Second International Symposium on Semantic Mining in Biomedicine (SMBM 2006), 7,* 85-89.

Gao, L. a. (2017). *Preliminary Exploration of Formula Embedding for Mathematical Information Retrieval: can mathematical formulae be embedded like a natural language?* arXiv preprint arXiv:1707.05154.

Gao, L. a. (2014). *ICST Math Retrieval System for NTCIR-11 Math-2 Task.* NTCIR.

Geeks for Geeks. (n.d.). Available at https://www.geeksforgeeks.org/integration-of-blockchain-and-ai/#:~:text=AI%20and%20blockchain%20are%20proving,media%20royalties%20and%20financial%20security

Gerlach, C. A. M. (2020). *MIT and others SpyderIDE.* http://docs.spyder-ide.org/current/panes/editor.html

Gill, S. S., Tuli, S., Xu, M., Singh, I., Singh, K. V., Lindsay, D., Tuli, S., Smirnova, D., Singh, M., Jain, U., Pervaiz, H., Sehgal, B., Kaila, S. S., Misra, S., Aslanpour, M. S., Mehta, H., Stankovski, V., & Garraghan, P. (2019). *Transformative Effects of IoT, Blockchain and Artificial Intelligence on Cloud Computing: Evolution.* Vision, Trends and Open Challenges, Internet of Things.

Goodfellow, I., Pouget-Abadie, J., Mirza, M., Xu, B., Warde-Farley, D., Ozair, S., Courville, A., & Bengio, Y. (2014). *Generative Adversarial Nets.* arXiv preprint:arXiv:1406.2661v1.

Grego, T., Pęzik, P., Couto, F., & Rebholz-Schuhmann, D. (2009). *2009. Identification of chemical entities in patent documents.* Distributed Computing, Artificial Intelligence, Bioinformatics, Soft Computing, and Ambient Assisted Living.

Greiner-Petter, A. a. (2020). Discovering mathematical objects of interest—a study of mathematical notations. *Proceedings of The Web Conference 2020,* 1445-1456. 10.1145/3366423.3380218

Greiner-Petter, A., Youssef, A., Ruas, T., Miller, B. R., Schubotz, M., Aizawa, A., & Gipp, B. (2020). Math-word embedding in math search and semantic extraction. *Scientometrics, 125*(3), 3017–3046. doi:10.100711192-020-03502-9

Guera, D., & Delp, E. J. (2018, Nov). Deepfake video detection using recurrent neural networks. In *15th IEEE International Conference on Advanced Video and Signal Based Surveillance (AVSS), Auckland, New Zealand* (pp. 1-6). IEEE. 10.1109/AVSS.2018.8639163

Guoa, J., Fana, Y., Liang, P., Yang, L., Ai, Q., Zamani, H., & Wua, C. (2019). A Deep Look into Neural Ranking Models for Information Retrieval. *Journal of Information Processing and Management.*

Gupta, D., & Siddiqui, S. (2014). Big Data Implementation and Visualization. *IEEE International Conference on Advances in Engineering & Technology Research, ICAETR - 2014.*

Guru99. (n.d.). Available at https://www.guru99.com/blockchain-tutorial.html

Hacioglu. (n.d.). *Digital Business Strategies in Blockchain Ecosystems-Transformational Design and Future of Global Business.* Springer.

Haoa, S., & Lee, D.-H. (2019). Sequence to sequence learning with attention mechanism for short term passenger flow prediction in large-scale metro system. Transportation Research Part C: Emerging Technologies, 107, 287-300.

Hardeniya, N., Perkins, J., Chopra, D., Joshi, N., & Mathur, I. (2016). *Natural Language Processing: Python and NLTK*. books.google.com

Hawizy, L., Jessop, D. M., Adams, N., & Murray-Rust, P. (2011). ChemicalTagger: A tool for semantic text-mining in chemistry. *Journal of Cheminformatics, 3*(1), 17. doi:10.1186/1758-2946-3-17 PMID:21575201

Hettne, K. M., Stierum, R. H., Schuemie, M. J., Hendriksen, P. J., Schijvenaars, B. J., Mulligen, E. M., Kleinjans, J., & Kors, J. A. (2009). A dictionary to identify small molecules and drugs in free text. *Bioinformatics (Oxford, England), 25*(22), 2983–2991. doi:10.1093/bioinformatics/btp535 PMID:19759196

Hinton, G. E., Krizhevsky, A., & Wang, A. S. D. (2011). *Transforming auto-encoders* (Vol. 6791). Springer. doi:10.1007/978-3-642-21735-7_6

Hirschberg, J., & Manning, C. D. (2015). *Advances in natural language processing*. American Association for the Advancement of Science (AAAS).

Hirtan, L., Dobre, C., Krawiec, P., & Batalla, J. M. (2019). *Blockchain-based approach for e-health data access management with privacy protection*. IEEE. doi:10.1109/CAMAD.2019.8858469

Hoffart, Yosef, Bordino, Fürstenau, Pinkal, Spaniol, Taneva, Thater, & Weikum. (2011). Robust disambiguation of named entities in text. *EMNLP*, 782–792.

Hsu, C. C., Zhuang, Y. X., & Lee, C. Y. (2020). Deep fake image detection based on pairwise learning. *Applied Sciences (Basel, Switzerland), 10*(1), 370. doi:10.3390/app10010370

Hügle. (2020). *Applied machine learning and artificial intelligence in rheumatology*. Rheumatol Adv Pract.

Huilgol, P. (2020). *Precision vs. Recall – An Intuitive Guide for Every Machine Learning Person*. https://www.analyticsvidhya.com/blog/2020/09/precision-recall-machine-learning/

Hu, X. a. (2013). Wikimirs: a mathematical information retrieval system for wikipedia. *Proceedings of the 13th ACM/IEEE-CS joint conference on Digital libraries*, 11-20. 10.1145/2467696.2467699

Intech Open. (n.d.). Available at https://www.intechopen.com/online-first/natural-language-processing-applications-in-business

Jabeen, H. (2018). *Stemming and Lemmatization in Python*. https://www.datacamp.com

Jaiman, A. (2020). *Positive Use Cases of Deepfakes*. https://towardsdatascience.com/positive-use-cases-of-deepfakes-49f510056387

Javed, M. U., Rehman, M., Javaid, N., Aldegheishem, A., Alrajeh, N., & Tahir, M. (2020). *Blockchain-Based Secure Data Storage for Distributed Vehicular Networks*. MDPI. doi:10.3390/app10062011

Jayashree, G. & Priya, C. (2019). *Design of Visibility for Order Lifecycle using Datawarehouse*. DOI: .F9171.088619 doi:10.35940/IJEAT

Jayashree, G., & Priya, C. (2019). Comprehensive Guide to Implementation of Datawarehouse in Education. *Proceedings of ICTIDS 2019.*

Jayashree, G., & Priya, C. (2020). Data Integration with XML ETL Processing. *Proceedings of ICCSEA 2020.*

Jha, R. Prakash, & Kanagachidambaresan. (2021). Tensorflow Basics. In Programming with Tensorflow (pp. 5-13). EAI/Springer Innovations in Communication and Computing.

Ji, Sun, Cong, & Han. (2016). Joint recognition and linking of fine-grained locations from tweets. *WWW*, 1271–1281.

Jiang, Z., Zhu, H., Peng, L., Ding, W., & Ren, Y. (2020, October). Self-Supervised Spoofing Audio Detection Scheme. *Proc. Interspeech*, *4223-4227*, 4223–4227. Advance online publication. doi:10.21437/Interspeech.2020-1760

Johnson, M., Schuster, M., Le, Q. V., Krikun, M., Wu, Y., Chen, Z., Thorat, N., Viégas, F., Wattenberg, M., Corrado, G., & Hughes, M. (2017). *Zero-Shot Translation with Google's Multilingual Neural Machine Translation System.* https://direct.mit.edu/tacl/article/doi/10.1162/tacl_a_00065/43400/Google-s-Multilingual-Neural-Machine-Translation

Kalmykov, M. (2019). *Positive Applications for Deepfake Technology.* https://hackernoon.com/the-light-side-of-deepfakes-how-the-technology-can-be-used-for-good-4hr32pp

Kanakaraj, M., & Guddeti, R. M. R. (2015, February). Performance analysis of Ensemble methods on Twitter sentiment analysis using NLP techniques. In *Proceedings of the 2015 IEEE 9th International Conference on Semantic Computing (IEEE ICSC 2015)* (pp. 169-170). IEEE.

Kapur, J. N. (1989). *Maximum-entropy models in science and engineering.* John Wiley & Sons.

Kate, A., Kamble, S., Bodke, A., & Joshi, M. (2018). Conversion of Natural Language Query to SQL Query. *IEEE Second International Conference on Electronics, Communication and Aerospace Technology, ICECA - 2018.*

Kazama & Torisawa. (2007). Exploiting wikipedia as external knowledge for named entity recognition. *EMNLP-CoNLL.*

Khalil, S. S., Youssef, S. M., & Saleh, S. N. (2021). iCaps-Dfake: An Integrated Capsule-Based Model for Deepfake Image and Video Detection. *Future Internet*, *13*(4), 93. doi:10.3390/fi13040093

Kietzmann, J. H., Hermkens, K., McCarthy, I. P., & Silvestre, B. S. (2011). Social media? Get serious! Understanding the functional building blocks of social media. *Business Horizons*, *54*(3), 241–251. doi:10.1016/j.bushor.2011.01.005

Kim, Thiessen, Bolton, Chen, Fu, Gindulyte, Han, He, He, Shoemaker, Wang, Yu, Zhang, & Bryant. (2015). *Chem Substance and Compound Databases.* doi:10.1093/nar/gkv951

Klein, C. (2011). *Information Extraction from Text for Improving Research on Small Molecules and Histone Modifications* [Ph.D. thesis]. Bonn, Germany: Universitäts-und Landesbibliothek.

Klinger, R., Kolárik, C., Fluck, J., Hofmann-Apitius, M., & Friedrich, C. M. (2008). Detection of IUPAC and IUPAC-like chemical names. *Bioinformatics (Oxford, England)*, *24*(13), i268–i276. doi:10.1093/bioinformatics/btn181 PMID:18586724

Kohlhase, M. a. (2006). A search engine for mathematical formulae. In *International Conference on Artificial Intelligence and Symbolic Computation* (pp. 241-253). Springer. 10.1007/11856290_21

Koopman, M., Rodriguez, A. M., & Geradts, Z. (2018, August). Detection of deepfake video manipulation. In *The 20th Irish Machine Vision and Image Processing Conference (IMVIP)*. Ulster University.

Krallinger, M., Leitner, F., Rabal, O., Vazquez, M., Oyarzabal, J., & Valencia, A. (2013). Overview of the chemical compound and drug name recognition (CHEMDNER) task. BioCreative Challenge Evaluation Workshop, 2.

Krallinger, M., Leitner, F., & Rabal, O. (2013). Overview of the chemical compound and drug name recognition (CHEMDNER) task. *BioCreative Challenge Eval. Workshop*, 2, 2.

Krallinger, M., Rabal, O., Leitner, F., Vazquez, M., Salgado, D., Lu, Z., Leaman, R., Lu, Y., Ji, D., Lowe, D. M., Sayle, R. A., Batista-Navarro, R. T., Rak, R., Huber, T., Rocktäschel, T., Matos, S., Campos, D., Tang, B., Xu, H., ... Valencia, A. (2015). The CHEMDNER corpus of chemicals and drugs and its annotation principles. *Journal of Cheminformatics*, 7(S1, Suppl 1), S2. doi:10.1186/1758-2946-7-S1-S2 PMID:25810773

Krishnachalitha & Priya. (2021). A Novel Approach for the Early Detection of Rheumatoid Arthritis on Hand and Wrist Using Convolutional Reinforcement Learning Techniques. *Annals of the Romanian Society for Cell Biology.*

Krishnan & Manning. (2006). An effective two-stage model for exploiting non-local dependencies in named entity recognition. *ACL*, 1121–1128.

Krstovski, K. a. (2018). *Equation embeddings.* arXiv preprint arXiv:1803.09123.

Kumar, N. (2017, December). Sentiment Analysis of Twitter Messages: Demonetization a Use Case. In *2017 2nd International Conference on Computational Systems and Information Technology for Sustainable Solution (CSITSS)* (pp. 1-5). IEEE.

Kumar, Wang, Kumar, Yang, Khan, Ali, & Ali. (2020). *An Integration of Blockchain and AI for Secure Data Sharing and Detection of CT images for the Hospitals.* Academic Press.

Kumar, A., & Jaiswal, A. (2019). Systematic literature review of sentiment analysis on Twitter using soft computing techniques. *Concurrency and Computation*, 32(1), e5107.

Kumar, O., & Goyal, A. (2016). Visualization: A novel approach for big data analytics. *Second International Conference on Computational Intelligence & Communication Technology.*

Kushman, N. a. (2014). Learning to automatically solve algebra word problems. In *Proceedings of the 52nd Annual Meeting of the Association for Computational Linguistics (Volume 1: Long Papers)*, (pp. 271-281). 10.3115/v1/P14-1026

Larson, R. R. (2013). *The Abject Failure of Keyword IR for Mathematics Search: Berkeley at NTCIR-10 Math.* NTCIR.

LeCun, Y., Bengio, Y., & Hinton, G. (2015). Deep learning. *Nature*, 521(7553), 436–444. doi:10.1038/nature14539 PMID:26017442

Liao & Veeramachaneni. (2009). A simple semi-supervised algorithm for named entity recognition. *NAACL-HLT*, 58–65.

Li, J., Song, Y., Wei, Z., & Wong, K. F. (2018). (2018, December). A joint model of conversational discourse and latent topics on microblogs. Computational Linguistics, MIT Press Journal. *Computational Linguistics*. Advance online publication. doi:10.1162/coli_a_00335

Li, J., Sun, Y., Johnson, R. J., Sciaky, D., Wei, C.-H., Leaman, R., Davis, A. P., Mattingly, C. J., Wiegers, T. C., & Lu, Z. (2016). BioCreative V CDR task corpus: A resource for chemical disease relation extraction. *Database (Oxford)*, 2016, baw068. Advance online publication. doi:10.1093/database/baw068 PMID:27161011

Liu, Z., Chi, Z., Osmani, M., & Demian, P. (2021). *Blockchain and Building Information Management (BIM) for Sustainable Building Development within the Context of Smart Cities.* MDPI.

Livska, M. a. (2013). Similarity search for mathematics: Masaryk university team at the ntcir-10 math task. *Proceedings of the 10th NTCIR Conference on Evaluation of Information Access Technologies*, 686-691.

Livska, M. a. (2015). Combining text and formula queries in math information retrieval: Evaluation of query results merging strategies. In *Proceedings of the First International Workshop on Novel Web Search Interfaces and Systems*, (pp. 7-9). 10.1145/2810355.2810359

Li, Y., & Lyu, S. (2019). Exposing deepfake videos by detecting face warping artifacts. *Proceedings of the IEEE Conference on Computer Vision and Pattern Recognition Workshops*, 46-52.

Loc, T., Michael, T., Sirisha, R., & Yan, L. (2021). Interpretable and Trustworthy Deepfake Detection via Dynamic Prototypes. *Proceedings of the IEEE/CVF Winter Conference on Applications of Computer Vision (WACV), 1*(1), 1973-1983. https://openaccess.thecvf.com/content/WACV2021/papers/Trinh_Interpretable_and_Trustworthy_Deepfake_Detection_via_Dynamic_Prototypes_WACV_2021_paper.pdf

Loper, E., Klein, E., & Bird, S. (2009). *Natural language processing with Python: analyzing text with the natural language toolkit.* books.google.com

Lowe & Sayle . (2015). LeadMine: A grammar and dictionary driven approach to chemical entity recognition. *Proceedings of the fourth BioCreative challenge evaluation workshop*, 2.

Lucene, A. (2010). *Apache lucene-overview.* http://lucene. apache. org/iava/docs/

Luo, L., Yang, Z., Yang, P., Zhang, Y., Wang, L., Wang, J., & Lin, H. (2018). A neural network approach to chemical and gene/protein entity recognition in patents. *Journal of Cheminformatics, 10*(1), 65. doi:10.118613321-018-0318-3 PMID:30564940

Lyu, S. (2020). Deepfake Detection: Current Challenges and Next Steps. *IEEE International Conference on Multimedia & Expo Workshops (ICMEW)*, 1-6. 10.1109/ICMEW46912.2020.9105991

Malaria Must Die. (2019). *David Beckham speaks nine languages to launch Malaria Must Die Voice Petition.* https://youtu.be/QiiSAvKJIHo

Mansouri, B. a. (2020). DPRL Systems in the CLEF 2020 ARQMath Lab. *Working Notes of CLEF 2020-Conference and Labs of the Evaluation Forum.*

Mansouri, A., Affendey, L. S., & Mamat, A. (2008). Named entity recognition approaches. *Int J Comp Sci Netw Sec, 8*, 339–344.

Mansouri, B. a. (2019). Tangent-CFT: An Embedding Model for Mathematical Formulas. In *Proceedings of the 2019 ACM SIGIR international conference on theory of information retrieval*, (pp. 11-18). 10.1145/3341981.3344235

Marr, B. (2018). *How Much Data Do We Create Every Day? The Mind-Blowing Stats Everyone Should Read.* Forbes. https://www.forbes.com/sites/bernardmarr/2018/05/21/how-much-data-do-we-create-every-day-the-mind-blowing-stats-everyone-should-read/?sh=316adc3360ba

Mate & Kureshi (2020). Understanding CNN to Automatically Diagnose Rheumatoid Arthritis using Hand Radiographs. *International Journal of Advanced Science and Technology.*

Mattmann, C. (2021). Sequence-to-sequence models for chatbots. In *Machine Learning with TensorFlow* 2e. Manning. https://livebook.manning.com/book/machine-learning-with-tensorflow-second-edition/chapter-18/

McQueen, F. M., Stewart, N., & Crabbe, J. (1998). Magnetic resonance imaging of the wrist in early rheumatoid arthritis reveals a high prevalence of erosions at four months after symptom onset. *Annals of the Rheumatic Diseases.*

Mejia, N. (2019). *AI for Credit Scoring – An Overview of Startups and Innovation.* https://emerj.com/ai-sector-overviews/ai-for-credit-scoring-an-overview-of-startups-and-innovation/

Melnyk, L., Kubatko, O., Dehtyarova, I., Matsenko, O., & Rozhko, O. (2019). The effect of industrial revolutions on the transformation of social and economic systems. *Problems and Perspectives in Management, 17*(4), 381–391. doi:10.21511/ppm.17(4).2019.31

Menzenski. (2015). *Introduction to text analysis With Python and the Natural Language Toolkit.* Academic Press.

Mette Klarlund, M. (1999). Wrist and Finger Joint MR Imaging in Rheumatoid Arthritis. *Acta Radiologica.*

Miao, Y., Song, J., Wang, H., Hu, L., Hassan, M. M., & Chen, M. (2020). *Smart Micro-GaS: A Cognitive Micro Natural Gas Industrial Ecosystem Based on Mixed Blockchain and Edge Computing.* IEEE Xplore.

Mikheev. (1999). A knowledge-free method for capitalized word disambiguation. *ACL,* 159–166.

Miner, R. a. (2007). An approach to mathematical search through query formulation and data normalization. In *Towards Mechanized Mathematical Assistants* (pp. 342–355). Springer. doi:10.1007/978-3-540-73086-6_27

Mirza, M., & Osindero, S. (2014). *Conditional Generative Adversarial Nets.* arXiv preprint: arXiv:1411.1784v1.

Mivsutka, J. a. (2008). *Extending full text search engine for mathematical content.* Towards Digital Mathematics Library.

Mivsutka, J. a. (2011). System description: Egomath2 as a tool for mathematical searching on wikipedia.org. In *International Conference on Intelligent Computer Mathematics* (pp. 307-309). Springer.

Mnasri. (2019). *Recent advances in conversational NLP: Towards the standardization of Chatbot building.* https://arxiv.org/abs/1903.09025

Mohd Ali, S., Gupta, N., Nayak, G. K., & Lenka, R. (2016). Big data visualization: Tools and challenges. *IEEE-2nd International Conference on Contemporary Computing and Informatics, IC3I 2016.*

Mosley, T. (2019). *Perfect Deepfake Tech Could Arrive Sooner Than Expected.* https://www.wbur.org/hereandnow/2019/10/02/deepfake-technology

Mujtaba. (2020). *An Introduction to Bag of Words (BoW) | What is Bag of Words?* https://www.mygreatlearning.com

Murakami, Hatano, Tan, Kim, & Aoki. (2017). Automatic identification of bone erosions in rheumatoid arthritis from hand radiographs based on deep convolutional neural network. *Multimed. Tools Appl.*

Murakami, S., Hatano, K., & Tan, J. (2018). Automatic identification of bone erosions in rheumatoid arthritis from hand radiographs based on deep convolutional neural network. *Multimed Tools Appl.*

Nadeau, D., & Sekine, S. (2007). A survey of named entity recognition and classification. *Lingvisticae Investigationes, 30*(1), 3–26. doi:10.1075/li.30.1.03nad

Naik, R. R. (2015). A review on plagiarism detection tools. *International Journal of Computers and Applications, 125*(11).

Narayanaswamy, M., Ravikumar, K. E., & Vijay-Shanker, K. (2003). A biological named entity recognizer. *Pacific Symposium on Biocomputing,* 427.

Ndukwe, I. G., Daniel, B. K., & Amadi, C. E. (2019). A Machine Learning Grading System Using Chatbots. *International Conference on Artificial Intelligence in Education (AIED 2019): Artificial Intelligence in Education,* 365-368. https://link.springer.com/chapter/10.1007/978-3-030-23207-8_67

Netzer, O., Lemaire, A., & Herzenstein, M. (2018). *When words sweat: Identifying signals for loan default in the text of loan applications.* Columbia Business School Research Paper.

Nguyen, Nguyen, Nguyen, Nguyen, & Nahavandi. (2020). *Deep Learning for Deepfakes Creation and Detection: A Survey.* arXiv preprint: arXiv:1909.11573v2.

Nguyen, H. H., Tieu, N.-D. T., Nguyen-Son, H.-Q., Junichi Yamagishi, V. N., & Echizen, I. (2018). Modular convolutional neural network for discriminating between computer-generated images and photographic images. *Proceedings of the 13th International Conference on Availability, Reliability and Security, 1*(1), 10. 10.1145/3230833.3230863

Nguyen, H. H., Yamagishi, J., & Echizen, I. (2019, May). Capsuleforensics: Using capsule networks to detect forged images and videos. *2019 IEEE International Conference on Acoustics, Speech and Signal Processing (ICASSP)*, 2307-2311. 10.1109/ICASSP.2019.8682602

Novotny, V. a. (2020). Three is better than one. *CEUR Workshop Proceedings*.

Ota, Y., Maruyama, K., & Terada, M. (2012, December). Discovery of interesting users in twitter by overlapping propagation paths of retweets. In *2012 IEEE/WIC/ACM International Conferences on Web Intelligence and Intelligent Agent Technology* (Vol. 3, pp. 274-279). IEEE. 10.1109/WI-IAT.2012.110

Pathak, A. a. (2017). Mathirs: Retrieval system for scientific documents. *Computacion y Sistemas, 21*(2), 253-265.

Pathak, A. a. (2018). A formula embedding approach to math information retrieval. *Computacion y Sistemas, 22*(3), 819-833.

Pathak, A. a. (2019). Lstm neural network based math information retrieval. In *Second International Conference on Advanced Computational and Communication Paradigms (ICACCP)* (pp. 1-6). IEEE. 10.1109/ICACCP.2019.8882887

Pathak, A., Pakray, P., & Gelbukh, A. (2019). Binary vector transformation of math formula for mathematical information retrieval. *Journal of Intelligent & Fuzzy Systems, 36*(5), 4685–4695. doi:10.3233/JIFS-179018

Pattaniyil, N. a. (2014). *Combining TF-IDF Text Retrieval with an Inverted Index over Symbol Pairs in Math Expressions: The Tangent Math Search Engine at NTCIR 2014*. NTCIR.

Paul, K. (2020). *Twitter to label deepfakes and other deceptive media*. https://www.reuters.com/article/us-twitter-security-idUSKBN1ZY2OV

Petrovic, S., Osborne, M., & Lavrenko, V. (2011). Rt to win! predicting message propagation in twitter. *ICWSM, 11*, 586–589.

Pineau, D. C. (2016). *Math-aware search engines: Physics applications and overview*. arXiv preprint arXiv:1609.03457.

Programmer Backpack. (n.d.). Available at https://programmerbackpack.com/top-natural-language-processing-nlp-algorithms-and-techniques-for-beginners/

Radford, A., Metz, L., & Chintala, S. (2015). *Unsupervised representation learning with deep convolutional generative adversarial networks*. arXiv preprint:arXiv:1511.06434

Rahmouni, N., Nozick, V., Yamagishi, J., & Echizen, I. (2017). Distinguishing computer graphics from natural images using convolution neural networks. *2017 IEEE Workshop on Information Forensics and Security (WIFS), 1*(1), 1-6. 10.1109/WIFS.2017.8267647

Ramesh, K., Ravishankaran, S., & Joshi, A. (2017). A Survey of Design Techniques for Conversational Agents. In *International Conference on Information, Communication and Computing Technology (ICICCT 2017): Information, Communication and Computing Technology* (pp 336-350). Springer. 10.1007/978-981-10-6544-6_31

Ravin & Wacholder. (1997). *Extracting names from natural-language text*. IBM Research Report RC 2033.

Rebholz-Schuhmann, Arregui, Gaudan, Kirsch, & Jimeno. (2008). Text processing through Web services: calling Whatizit. *Bioinformatics, 24*(2), 296-298.

Reshma, E. U., & Remya, P. C. (2017). A Review of Different Approaches in Natural Language Interfaces to Databases. *Proceedings of the International Conference on Intelligent Sustainable Systems ICISS 2017.*

Roesslein, J. (2020). *Tweepy documentation.* Retrieved from https://www.tweepy.org/

Rout, J. K., Choo, K. K. R., Dash, A. K., Bakshi, S., Jena, S. K., & Williams, K. L. (2018). A model for sentiment and emotion analysis of unstructured social media text. Electronic Commerce Research. *Journal Electronic Commerce Research, 18,* 181–199. doi:10.100710660-017-9257-8

Sabir, E., Cheng, J., Jaiswal, A., Abd Almageed, W., Masi, I., & Natarajan, P. (2019). *Recurrent convolutional strategies for face manipulation detection in videos.* arXiv preprint: arXiv:1905.00582v3.

Sailunaz, K., & Alhajj, R. (2019). Emotion and sentiment analysis from Twitter text. *Journal of Computational Science, 36.* https://doi.org/ doi:10.1016/j.jocs.2019.05.009

Saini, A. (2019). A Novel Code-Switching Behaviour Analysis in Social Media Discussions Natural Language Processing. *2019 IEEE International Conference on Big Data.*

Salah. (2018). *Blockchain for AI: Review and Open Research Challenges.* IEEE.

Samaniego, Kassani, Espana, & Deters. (n.d.). *Access Control Management for Computer-Aided Diagnosis Systems using Blockchain.* Academic Press.

Sarkar, D. (2019). *Text analytics with Python: a practitioner's guide to natural language processing.* Apress. doi:10.1007/978-1-4842-4354-1_6

Sayle, R., Xie, P. H., & Muresan, S. (2012). Improved chemical text mining of patents with infinite dictionaries and automatic spelling correction. *Journal of Chemical Information and Modeling, 52*(1), 51–62. doi:10.1021/ci200463r PMID:22148717

Scharpf, P. a. (2019). AnnoMathTeX-a formula identifier annotation recommender system for STEM documents. *Proceedings of the 13th ACM Conference on Recommender Systems,* 532-533. 10.1145/3298689.3347042

Schett, G. (2012). Synovitis an inflammation of joints destroying the bone. *Swiss Medical Weekly.*

Schubotz, M. a. (2015). Challenges of mathematical information retrieval in the ntcir-11 math wikipedia task. *Proceedings of the 38th international ACM SIGIR conference on research and development in information retrieval,* 951-954. 10.1145/2766462.2767787

Schubotz, M. a. (2017). VMEXT: a visualization tool for mathematical expression trees. In *International Conference on Intelligent Computer Mathematics* (pp. 340-355). Springer. 10.1007/978-3-319-62075-6_24

Schwartz, M. (2018). *Who Killed the Kiev Protesters? A 3-D Model Holds the Clues.* https://www.nytimes.com/2018/05/30/magazine/ukraine-protest-video.html

Scott, A. J., & Gavin, J. (2018, April 11). Revenge pornography: The influence of perpetrator-victim sex, observer sex, and observer sexting experience on perceptions of seriousness and responsibility. *Journal of Criminal Psychology, 8*(2), 162–182. doi:10.1108/JCP-05-2017-0024

Sekine, S., & Ranchhod, E. (2009). *Named entities: recognition, classification and use* (Vol. 19). John Benjamins Publishing. doi:10.1075/bct.19

Seki, Y. (2016, May). Use of twitter for analysis of public sentiment for improvement of local government service. In *2016 IEEE International Conference on Smart Computing (SMARTCOMP)* (pp. 1-3). IEEE.

Sesagiri Raamkumar, A., Erdt, M., Vijayakumar, H., Rasmussen, E., & Theng, Y. L. (2018). *Understanding the Twitter usage of humanities and social sciences academic journals.* Academic Press.

Settles. (2004). Biomedical named entity recognition using Conditional Random Fields and rich feature sets. *ACL,* 104–107.

Sgantzos, K., & Grigg, I. (2019). *Artificial Intelligence Implementations on the Blockchain. Use Cases and Future Applications.* MDPI. doi:10.3390/fi11080170

Shahroz, T., Sangyup, L., & Simon, W. S. (2021). *One Detector to Rule Them All: Towards a General Deepfake Attack Detection Framework.* arXiv e-prints. https://ui.adsabs.harvard.edu/abs/2021arXiv210500187T

Sharma, P., & Moh, T. (2016). Prediction of Indian election using sentiment analysis on Hindi Twitter. *2016 IEEE International Conference on Big Data (Big Data),* 1966-1971. doi: 10.1109/BigData.2016.7840818

Sharma, P., & Moh, T. S. (2016, December). Prediction of Indian election using sentiment analysis on Hindi Twitter. In *2016 IEEE international conference on big data (big data)* (pp. 1966-1971). IEEE.

Sheela & Priya. (2020). *Enabling the efficiency of Blockchain Technology in Tele-Healthcare with Enhanced EMR.* IEEE Explore.

Shen, T., Liu, R., Bai, J., & Li, Z. (2018). *"Deep fakes" using Generative Adversarial Networks (GAN).* http://noiselab.ucsd.edu/ECE228_2018/Reports/Report16.pdf

Shukla, P., & Iriondo, R. (2021). *Natural Language Processing (NLP) with Python Tutorial on the basics of natural language processing (NLP) with sample coding implementations in Python.* Academic Press.

Siarohin, A., Lathuilière, S., Tulyakov, S., Ricci, E., & Sebe, N. (2020). *First Order Motion Model for Image Animation.* arXiv preprint: arXiv:2003.00196.

Singh, S. (2019). *How to Get Started with NLP – 6 Unique Methods to Perform Tokenization.* https://www.analytics-vidhya.com

Singh, G., & Solanki, A. (2016). An algorithm to transform natural language into SQL queries for relational databases. *International Academy of Ecology and Environmental Sciences (IAEES) Selforganizology, 3*(3), 100–116.

Singh, S., Sharma, P. K., Yoon, B., Shojafar, M., Cho, G. H., & Ra, I.-H. (2020). *Convergence of Blockchain and Artificial Intelligence in IoT Network for the Sustainable Smart City.* Elsevier.

Sojasingarayar, A. (2020). *Seq2Seq AI Chatbot with Attention Mechanism Artificial Intelligence.* IASchool/University, Boulogne-Billancourt, France. https://arxiv.org/ftp/arxiv/papers/2006/2006.02767.pdf

Sojka, P. a. (2011). The art of mathematics retrieval. *Proceedings of the 11th ACM symposium on Document engineering,* 57-60. 10.1145/2034691.2034703

Sojka, P. a. (2018). MIaS: math-aware retrieval in digital mathematical libraries. *Proceedings of the 27th ACM International Conference on Information and Knowledge Management,* 1923-1926. 10.1145/3269206.3269233

Stathopoulos, Y. A. (2018). *Variable typing: Assigning meaning to variables in mathematical text.* Academic Press.

Stathopoulos, Y. A. (2016). *Mathematical information retrieval based on type embeddings and query expansion.* International Committee on Computational Linguistics.

Statt, N. (2019). *Thieves are now using AI deepfakes to trick companies into sending them money.* https://www.theverge.com/2019/9/5/20851248/deepfakes-ai-fake-audio-phone-calls-thieves-trick-companies-stealing-money

Sutskever, I., Vinyals, O., & Le, Q. V. (2014). Sequence to sequence learning with neural networks. NIPS.

Szlosek, D., & Ferrett, J. (2016). *Using Machine Learning and Natural Language Processing Algorithms to Automate the Evaluation of Clinical Decision Support in Electronic Medical Record Systems.* www.semanticscholar.org

Tam, Y.-C. (2020). Cluster-based beam search for pointer-generator Chatbot grounded by knowledge. *Computer Speech & Language, 64,* 101094. doi:10.1016/j.csl.2020.101094

Tareaf, R. B., Berger, P., Hennig, P., Koall, S., Kohstall, J., & Meinel, C. (2018). Information Propagation Speed and Patterns in Social Networks: A Case Study Analysis of German Tweets. *JCP, 13*(7), 761–770. doi:10.17706/jcp.13.7.761-770

Thanaki, J. (2017). *Python natural language processing.* books.google.com

Thanaki, J. (2021). *Python Natural Language Processing.* O'Reilly. https://www.oreilly.com/library/view/python-natural-language/9781787121423/6f015f49-58e9-4dd1-8045-b11e7f8bf2c8.xhtml

Thanda, A. a. (2016). *A Document Retrieval System for Math Queries.* NTCIR.

Thejaswini, S., & Indupriya, C. (2019). Big Data Security Issues and Natural Language Processing. *Proceedings of the Third International Conference on Trends in Electronics and Informatics ICOEI 2019.*

Tian, X., & Wang, J. (2021). Retrieval of Scientific Documents Based on HFS and BERT. *IEEE Access: Practical Innovations, Open Solutions, 9,* 8708–8717. doi:10.1109/ACCESS.2021.3049391

Toral, A., & Munoz, R. (2006). A proposal to automatically build and maintain gazetteers for named entity recognition by using Wikipedia. *Workshop on NEW TEXT Wikis and blogs and other dynamic text sources.*

Tripathi, C. (2020). *Important use cases of Natural Language Processing.* https://ashutoshtripathi.com/2019/05/30/examples-nlp-natural-language-processing/

Trupthi, M., Pabboju, S., & Narasimha, G. (2017). Sentiment Analysis on Twitter Using Streaming API. *2017 IEEE 7th International Advance Computing Conference (IACC),* 915-919. doi: 10.1109/IACC.2017.0186

Tutorials Point. (n.d.). Available at https://www.tutorialspoint.com/artificial_intelligence/artificial_intelligence_natural_language_processing.htm

Tyagi, N. (2020). *Understanding the GINI index.* Medium. https://medium.com/analytics-steps/understanding-the-gini-index-and-information-gain-in-decision-trees-ab4720518ba8

Tyagi, P., & Tripathi, R. C. (2019, February). A review towards the sentiment analysis techniques for the analysis of twitter data. *Proceedings of 2nd International Conference on Advanced Computing and Software Engineering (ICACSE).*

Upadhyay, A. (2020). *What is correlation in Machine Learning.* Medium. https://medium.com/analytics-vidhya/what-is-correlation-4fe0c6fbed47

Vinyals, O., & Le, Q. V. (2015). A Neural Conversational Model, *Proceedings of the 31st International Conference on Machine Learning, 37)* https://arxiv.org/abs/1506.05869

Virmani, D. a. (2019). A text preprocessing approach for efficacious information retrieval. In *Smart Innovations in Communication and Computational Sciences* (pp. 13–22). Springer. doi:10.1007/978-981-10-8968-8_2

Vismaya & Reynald. (2017). Natural language processing using python. *International Journal of Scientific & Engineering Research, 8*(5).

Wang, J., Wu, Z., Chen, J., & Jian, G. Y. (2021). M2TR: *Multi-modal Multi-scale Transformers for Deepfake Detection.* CoRR, abs/2104.09770. https://arxiv.org/abs/2104.09770

Wang, Y. a. (2015). WikiMirs 3.0: a hybrid MIR system based on the context, structure and importance of formulae in a document. *Proceedings of the 15th ACM/IEEE-CS joint conference on digital libraries*, 173-182. 10.1145/2756406.2756918

Wang, Y., Xiao, J., Suzek, T. O., Zhang, J., Wang, J., & Bryant, S. H. (2009). PubChem: A public information system for analyzing bioactivities of small molecules. *Nucleic Acids Research*, *37*(Web Server), W623–W633. doi:10.1093/nar/gkp456 PMID:19498078

Weizenbaum, W. J. (1966). Eliza—A computer program for the study of natural language communication between man and machine. *Communications of the ACM*, *9*(1), 36–45. doi:10.1145/365153.365168

Westerlund, M. (2019). The Emergence of Deepfake Technology: A Review. *Technology Innovation Management Review*, *9*(11), 39–52. doi:10.22215/timreview/1282

Wodajo, D., & Atnafu, S. (2021). *Deepfake Video Detection Using Convolutional Vision Transformer* (Vol. abs/2102.11126). CoRR. https://arxiv.org/abs/2102.11126

Wu, B., & Shen, H. (2015). Analyzing and predicting news popularity on Twitter. *International Journal of Information Management*, *35*(6), 702–711. doi:10.1016/j.ijinfomgt.2015.07.003

Xuan, X., Peng, B., Dong, J., & Wang, W. (2019). *On the generalization of GAN image forensics*. arXiv preprint: arXiv:1902.11153. doi:10.1007/978-3-030-31456-9_15

Yan, Spangler, & Chen. (2012). Learning to Extract Chemical Names based on Random Text Generation and Incomplete Dictionary. *BIOKDD'12*.

Yang, W., Hui, C., Chen, Z., Xue, J. H., & Liao, Q. (2019). FV-GAN: Finger vein representation using generative adversarial networks. *IEEE Transactions on Information Forensics and Security*, *14*(9), 2512–2524. doi:10.1109/TIFS.2019.2902819

Yasunaga, M., & Lafferty, J. D. (2019). Topiceq: A joint topic and mathematical equation model for scientific texts. *Proceedings of the AAAI Conference on Artificial Intelligence*, *23*, 7394–7401. doi:10.1609/aaai.v33i01.33017394

Ye, S., & Wu, S. F. (2010, October). Measuring message propagation and social influence on Twitter. com. In *International conference on social informatics* (pp. 216-231). Springer. 10.1007/978-3-642-16567-2_16

Yoo, S., Song, J., & Jeong, O. (2018, March). Social media contents based sentiment analysis and prediction system. Expert Systems with Applications. *Journal Expert Systems with Applications, 105*, 102-111.

Yue, L., Chen, W., Li, X., Zuo, W., & Yin, M. (2018, July). A survey of sentiment analysis in social media. Knowledge and Information Systems. *Journal Knowledge and Information Systems, 60*(2), 617–663. doi:10.100710115-018-1236-4

Zanibbi, R. a. (2016). *NTCIR-12 MathIR Task Overview*. NTCIR.

Zhang, Y., Zheng, L., & Thing, V. L. (2017). Automated faceswapping and its detection. *2017 2nd IEEE International Conference on Signal and Image Processing*. 10.1109/SIPROCESS.2017.8124497

Zhao, H., Zhou, W., Chen, D., Wei, T., Zhang, W., & Yu, N. (2021). *Multi-attentional Deepfake Detection*. CoRR, abs/2103.02406(1). https://arxiv.org/abs/2103.02406

Zhou & Su. (2002). Named entity recognition using an HMM based chunk tagger. *ACL*, 473–480.

Zhu, J., Uren, V., & Motta, E. (2005). *Espotter: Adaptive named entity recognition for web browsing. In WM*. Springer.

About the Contributors

Poonam Tanwar received the B.Tech & M.Tech in Computer Science & Engineering from Maharishi Dayanand University, India in year 2001 & 2009 respectively and Ph.D. degree in computer science & Engineering from the Uttarakhand Technical University, India in 2015. Dr. Poonam Tanwar has 18 years of teaching experience working as associate Prof. in Manav Rachna International Institute of Research & Studies, Faridabad, India. She has published more than 50 research papers in various International Journals and Conferences. She has one copyright and filled 6 patents. She has edited book titled "Big Data Analytics and Intelligence: A Perspective for Health Care" in 2019 under the banner of emerald. She was Guest Editor for Special issue of "Advancement in Machine Learning (ML) and Knowledge Mining (KM)" for International Journal of Recent Patents in Engineering (UAE) & one more is in process. She has been awarded woman researcher award by VDGOODS Academy Chennai. She has organized various Science & Technology awareness program for rural development. She received Certificate of Recognition (Silver Category) for Outstanding Contribution to Campus Connect Program for all academic years since 2011 to 2017 by INFOSYS, Chandigarh. Beside this she is Technical program committee member for various International Conferences Like ICIC 2018, ICFNN, Rome (Italy), European Conference on Natural Language Processing and Information Retrieval, Berlin (Europe) Etc.

C. Priya, PhD, is currently working as Associate Professor, Department of Information Technology, School of Computing Sciences, Vels Institute of Science, Technology and Advanced Studies (VISTAS), Chennai, India. She has a seventeen years of teaching experience in Engineering, UG and PG level. Her research interest includes Cloud Computing, IoT, Block Chain Technology, Big Data Analytics, Deep Learning, NLP and Artificial Intelligence. Under her guidance two M.Phil research scholars were awarded and eight Ph.D scholars pursuing their research. She has published more than 50 research papers in SCI, IEEE, SCOPUS, ELSEVIER journals. She also published of 20 Book Chapters in SPRINGER, ELSEVIER, CRC Press, BPI Publications. She serves as Editorial Board Member and Reviewer in various International Journals. She has authored or co-authored more than 40 research articles published in National and International Conference Proceedings. She is an active member in Professional Bodies like ISTE, CSI, IACRD(USA), IRDP, IARA. She serves as Question Paper setter in various universities in India and Departmental Selection Committee Member for M.Phil and Ph.D Scholars at VISTAS. She is a Doctoral Committee member for P.hD., Researchers in various universities. She is an Author of 3 books, namely, 1. Selenium IDE 2. Let us C - Authentic guide to C Programming 3. PyCharmIDE-A Handbook of Python Programming. She serves as a Technical Session Chair, Keynote Speaker, Advisory Board, Technical Program Committee Member, Resource Person in many International Conferences in India and Malaysia. She has received Seven Awards such as 1. "National Eminent Educator Award" from International Institute of Organized Research (I2OR) on December 2020 2. "Global Teacher Award" at DELHI from AKS awards September 2019 3."Teacher's Day award for Book Published" on 5th September 2019 at VISTAS 4."International Best Researcher Award" from International American Council for Research and Development on June 2019 5."Dr. A. P. J. Abdul Kalam Life Time Achievement National Award" from Innovative Research Developers and Publishers Awards October 2018 6." Excellence Teaching In Higher Education" at Bengaluru from International Women Researchers Connect and Awards 2018 on Women's day 7."Best Teacher Award" on April 2009 at Saveetha Engineering College, India.

Arti Saxena Research Area: Fixed Point Theory, Machine Learning, Mathematical Modeling. About research contribution: After award of Ph.D. in 2009, from Dayalbagh Educational Institute, Deemed to be University, Agra, Under the head of Manav Rachna, till date I have 30 research publications whereas in the last three Years, 13 publications in various national and international journals have been added in the account. In addition to this, I have 4 chapters in edited books and 3 Research Books Published. I attended more than 20 FDPs and more than 10 MOOC Courses and Courseera certifications. I completed many coding assignments and projects too involving skills of Python, R, Matlab, Mysql. Got Director's Medal for securing highest marks in M. Sc. Mathematics specialization in Computer Applications. I got many appreciations during my research and afterwards. I was rewarded as Er. Vivek Mohan Memorial Young Scientist Award at the 9th conference of the International Academy of Physical Sciences Allahabad (CONIAPS IX) 2007. I got a position in top 32% in NIIT National IT Aptitude test (NITAT) 2004. Successfully organised a National Conference on "Recent Trends in Mathematical Modeling and Soft Computing Techniques" Department of Mathematics, on 29th March 2014, FET, MRIU. Many more educational workshops and seminars organized in department.

* * *

V. Ajantha Devi is working as a Research head in AP3 Solutions, Chennai, Tamil Nadu, India. She received her PhD from University of Madras in 2015. She has worked as Project Fellow under UGC Major Research Project. She has been certified as "Microsoft Certified Application Developer" (MCAD) and "Microsoft Certified Technical Specialist" (MCTS) from Microsoft Corp. She has more than 30 papers in international journals and conference proceedings to her credit. She has written, co-authored, and edited a number of books in the field of computer science. Associated a s a member of the Program Committee/Technical Committee/Chair/Review Board for a variety of international conferences. She has five Australian Patents and one Indian Patent to her credit in the area of Artificial Intelligence, Image Processing and Medical Imaging. Her work in Image Processing, Signal Processing, Pattern Matching, and Natural Language Processing is based on artificial intelligence, machine learning, and deep learning techniques. She has won many Best paper presentation awards as well as a few research-oriented international awards.

V. Belsini Gladshiya is working as Assistant Professor, Department of Computer Science at Agurchand Manmull Jain College and pursuing Ph.D degree at School of Computing Sciences, Vels Institute of Science and Technology and Advance Studies (VISTAS), Chennai under the guidance of Dr. K. Sharmila, Associate Professor, School of Computing Science,(VISTAS). She has 14 years of experience in teaching in UG and PG level. She received "Excellence in Teaching Award" from Sri Karunanadar Charitable Trust. She has published two books namely "Data Communication and Networking " for UG students and "Big Data Analytics for PG students.

Sharmila K. GladShiya received her M.Sc from Alagappa University, M.Phil Degree from Bharathidasan University, and Ph.D in Computer Science from VISTAS University, Tamilnadu, India. She is currently working as Associate Professor, School of Computing Sciences, Vels Institute of Science and Technology and Advance Studies (VISTAS), Chennai, Tamilnadu, India. She has 10 years of teaching experience in both UG and PG level. Her research interest includes Big Data Analytics, Cloud computing, Machine Learning and Block chain Technology. She has produced four M.Phil Research scholars. She has published 55 research papers in various International Journals such as Scopus and UGC referred journal. She has published four books, Software Testing, Python Programming for beginners, Data Communication and Networks and Big Data Analytics. She received "Best Young Scientist" Award by GRABS Educational Charitable Trust for her outstanding contribution to research and "Lifetime Achievement Award" for Education by SRI KARUNANADAR CHARITABLE TRUST. She has also filled National patent title "The Smart Network Optimization Technique to Retrieve data Over Cloud By Uploading The Related Images" during 2021.

R. Hema completed M.C.A. from Bharathidasan University in the year 1996. She then started her career as Lecturer in Tagore Engineering College, Chennai and worked in various Engineering colleges in South and North regions of India. Later she completed her Ph.D in the area of Text Mining from Anna University, Chennai in the year 2018 and in the same year, she joined as Assistant Professor in Department of Computer Science, Institute of Distance Education, University of Madras, Chennai. She has guided many projects in the post graduate level and her area of interests include Natural Language Processing, Big Data Analytics, Deep Learning and Image Processing.

Sudarshana Kerenalli has obtained his UG and PG degrees from Visvesvaraya Technological University Belagavi. His areas of research interest include Machine Learning, Data Analytics, Precision Agriculture, and Cyber-Forensics. Currently, he is a Research Scholar at GITAM School of Technology, Bengaluru, Karnataka, India.

Parvathi R. is an Associate Professor of School of Computing Science and Engineering at VIT University, Chennai since 2011. She received the Doctoral degree in the field of spatial data mining in the same year. Her teaching experience in the area of computer science includes more than two decades and her research interests include data mining, big data and computational biology.

Mylara Reddy is an Assistant Professor at the Department of Computer Science and Engineering, GITAM University, Bangalore, Karnataka, India. He received M. Tech. degree and Ph. D. from Visvesvaraya Technological University, Belagavi, in 2006 and 2019, respectively. His research interest includes cloud computing, fault tolerance, Computer networks, and file structures.

Pattabiraman Venkatasubbu obtained his Bachelor's from Madras University and Master's degree from Bharathidasan University. He completed his PhD from Bharathiar University, India. He has a total Professional experience of more than 16 years working in various prestigious institutions. He has published more than 30 papers in various National and International peer reviewed journals and conferences. He visited various countries namely few China, Singapore, Malaysia, Thailand and South Africa etc. for presenting his research contributions as well as to giving key note address. He is currently an Associate Professor and Program-Chair for Master's Programme at VIT University-Chennai Campus, India. His teaching and research expertise covers a wide range of subject area including data structures, knowledge discovery and data mining, database technologies, big data analytics, network and information security, etc.

Index

A

Artificial Intelligence 1, 28, 68, 71, 89-90, 92-93, 120, 122-124, 127, 165, 167-168, 171, 189, 191, 202, 204-206, 210-219
authentication 204, 217
Auto Encoders 1, 28

B

Bag of Words 3, 14, 93, 107-109, 118, 142-143, 153-154
Business Intelligence 169, 171, 174-178, 187

C

Chatbots 116, 143, 165-167, 169-170, 173, 209
Chemical Named Entity Recognition 59-60, 62, 71
classification 3-4, 7-8, 30-31, 59, 61-62, 73, 93-95, 98, 112, 114-115, 117-118, 130, 132, 141, 143, 154, 156, 171, 173, 178, 192, 197, 207, 217
closeness centrality 50-53
consensus 204, 209-213, 215, 217
Convolutional Neural Networks 189, 192
credit score 120-124, 130, 140
Creditworthiness Assessment 120-121, 126-127, 140, 209
Customer Behavior 169
Cyber Forensics 1, 23, 28

D

Data Generation 126
Decentralization 204, 209-211, 215
deep learning 1-3, 8, 12, 15, 18, 24, 26, 28, 48, 59-60, 62, 65-67, 69-72, 94, 97, 110, 118, 120, 125-126, 137-138, 140-141, 143, 146-147, 155, 166-167, 189-192, 195
deep learning techniques 1, 3, 48, 59, 65-66, 167
deep neural network 68, 142-144

D

deepfakes 1-5, 7, 10, 12, 15, 20-28
degree centrality 50-52
Democratization 176
Deocder 142
digital environment 204, 206
digital footprints 120-121, 127
digital mathematical library 74, 81, 85

E

encoder 5-8, 19, 87, 142, 144, 156-159, 161-162
encryption 204, 210, 213, 217

F

fake news 1, 22, 25, 28-30, 47
Features of Chemical Names 59

G

Generative Adversarial Networks (GAN) 1, 8, 27-28

H

hashing 78, 90, 204, 209-210, 217
hashtags 29, 31, 36, 38, 40, 44, 47, 52

I

immutable 204, 209
indexing 74, 76, 78, 80, 82, 84, 86-87, 89, 101, 172, 217
information retrieval 74-76, 78-81, 85-87, 89-92, 143, 204-205, 207, 215, 217-218

L

Language translation 98, 113-114
Latent Dirichlet Allocation 178, 181
Logistic Regression 112, 130, 132-133, 138, 143
LSTM 16-17, 67, 69, 78, 91, 142-144, 156-159, 161, 171

M

machine learning 8, 14, 36, 48, 51, 59-60, 65-66, 69-70, 93-94, 105-107, 109-110, 112, 115, 118-120, 122, 124-126, 128, 130, 136-138, 140-141, 143, 146-147, 150, 153-155, 167-171, 177-178, 189-191, 202
Machine learning techniques 66
mathematical information retrieval 74-76, 80, 89-92
microblogging 29-31, 40, 44, 47
modularity 50, 53-54, 56, 97
Multimedia Content 28

N

Natural Language Processing 2, 38, 49, 59, 62, 67, 75, 78, 85, 89, 93-94, 98, 107, 114-122, 124-125, 127, 140-144, 147, 154-155, 159, 167-170, 172, 175, 177, 188, 206-208

P

pandemic 29, 173
polarity 29-31, 38, 42, 47
POS tagging 93, 110, 154
Power BI 177-183
propaganda 29

R

Random Forest 14, 130, 133-134, 138, 141, 143, 192
recurrent neural network 28, 142-143, 146, 155-156, 161, 167
Reinforcement Learning 189-190, 192, 194-196, 200, 202
rheumatoid arthritis 189, 192-195, 197, 202-203
Rheumatology 194, 202

S

Semantic analysis 93-94, 114-115, 178, 208
sentiment analysis 30-31, 48-52, 95, 115, 154, 208
social network 1, 25, 29, 51, 55, 122
Sparse Networks 50, 53
Stemming 81, 93, 95, 102, 104-107, 118, 143, 154, 206

T

text processing 69, 73, 93-95, 98, 108
Textblob 36, 38, 42, 97
tokenization 38, 60, 62, 82, 85, 93-95, 102-103, 105, 107-108, 118, 143, 154, 178
tweets 29-31, 36, 38, 40-42, 44-47, 50-52, 55, 58, 72, 115, 126
Twitter 22-23, 27, 29-31, 36-41, 43-44, 46-53, 55, 58, 126, 187
Twitter API 29-30, 37-38, 47

U

unstructured data 69, 94, 116, 127, 154, 169, 175, 187, 206

V

Voice Assistant 117, 169
Voice Phishing 22, 28

www.igi-global.com

Publisher of Peer-Reviewed, Timely, and
Innovative Academic Research Since 1988

IGI Global's Transformative Open Access (OA) Model:
How to Turn Your University Library's Database Acquisitions Into a Source of OA Funding

Well in advance of Plan S, IGI Global unveiled their OA Fee Waiver (Read & Publish) Initiative. Under this initiative, librarians who invest in IGI Global's InfoSci-Books and/or InfoSci-Journals databases will be able to subsidize their patrons' OA article processing charges (APCs) when their work is submitted and accepted (after the peer review process) into an IGI Global journal.

How Does it Work?

Step 1: **Library Invests in the InfoSci-Databases:** A library perpetually purchases or subscribes to the InfoSci-Books, InfoSci-Journals, or discipline/subject databases.

Step 2: **IGI Global Matches the Library Investment with OA Subsidies Fund:** IGI Global provides a fund to go towards subsidizing the OA APCs for the library's patrons.

Step 3: **Patron of the Library is Accepted into IGI Global Journal (After Peer Review):** When a patron's paper is accepted into an IGI Global journal, they option to have their paper published under a traditional publishing model or as OA.

Step 4: **IGI Global Will Deduct APC Cost from OA Subsidies Fund:** If the author decides to publish under OA, the OA APC fee will be deducted from the OA subsidies fund.

Step 5: **Author's Work Becomes Freely Available:** The patron's work will be freely available under CC BY copyright license, enabling them to share it freely with the academic community.

Note: This fund will be offered on an annual basis and will renew as the subscription is renewed for each year thereafter. IGI Global will manage the fund and award the APC waivers unless the librarian has a preference as to how the funds should be managed.

Hear From the Experts on This Initiative:

"I'm very happy to have been able to make one of my recent research contributions *freely available* along with having access to the *valuable resources* found within IGI Global's InfoSci-Journals database."

– Prof. Stuart Palmer,
Deakin University, Australia

"Receiving the support from IGI Global's OA Fee Waiver Initiative *encourages me to continue my research work without any hesitation.*"

– Prof. Wenlong Liu, College of Economics and Management at Nanjing University of Aeronautics & Astronautics, China

Printed in the United States
by Baker & Taylor Publisher Services